*The American Civil War
and the British Press*

The American Civil War and the British Press

by ALFRED GRANT

with a foreword by PHIL LeCUYER

McFarland & Company, Inc., Publishers
Jefferson, North Carolina, and London

Library of Congress Cataloguing-in-Publication Data

Grant, Alfred, 1918–
    The American Civil War and the British press / by Alfred Grant;
with a foreword by Phil LeCuyer.
        p.   cm.
    Includes bibliographical references and index.
    ISBN 0-7864-0630-5 (library binding : 50# alkaline paper) ∞
    1. United States — History — Civil War, 1861–1865 — Press coverage.
2. War — Press coverage — Great Britain — History — 19th century.
3. Press and politics — Great Britain — History — 19th century.
4. British newspapers — History — 19th century.   5. Journalism —
Great Britain — History — 19th century.   I. Title.
    E609.G73   2000
    973.7'8 — dc21   99-47689
                                                                                      CIP

British Library Cataloguing-in-Publication data are available

Manufactured in the United States of America

*McFarland & Company, Inc., Publishers
    Box 611, Jefferson, North Carolina 28640
    www.mcfarlandpub.com*

To Rita

Table of Contents

While interest is felt and attention is attracted, it is to be feared that in too many instances a true estimate has not been formed of the cause of the conflict, and the objects for which it is waged. Prevalent ignorance upon this matter leaves the public open to the exceeding danger of according the national sympathy, the moral, and possibly, active support to the wrong side; and when we remember the immense weight of English opinion in America, and the momentous consequences hanging on the event of war, this will be confessed a dreadful evil. The British public have, for the most part, seemed satisfied to possess some dim notion of these things, swallowing complacently such pills as their favourite organ may, from time to time, have prepared for them, and thus saving themselves the trouble of mastication. Thus has it followed that venal prints and unprincipled men have, to a lamentable extent, misled the public of this country into deplorable confusion and error in the matter.[1]

Foreword

by Phil LeCuyer

This book deals with the journalistic treatment of America's Civil War in the British press of that time. The author has sorted and sifted through reams of material: all of Britain's major newspapers, her principal monthly and quarterly magazines, a broad collection of pamphlets from the year 1859 until the assassination of President Lincoln in April of 1865, as well as book-length commentaries on the situation in America. From all this material he has selected the most significant and telling documents — and then wisely allowed them to speak for themselves.

Mr. Grant weaves the material together with concise introductory comments that point with deadly accuracy to the conceptual heart of each selection. He does not, on a page by page basis, argue. Rather, he presents the selections and points to the critical and revealing details in them, thereby allowing the argument to emerge of its own accord.

As straightforward and unpostured as Mr. Grant's procedure may appear, the argument that does develop through these pages is powerful and complex. It is inescapable. The British press — both the dominant institutions thereof and the leading players therein — misinformed their aggregate readership about the nature and progress of the conflict in America, and they did this on behalf of Britain's antidemocratic ruling class. The pervasive and sustained campaign of misinformation conducted on the pages of Britain's papers, magazines, and pamphlets of the period 1859–1865 can in the end only be deemed a thoroughly corrupt and cynical abrogation of journalistic responsibility. Thoroughly, but not quite completely. Amid the widespread debacle there were a few authors and publications that maintained a high standard of perspicacity and integrity. It is these very few exceptions that bring into sharpest relief the journalistic failure, and one might perhaps say, depravity of the British press taken altogether.

The selections from these honest pens project a sense of truth, albeit highly embattled and ineffectual to the point of political irrelevance. Perhaps one of the most notable and noble of those who wrote to reveal the situation rather than to persuade in support of government policy was Count Agénor de Gasparin in his book *The Uprising of the Great People: The United States in 1861*, which was published in London in 1861. But Gasparin, lucid and enlightened as he was, addressed British readers as a foreigner. Also, one must mention the honest reporting of *The Daily News*. This small newspaper, written for working men, was another remarkable example of editorial responsibility almost without resonance in the larger and more important organs of the British press.

The vast amount of evidence presented by Mr. Grant has been marshaled in an interesting way. His selections in the first section of the book establish the all-encompassing economic importance of America's cotton crop to Britain. The underlying dependency of Britain's mills on Confederate cotton is carefully contoured and quantified. This economic bond, a major constituitive ingredient in Britain's mid-nineteenth century prosperity, remains by and large uncommented upon by the British press. It brings to mind an addict attempting to justify and judge behavior without taking into account his addiction.

To produce cotton, slaves were indispensable. Britain had been in what seemed at the time an analogous situation vis-à-vis the sugar crop in her Caribbean colonies some three decades earlier. Mr. Grant allows his sources, in this case primarily pamphleteers, to expose the falseness and misuse of this analogy for the purpose of self-delusion.

Perhaps the deepest underlying reality informing the attempt of the British press to cover the American Civil War was political in the most profound sense. The North embodied the idea, revolting in class-based British society, of broad (even universal) democracy. It was the deep hope of many of the most articulate writers presented to use by Mr. Grant that the nation "dedicated to the proposition that all men are created equal" would indeed perish from the earth.

The second section of this book is comprised of six case studies. Here we see in a more particular way how the British press reported (1) the Battle of Gettysburg, (2) the campaigns and generalships of Sherman and Grant, (3) General Butler's order concerning the women of New Orleans, (4) the Trent Affair, in which Britain's own sovereign rights were at issue, (5) the awkward combination of Britain's official policy of neutrality and her practice of partisanship, and (6) the efficacy and justification of the Union's blockade. The subject matters of these several case studies vary from strategic and decisive (Gettysburg and the blockade) to what Mr. Grant calls "comic opera" (the Trent affair and Butler's edict). This range of case studies establishes how unmitigated and irrecoverable was the essential corruption of Britain's press.

The third section of Mr. Grant's book has within it two parts. The first is a detailed description of *The Times*, which enjoyed a subsidized circulation of 65,000. We are treated to biographical sketches of the editors and their American correspondents. We read not only what they wrote and published, but also some of their private correspondence to each other. Also, Mr. Grant, working here as must needs be from the recognized work of other scholars, shows us the composition and profile of the readership of this journalistic bastion. Here, Mr. Grant's claim that the newspaper was serving up what was called for, rather than what was objectively the case, receives its finishing touch.

The second part of this third section is perhaps of greatest use with regard to the present. In these pages Mr. Grant lays bare not the fact of self-deception, which at this stage in his presentation has been well established, but rather the techniques involved. These techniques, like symptoms of mental illness writ large, have enduring diagnostic value. We see the British press presenting its positions as based on "humanitarian concerns"—even for the slaves. These pseudo-concerns serve to efface genuine moral argument and honest analysis of economic interests. The second symptom is distraction, as exemplified by trumping up the issue of tariffs into a sufficient justification for secession. The third symptom might be called indirect narcissism. The text and subtext of British reporting on the society and culture of the American South was that "they embody our aspirations." There were, as Mr. Grant adduces, isolated Kent-like voices that could "tell an honest tale without marring it" about life in the South. The truth could be spoken, but it could not be countenanced.

These three techniques whereby a nation may delude itself—vague humanitarian concerns in place of moral analysis; substitution of red-herring issues for real ones with ensuing distraction and obfuscation; and indirect narcissism—have not perished from the earth any more than has the American Union. Our awareness of these techniques as they were applied (cynically or not) 140 years ago should sensitize us as readers of today's papers, and it should raise our level of immune response against self-serving argument presenting itself as the public interest.

The final section of the book is a simple juxtapositioning of the British press's portrayal of Abraham Lincoln during the war years and then after his death at the hand of an assassin. By this point the reader readily perceives the truth: There are those whose published language and thought has become so debauched that their praise of the noble dead conveys only the spectacle of newsprint as a meaningless void.

Preface and Acknowledgments

This is a history of the British Press during the American Civil War, 1861–1865. It is an investigation of the British press, which, in the main, ardently supported a government primarily concerned with maintaining a most undemocratic regime. Motivated by a fear of democracy and a multitude of similar emotions, the British papers were champions of the Confederacy.

My interest in the British press originated many years ago at the University of Edinburgh and resulted in my first book, a narrative of the British Press in the American Revolution, entitled *Our American Brethren*. The present work is a continuation of the exploration of the British Press.

This treatise draws on British newspapers, periodicals and pamphlets of the era. Special attention is paid to the work of the pamphleteers, whose message in most cases ran contrary to the thoughts of those in control of the media and therefore could not find a place of publication in newspapers or periodicals of the day.

I would like to offer my appreciation to the Scottish National Library, the Library of the University of Edinburgh, the Zimmerman Library of the University of New Mexico, and the Library of St. Johns' at Santa Fe, and to Laura Cooley, whose efforts to scour the countryside for secure secondary sources have been "above and beyond."

To Ed Dee of the Computing Services of Edinburgh University for the help he rendered to a writer who is computer ignorant. To professor Harry T. Dickinson of Edinburgh University and Phil LeCuyer of St. Johns' for their patience and advice, I owe the highest debt of gratitude.

Introduction

It was the fear of democracy that most influenced the ruling class of Britain in its relationship with America during the middle Victorian period. The Reform Act of 1832 did more than open Parliament to the wealthy industrialists of central England. It did little for the common man. The House of Commons and the House of Lords were still controlled by the aristocracy and those related to it. One in seven Englishmen had the franchise. Men like John Bright, MP from Manchester, who voiced the opportunities of democracy were treated with scorn and ridicule.

Although the cotton industry was the largest in England, the threat of curtailment of cotton from the American South was not of immediate concern. The textile mills had vastly overproduced in the late 1850s. The inventories of finished goods were enormous. The market was glutted. The fact that the Confederacy attempted an embargo on cotton during the years of 1861 and 1862 was of little concern to the mill owners. In truth, it was welcome. Old inventory was being sold at the new higher price of cotton. With mills in the Manchester area closed or working restricted hours, raw cotton was exported to the Union.

English industry prospered during the years of the American Civil War. The ship building trade, the shipping industry, the woollen industry and the linen industry all thrived. Shipyards on the Clyde and Mersey were building privateers for the Confederacy and small speedy vessels aimed at breaking the Union blockade of Southern ports. Liverpool became the center of a thriving industry of blockade runners. At the same time, the British shipping industry benefited from the vast increase of insurance that the Union shippers were forced to pay as a result of the Confederate privateers. Until the Confederate uprising and the feats of the privateers, United States shippers — nearly all located in the North — had carried more cargo between America and Britain than the carriers of Great

8   INTRODUCTION

Britain. With the war-related increase in insurance, however, many Union shippers were compelled to close shop. The shipping industry of Britain purchased 40 percent of the defunct American fleet.

The English prided themselves — and freely praised themselves in the press — upon the emancipation of the slaves of the British West Indies in the 1840s. Yet the emancipation did not imply immediate freedom. Negroes were to be indentured servants for many years. And was emancipation an act of humanitarianism, or one that sought to rid England of a set of colonies that were more of a burden than an asset? The sugar plantations in the British West Indies were facing increased competition from Saint Domingue (Haiti) and Cuba, and their importance was waning in the new industrial economy. Furthermore, British support of the West Indian sugar monopoly meant that Britain paid high prices for sugar that could have been obtained more cheaply elsewhere. By "liberating" the West Indian slaves, the British pulled their support out from under the West Indian planters and freed themselves from a system that no longer worked to their benefit.

Another part of British pride and self-congratulation was the untiring effort to end the slave trade in Africa. It is worth noting, however, that with the industrial revolution had come a great need for machinery lubricants, and one of the best was palm oil, produced in western Africa. Palm oil in fact became one of the prime factors in the economy of Liverpool, and British squadrons stationed off the western coast of Africa, ostensibly engaged in preventing the slave trade, were in an excellent position to prevent competition for palm oil as well.

Still the British papers believed themselves and their nation the exemplars of neutrality. In May 1861, Queen Victoria had issued a Proclamation of Neutrality, which was all shadow and little substance. The press continued to enjoy and build upon the message, but it had little meaning. It was and had been the policy of the British press to show more interest in the sound of words than their meaning. And so it was in the nineteenth century with neutrality.

Slavery, the press agreed, was an abomination; it was odious, hateful, loathsome, despicable. It was evil, iniquitous, wicked, unvirtuous, and immoral. But to free the Negro was not that simple. President Lincoln's Emancipation Proclamation would lead to a servile revolt. Innocent women and children would be slaughtered by rampaging blacks. And was there a need to free the Negro slave? Was he not better to live as a slave and to reap the benefits of loving slave holders? And to be instructed in Christianity? Was it not better to live in the Confederacy and be a slave than a free man in the North and not be invited to a family dinner or be welcomed at the community church.

British newspapers and journals portrayed the Confederacy not only as a land of virtuous aristocrats, but also as a homogeneous and patriotic entity. The problems of conscription, of army desertions, of peace societies and enemy sympathizers were difficulties of the North and not present in the South. All of the above was untrue. The Confederacy had introduced conscription one year before the North. It presented the same advantage to the wealthy: the privilege of purchasing a substitute. Army desertions were only slightly less than the North but more burdensome. The Confederacy had fewer men to call upon. Peace societies flourished in the mountain areas, and it was not unknown for draft officers to be murdered in those areas.

The duplicity of the British press was clearly exhibited in their view of President Lincoln. He was "the worst failure that America had ever produced"; he had the respect of nobody; his reelection would send down the last and worst president of the United States; "with singular bad taste, he was manifestly unfit"; his addresses were "riddled with confused grammar and blundering metaphors."

Yet when President Lincoln was assassinated the British press heaped laurels upon him: "The intimate connexion of wisdom and goodness of disposition has seldom been more forcibly illustrated." "Mr. Lincoln had shown signs of a moderate and conciliatory disposition." *The Times* managed three eulogies and, without blinking an eye, filled its columns with Lincoln the Great.

Overall, it is clear that the conflict in America became the rallying call for all Englishmen fearing an extended franchise, democracy, and the growing commercial power of America. The claim that a Confederate victory would lead to the amelioration and emancipation of the Negro because of the "moral pressure of Europe" was disingenuous at best. In its coverage of the Civil War in America, the British press simply provided, in the oldest tradition of the Fourth Estate, exactly what its readers demanded.

PART ONE

The Issues in Dispute

1. Cotton, Slavery and Christianity

Cotton and slavery, in combination, performed to the great advantage of both Southern America and Great Britain. From early colonial days, when cotton was hardly to be considered as a significant crop, it grew steadily to become the primary supplier of England's major industry. Unfortunately, cotton and slavery were inseparable in America. And the association led to an appalling Civil War in that country.

Prior to 1787 the planters of the Southern states had been engaged principally in the cultivation of rice and indigo, then the best-paying crops; but the profits of the trade were lessening yearly in consequence of competition from India. The cotton plant was then only cultivated to a limited extent; the process of cleaning the fiber being so slow and expensive as to render the production of the plant, on a large scale, impossible. Notwithstanding the increased demand for cotton from England, consequent upon the then-recent great improvements in the machinery for spinning, the exports from the United States in 1793 only amounted to 187,000 lbs., while the imports into England from the West Indies, Turkey, India, and other countries during the previous year reached 28,706,675 lbs.

James Hargreaves' "Jenny" was invented in 1767, Sir Richard Arkwright's "Throstle" in 1769, and Samuel Crompton's "Mule" in 1775, in which year, likewise, steam power was for the first time applied to cotton machinery. In 1787 Dr. Edmund Cartwright brought out his "power loom." One year later, the textile trade, becoming alarmed about the future supplies of raw cotton, had called the attention of the East India Company to the increasing requirements of the manufacture, and the capability of India for meeting those wants. No one, for a moment, expected that any assistance would come from America.

From 1764 to 1798 prices for raw cotton increased, notwithstanding the increased supplies. The receipts from North America in 1764 were about 1,000 lbs.; in 1770 about 2,000 lbs.; in 1784 about 14,000 lbs., and in 1791, 189,316 lbs. The invention of the cotton gin by Eli Whitney in 1793, introduced a new order of things. By the primitive rollers, one hand could clean only a few pounds daily; but by means of the new gin three to four hundred pounds could be turned out in the same space of time. The effect of Whitney's ingenuity was instantaneous: the export of cotton during 1794 — that is, one year after the invention — reached 1,601,760 lbs. against only 187,000 in 1793! In 1800 the shipments were 17,789,800 lbs. and in 1806 nearly one half of the cotton imported into Great Britain was the produce of the United States. Not only was the supply large, but it was in quality superior to anything British spinners had experienced. In the meantime the trade was making rapid progress all over Europe. Cotton machinery on the English principle was introduced into France in 1789; in Saxony in 1799; in Belgium in 1804, and in Holland a few years later. The first mill was erected in the United States in 1791; cotton goods were manufactured at Boston in 1808, and in 1815 the power loom was in full play there. The export of cotton wool from America increased from 17,789,800 lbs. in 1800 to 93,900,000 lbs. in 1810, and 127,800,000 lbs. in 1820.[2]

The South supplied Great Britain with three-fourths to five-sixths of her cotton needs:

	Total Imports to Great Britain (lbs.)	Imports from U.S. South (lbs.)
1840	592,488,010	487,856,504
1841	487,992,335	358,240,964
1842	531,750,086	414,030,779
1843	673,193,116	574,738,520
1844	646,111,340	517,218,662
1845	721,979,953	626,650,412
1846	467,856,274	401,949,393
1847	474,707,615	364,599,291
1848	713,020,161	600,247,488
1849	755,496,012	634,504,050
1850	663,576,861	493,153,112
1851	757,379,749	596,638,962
1852	929,782,448	765,630,544
1853	895,278,749	658,451,796
1854	887,333,149	722,151,346
1855	891,751,952	681,629,424
1856	1,023,866,304	780,040,016
1857	969,318,896	654,758,048
1858	932,847,056	732,403,840

England remained supreme in textile manufacture:

	Number of Spindles	*Bales of Cotton*
Great Britain	30,000,000	2,663,000 (50,000 per week)
United States	4,300,000	650,000 (12,000 per week)
France	4,000,000	621,000 (11,941 per week)
Germany	2,000,000	307,000 (5,904 per week)

Slavery, though unremunerative for general industrial purposes, was highly profitable as a labor-producing system for the new and fertile lands of the South and West. Some idea of the extent and value of this "export" business may be found by a glance at the following figures: From 1850 to 1860 the total slave population of the South increased from 3,200,304 to 3,949,557, an increase of 23.4 percent.

The slave population of the states where agriculture was principally cotton increased 41.1 percent during the same period 1850–1860. The difference in the number of slaves in the cotton producing states, a total of 263,301, were those imported from the slave breeding territories. Thus in round numbers, 263 slaves, valued at $263,000,000, were purchased by the seven cotton growing states in ten years![3]

	1850	*1860*
Alabama	342,844	435,132
Arkansas	47,100	111,104
Florida	39,310	61,753
Georgia	381,682	462,230
Louisiana	244,809	332,550
Mississippi	309,878	436,696
Texas	58,161	180,388
TOTAL	1,423,784	2,019,853

Such were the reckonings and the statistics which drove the production of cotton and so stimulated the torrent of slavery which was to inundate the American South. The textile industry was a major, if not the principal enterprise, of Great Britain. But the English had long prided themselves on the humanity of their island. After all the back slapping and self-aggrandizement over the emancipation of the Negro slave in the British West Indies and for the spirited resolve to end the slave trade from West Africa, how would civilized, benevolent, and Christian England deal with slavery in America? If the commentaries which appeared in the newspapers, journals, and pamphlets were to represent the views of their readers, and they unfailingly did, it could be rightly judged that many Englishmen were neither Christian nor filled with all the goodness and virtue their religion represented.

Christianity, however, was not to be denied in Victorian England. Surely there was not a nation more imbued with the value of Christianity and the Bible.

Alexander James Beresford-Hope was a major spokesman for the support of Christianity, the Confederacy, and the class structure of Britain. His aversion to slavery was the touchstone for the English ruling classes. Following his precepts, it would have been unsuitable and unchristian to have voiced approval of such a sinful creation as slavery. Unfortunately his regrets were invariably followed by a multiplicity of qualifications, and criteria which were, in essence, the English time-honored "but" to the malfeasance of slavery.

Haplessly Beresford-Hope could not distinguish between the unchristian prejudice of refusing to accept a man at one's dinner table and the cruelty of dealing with him like an animal: "In the free States the negro is treated with unchristian cruelty, excluded from the same church, from the same table, from the same railway carriage, from the same altar of God, as a loathsome beast of the field, in the slave States this terrible aversion has no existence, nor is found in a much milder degree."[4]

Beresford-Hope did acknowledge slavery to be "a curse and a misfortune," but in advocating the manner in which the chains were to be lightened remained sans clue. Could it be that the turning from heathen to Christian would do the deed?

"Slavery, I repeat," wrote Beresford-Hope, "is a curse and a misfortune to the country in which it exists, but the best of the slave owners make its chains as light as *possible* — they educate their blacks, they make them Christians, while in Africa they would have remained untaught and uncivilized."[5]

Beresford-Hope assured his readers that with victory the Confederacy would be compelled to change its ways as the result of intimate relations with Europe. He made no mention of the colonial escapades of the French and English and their treatment of the indigenous peoples:

> Once let the South be released from the harassing contest it has hitherto had to maintain with the North, and it must perforce be brought into intimate relations with Europe, upon whom it must rely for its manufactures, education and literature. It will be brought into direct contact with the public opinion of Europe, which will irresistibly compel it to change its course in regard to slavery; the better and more enlightened men in the South will be led to comprehend the vices of the slave system, and to imbibe higher and more Christian ideas on the subject: and these will, in turn, constrain the more bigoted and ignorant to follow their line of policy.[6]

Beresford-Hope, in the true Christian spirit, writes of the human family and of the Anglo-Saxon moral fiber. To have the Anglo-Saxon race dominated by a rabble of Negroes would be unthinkable:

> Believing, as I most fully do, in the unity of the human family, yet I cannot so far abjure my common sense as not to recognize that the cumulative accidents of rolling centuries have endowed some races with greater capacity of knowledge, greater acquirements, greater flexibility of mind and strength of will, and greater delicacy of moral fiber than others. I respect the proud standing of the Anglo-Saxon race among the nations of the world, and I cannot but own that the Negro — no matter by whose fault — stands, it may be, the last. So, while I wish to knock the fetters off his arm, I yet dare, in the face of false philanthropy, to deprecate in the name of Heaven the subjugation of millions of our Anglo-Saxon brethren by a rabble of Negroes let loose. Anything more loathsome or unnatural than such a revolution it would be impossible to conceive.[7]

Beresford-Hope could not remain serene with the fear of encroaching democracy. Clearly, his support of the Confederacy was not without concern of an extended franchise, not to the slave, but to the Englishman who might challenge the ruling class of Britain.

> The slave trade is utterly unjustifiable, and the middle passage is damnable, although we must own that the Negroes of America, descended as they are from the kidnapped victims of that horrible system, are not only Christianized, but also educated and civilized, as those in Africa cannot be; but yet their civilization is not one which should entitle them to place their feet upon the white man's neck, as they do if the "abolitionists" permit a reign of universal suffrage.[8]

There was no end of support for the cause of Christianity, the Confederacy, and slavery in Britain's pamphlet literature. Those championing the Confederacy were outraged at the Northern "war-crusaders" but failed to mention that the first aggressive act was the Confederate shelling of Fort Sumter.

> Should the war crusaders succeed, with their gospel of torches, faggots, fire, and sword, in conquering and divesting the South, the slaves whom they had freed from the galling tyranny of their masters would not feel themselves, amidst Northern treatment, to be "a heap much more men," when sold on the auction block in Northern cities as paupers — recently illustrated in the case of a number of fugitive slaves in Illinois — neither would they lift up their hands in blessing and shout, "Blessed be de Lord dat brought us to see dis first happy day of our lives," if shipped out of the country by the chivalrous white men on their landing in Africa. Such a state of things may be in accordance with strong delusion, Judaical blindness, and

hardness of heart, but certainly not with the doctrines of our Lord and Sav-iour Jesus Christ, the teachings of His most holy Word, or the merciful spirit of Christianity; and yet these wilful and chosen delusions are spread-ing in this country as well as in America, shown in the vigorous attempts now being made to manufacture public opinion in honour of these war crusaders in America, who charge the British with "a decline of anti-slav-ery fire." It is to be hoped that the people of this country will not be blinded by the subterfuges resorted to in dwelling upon the black picture of the South, in order to heighten the virtues of the North, when, by its double dealing, it has excited the pity and deserves the execrations of mankind.... May it ever be the exalted privilege and happiness of this highly favoured nation to endorse a gospel of emancipation founded on reason and argu-ment, and not on one of physical force associated with rash and bloody hands — the folly that seeks, through evil, good.[9]

As in the above example, Christian government and the immorality of such policies in the face of the anticipated servile rebellion was debated in the House of Commons. One pamphlet quoted a fragment of that debate, the remarks of a Mr. Horseman:

There is yet a greater crime than slavery — for a crime it is of a deeper and more unpardonable dye — for a white man and a Christian to invite a negro to achieve his freedom by a carnival of crime.... I say it is the very highest iniquity in the chief of a Christian Government to excite the negro, with the ferocity of the tiger, to the perpetuation of cruelties that cannot be numbered, and crimes which I dare not even name, with no possible ter-mination to that desperate and deadly strife of races but in the extermina-tion of the weaker and the vanquished.[10]

Contrary to the position of the ruling class of Britain and its press, there was a strong revulsion among many Britons over the question of slavery in Amer-ica. Such sentiment was not to be found in the primary newspapers or journals, but mainly in the pamphleteer literature which was so popular in 19th century Britain. There was a call to Britishers to remember their past and reflect on their present:

We blush for Britons who have sympathized with the attempted establish-ment of a slave power. Do we not feel a manly pride that a slave is a slave no longer when he touches British soil? Is not hatred of slavery an heir-loom which we are bound to preserve in all its integrity, and hand down unimpaired to our children? Ought we not, then, to give our fullest moral support to the United States' Government, in its effort to crush a rebellion based upon that institution which we loathe? In a war of Law against Licence — of Freedom against Slavery — of Civilization against Barbarism, shame upon Christian Britain if she waver in her choice![11]

The Times, 6 January 1863, mounted an attempt to support the Confederacy by maintaining that the Bible sanctioned slavery:

> These gentlemen (Lincoln and his men) preach not for an infallible Church, for no such Church has yet ventured to be as dogmatic and positive on this point as they are. They preach with the Bible in their hands. In that book there is not one single text that can be perverted to prove Slavery unlawful, though there is much which naturally tends to its mitigation, its elevation, and its final extinction. In the New Testament we have an Epistle written by the man who represents the last revealed phase and development of the Gospel, sent by the hand of a runaway slave, who had sought refuge with the writer, to his lawful master, to the purport that the master and his slave were to get on better, and do their duty to one another more thoroughly for the future. The same writer tells his recent converts that if they are slaves they must make the best of that condition, and not try to escape it, at least by any means contrary to the laws of the country. The context which says that a faithful and dutiful Christian slave becomes the freedman of HIS HEAVENLY MASTER clearly proves that a slave who refuses the offer of freedom has a high scriptural argument for his choice. If it be said that Slavery is at variance with the spirit of the Gospel, so also are a good many things which are not yet laid under the ban of Abolition, or threatened with the "War Power." Sumptuous fare, purple and fine linen, wealth, ecclesiastical titles, unmarried clergy, good clerical incomes, and many other things are contrary to the spirit of the Gospel, or, at least, can be proved so as easily as Slavery. But the Roman Catholics have just as much to say for any one of their peculiar doctrines as the Abolitionists have for their one article of a standing or falling community. Whether the Confederates have done right to throw off the Union is a distinct question, but they cannot have a better defense than a proclamation of war to the knife, a solemn invocation of the "War Power" against every slave owner who still claims the duty of his slave.

The Times article found little support among the readers of that newspaper and was never repeated. But it did stir up a nest of disquiet among pamphleteers, as the following example shows.

> And are we to be told that the Bible sanctions slavery? The Bible sanctions slavery?— sanctions the dragging of human beings from their homes, and disciplining them under the scourge into machines for labour: — sanctions man to live without knowledge and without the capacity to make anything his own, and to toil that another may reap?— sanctions driving men and women to work like beasts of burden under the lash?— sanctions the prohibition of holy wedlock — the separation of all ties of God's ordaining at the caprice of man — the total prostration of body, and, as far as force can effect it, of soul, beneath the irresponsible power of any villain, however base, who has money to purchase it? The claim, whether

expressed or not, to insult, torture, scourge to death, if such be his pleasure, a man or a woman, a son or a daughter, it may be, of the Lord God
Almighty? (the Bible sanction such a system as this?) I have proved the sup-
position to be an error, and the error results in a blasphemy foul enough
to make the angels weep. What do Christian men and Christian ministers
mean by speaking gently of such a system? The Bible condemns it from
beginning to end. Woe to us if we sympathize with crime, and take pleasure in those who commit it. We have too much to answer for in this matter. It is we who have planted American slavery, fostered it by our commerce, and are upholding it by our sympathy. God is just. He is showing
this in America today, let us beware of provoking Him to show it in England to-morrow.[12]

That slavery and Christianity do not coexist is enunciated in the New Testament:

Can we be astonished that in the midst of such a community [the American South] the spirit and principles of Christianity, the nominal religion
of the nation, are virtually set aside, and the precepts of an inferior and
abrogated code of ethics adopted as a standard of conduct? The Bible as a
whole, if honestly interpreted, is an anti-slavery book; and though there
are certain passages contained in the Old Testament which permitted slavery in a semi-civilized age, there are none which recommend the institution to the adoption of a people; whilst, should there be any capable of
such a construction, they are clearly nullified, so far as Christians are concerned, by the doctrines enunciated in the New Testament. True, our Sav-
iour did not denounce the institution by name, for probably he was never
brought into direct contact with it; but it is unquestionable that the existence of practical Christianity is impossible where slavery exists.[13]

Equally, the Jewish Talmud was cited:

To begin with the Talmud, the following quotation may suffice: — First, "He
who buys a Hebrew bondsman buys for himself a master"; a sentence not to
be construed so as to mean merely that ofttimes the servant becomes the
master; but to be taken as showing the master to have been so bound by man-
ifold legal obligations in relation to the rights of the servant, as in a sense to
instate the latter in a certain mastery.... Second, No Jubilee, no Hebrew slavery, proves decisively that there was no slavery tolerated by the Jewish law
that did not include in it the certainty of emancipation.... The Midrash is of
opinion that the exodus from Egyptian bondage was granted on condition
that the Israelites should never more allow themselves to sink into a state of
servitude. Maimonides says that all the enactments with regard to slaves are
intended to call forth mildness and mercy toward the unfortunate. The
statute, says he, forbidding the giving up a runaway slave to his master, is
the most merciful law in a code of laws distinguished for their mercy.[14]

Some in Britain found it difficult to understand the attitudes of the people of that island toward the conflict in America:

> It is not very easy to balance in equal scales the respective evils of Slavery on the one hand, and of War and Anarchy on the other. The chronic suffering of the slave, and the permanent demoralization of the slave holder, present pictures far less exciting to our imaginations than the acute agonies of a field of battle, or the furious crimes of a servile insurrection. When to these causes we add the readier sympathies which, alas! inevitably arise for the woes of men and women of our own race and social standing, over those of another colour and class, we shall doubtless obtain a clue to much of that misapplication of English feeling at this moment on the subject of America. Thus it came to pass, that we are now sympathizing with the slave holders struggling against the righteous punishment of ruin which their long suppressions have provoked, rather than with the unoffending victims escaping at last from the ten-fold evils of cruel servitude. Thus at this moment, in our land, lamentations over the horror of "a fratricidal war" have utterly drowned the cry which once arose from the heart of England against the giant Wrong which that war must terminate. Thus the threat of the possibility of a "renewal of St. Domingo massacres" is continually used by the advocates of the Southern cause, as if it were alone sufficient to condemn, beyond appeal, the policy of President Lincoln — nay, to place him altogether outside the pale of the sympathies of a Christian community. The anticipation that the Emancipation Proclamation will lead to a "carnival of crime," or that the negro will display "the ferocity of a tiger" when delivered from the lash of his oppressors have little plausible grounds.... The real danger to the white population lies in attempting to re-solder the fetters of the slaves, and not in completing the work of their liberation. Those very "St. Domingo massacres" which are perpetually held up before us as warnings against emancipation, are, in fact, the strongest arguments in favour of its speedy and final completion, inasmuch as they only took place, when, after eight years of peaceful and industrious freedom enjoyed by the negroes, Buonaparte sent an army to reduce them once more into slavery. If the North should be finally driven back, and the South enabled by European countenance and aid, to "found its commonwealth on the corner-stone of slavery," then, indeed, may come the danger of similar scenes of reckless fury and despair. As yet, and in the event of the final triumph of the North, no such catastrophe need be dreaded.[15]

Count Agénor de Gasparin was a frequent writer on the English scene in the Victorian era. His comments on "English Christianity" and slavery are well worth reproducing:

> "Let us beware of calumniating the generous movements of humanity, when, here and there, they show themselves in the current of history. There is a shrewd scepticism which looks at moral grandeur only to condemn it,

which estimates all noble impulses with cool calculation of their money value. The Christian public opinion of Britain wrenched from Parliament the Act of Emancipation some thirty years ago; yet have there been wanting voices to insinuate that this act, the glory of the century, was, at bottom, nothing but a Machiavellian calculation? Have we forgotten the resistance made to that act by vested interests, not simply in the colonies, but in the city of London? Was it not opposed by some of the leading representatives of the traditional party of England? Did not predictions of ruin abound — ruin to the planters, ruin to English manufactures, ruin to British seaports? And was it not, at last, in full view of these sinister prophecies, a measure accomplished by the combined and persevering efforts of churches, of societies, of philanthropists, by multitudinous prayers and petitions of men, and women, and children, rather than by the deliberate will of statesmen? Yet the summary judgement may still be heard, "The emancipation of the negroes was a chef d'oeuvre of British perfidy."[16]

The author reflects further in a subsequent commentary:

Yes, for long months, English Christians have not had, as it were, a single word of encouragement to place at the service of those who were combating and suffering for a noble cause. Not a meeting, not an address; the journals which serve as organs to the principal churches have almost all made it their study to discredit the movement, to point out with an accent of triumph the mortifications of the republic, to exaggerate the successes of the South, and deprecate those of the North, to deny that slavery was in question, to legitimatize the separation, to present as a desirable ideal the definitive maintenance of a Southern Confederacy…. The silence of English Christians is a universal calamity.

One would say at times that political England alone remained, while Christian England had disappeared. English Christians have succeeded in persuading themselves that slavery is not the question in the United States. How? Truly, I cannot yet succeed in comprehending. The fact is certain, notwithstanding, and it alone explains the attitude which has grieved us so deeply. By virtue of a marvelous transformation, the same men whom English opinion formerly condemned with just severity, have become almost interesting since, by treason and perjury, by pillaging public property, and repudiating private debts; taking care, moreover, to proclaim the sanctity of slavery, they have endeavoured to overthrow their free constitution, and have supplicated foreign powers to aid in the destruction of their country.

Whence comes such a metamorphosis? Whence comes it that the question of slavery, which formerly figured alone in the debates of the North and South, and which also figured alone in the ordinance of secession, fades away all at once, and passes in the eyes of English Christians as preserving only a secondary part? I need not again inquire how. I limit myself to affirming, and no one will contradict me, that if, before the too well received sophisms of these last years, it has been announced to Europe that a President opposed to the extension of slavery was about to be elected, the English Christians would have manifested the liveliest joy. And if it had then been added, that the South would break the Union on account of such an election, it would have been thence concluded that slavery was alone in question, since the mere threat of arresting its extension sufficed to precipitate the South into an armed revolt.[17]

Such were Europeans writing of American slavery. No account of slavery in America, however, would be complete without a reference to the writings of Frederick Douglass.

Frederick Augustus Washington Bailey was born on February 7, 1817, at Tuckahoe, Maryland, the son of a Negro female slave, and of a father unknown but thought to be white. He escaped from slavery in 1838 and fled to New York City and then to New Bedford, Massachusetts, where he worked as a laborer and managed to elude slave hunters. He changed his name to Douglass in an effort to mislead his stalkers.

Douglass was befriended by abolitionists and became the spokesman for the Negro slave. His autobiography, *Narrative of the Life of Frederick Douglass — An American Slave*, appeared in 1845 to considerable reaction, and Douglass became a militant anti-slavery leader.

In August, 1832, my master attended a Methodist camp-meeting held in the Bay-side, Talbot county, and there experienced religion. I indulged a faint hope that his conversion would lead him to emancipate his slaves, and that, if he did not do this, it would, at any rate make him more kind and humane. I was disappointed in both these respects. It neither made him to be humane to his slaves, nor to emancipate them. Prior to his conversion, he relied upon his own depravity to shield and sustain him in his savage barbarity; but after his conversion, he found religious sanction and support for his slave holding cruelty. He made the greatest pretensions to piety. His house was the house of prayer. He prayed morning, noon, and night. He very soon distinguished himself, among his brethren, and was soon made a class-leader and exhorter....[18]

Were I to be again reduced to the chains of slavery, next to that of enslavement, I should regard being a slave of a religious master the greatest calamity that could befall me. For of all the slave holders with whom I have ever met, religious slave holders are the worst. I have ever found them the meanest and basest, the most cruel and cowardly, of all others.

My blood boils as I think of the bloody manner in which Messrs. Wright Fairbanks and Garrison West, both class-leaders, in connection with many others, rushed in upon us with sticks and stones, and broke up our virtuous little Sabbath school, at St. Michael's — all calling themselves Christians! humble followers of the Lord Jesus Christ!

We have men-stealers for ministers, women-whippers for missionaries, and cradle-plunderers for church members. The man who wields the blood-clotted cowskin during the week fills the pulpit on Sunday, and claims to be a minister of the meek and lowly Jesus. The man who robs me of my earnings at the end of each week meets me as a class-leader on Sunday morning, to show me the way of life, and the path of salvation. He who sells my sister, for purposes of prostitution, stands forth as the pious advocate of purity. He who proclaims it as a religious duty to read the Bible denies me the right of learning to read the name of God who made me. He who is the religious advocate of marriage robs whole millions of its sacred influence, and leaves them to the ravages of wholesale pollution. The warm defender of the sacredness of the family relation is the same that scatters whole families, — sundering husbands and wives, parents and children, sisters and brothers, — leaving the hut vacant, and the hearth desolate. We see the thief preaching against theft, and the adulterer against adultery. We have men sold to build churches, women sold to support the gospel, and babes sold to purchase Bibles for the poor heathen! all for the glory of God and the good of souls! The slave auctioneer's bell and the church-going bell chime in with each other, and the bitter cries of the heart-broken slave are drowned in the religious shouts of his pious master. Revivals of religion and revivals of the slave-trade go hand in hand together. The slave prison and the church stand near each other. The clanking of fetters and the rattling of chains in the prison, and the pious psalm and solemn prayer in the church, may be heard at the same time. The dealers in the bodies and souls of men erect their stand in the presence of the pulpit, and they mutually help each other. The dealer gives his blood-stained gold to support the pulpit, and the pulpit, in return, covers his infernal business with the garb of Christianity. Here we have religion and robbery the allies of each other — devils dressed in angels' robes, and hell presenting the semblance of paradise....[19]

Is this the Christianity of our history? Is this the companion of God?

2. Emancipation

In his annual message to Congress on the 1 December 1862, President Lincoln outlined his intention to emancipate the Negroes of America:

> I recommend the adoption of the following resolution and articles amendatory to the Constitution of the United States: "Every State, wherein slavery now exists, which shall abolish the same therein, at any time, or times, before the first day of January, in the year of our Lord one thousand and eight hundred and sixty three, shall receive compensation from the United States.... As to the first article, the main points are: first, emancipation; secondly, the length of time for consummating it — thirty-seven years; and thirdly, the compensation. The emancipation will be unsatisfactory to the advocates of perpetual slavery; but the length of time should greatly mitigate their dissatisfaction. The time spares both races from the evils of sudden derangement — in fact, from the necessity of any derangement — while most of those whose habitual course of thought will be disturbed by the measure will have passed away before its consummation. They will never see it. Another class will hail the prospect of emancipation, but deprecate the length of time. They will feel that it gives too little to the now living slaves. But it really gives them much. It saves them from the vagrant destitution which must largely attend immediate emancipation in localities where their numbers are very great; and it gives the inspiring assurance that their posterity shall be free forever. The plan leaves to each State, choosing to act under it, to abolish slavery now, or at the end of the century, or at any intermediate time, or by degrees, extending over the whole or any part of the period; and it obliges no two states to proceed alike. It also provides for compensation, and generally the mode of making it. This, it would seem, must further mitigate the dissatisfaction of those who favor perpetual slavery, and especially of those who are to receive the compensation.

Doubtless some of those who are to pay, and not to receive will object. Yet the measure is both just and economical. In a certain sense the liberation of slaves is the destruction of property — property acquired by descent, or by purchase, the same as any other property. It is no less true for having been often said, that the people of the south are more responsible for the original introduction of this property, than are the people of the north; and when it is remembered how unhesitatingly we all use cotton and sugar, and share the profits of dealing in them, it may not be quite safe to say, that the south has been more responsible than the north for its continuance. If then, for the common object, this property is to be sacrificed is it not just that it be done at a common charge?

On 1 January 1863, a second proclamation was issued by Lincoln:

Whereas, in the twenty-second day of September, in the year of our Lord one thousand eight hundred and sixty-two, a proclamation was issued by the President of the United States, containing, among other things, the following, to wit:

That on the first day of January, in the year of our Lord one thousand eight hundred and sixty-three, all persons held as slaves within any state or designated part of a state, the people whereof shall then be in rebellion against the United States, shall be then, thenceforward, and forever, free; and the Executive Government of the United States, including the military and naval authority thereof, will recognize and maintain the freedom of such persons, and will do no act or acts to repress such persons, or any of them, in any efforts they may make for their actual freedom.

Now, therefore, I, Abraham Lincoln, President of the United States, by virtue of the power in me vested as commander-in-chief of the army and navy of the United States, in time of actual armed rebellion against the authority and government of the United States, and as a fit and necessary war measure for suppressing said rebellion, do, on this first day of January, in the year of our Lord one thousand eight hundred and sixty-three, and in accordance with my purpose so to do, publicly proclaim for the full period of one hundred days from the day first above mentioned, order and designate as the states and parts of states wherein the people thereof, respectively, are this day in rebellion against the United States....

And by the virtue of the power and for the purpose aforesaid, I do order and declare that all persons held as slaves within the designated states are, and henceforward shall be, free; and that the Executive Government of the United States, including the military and naval authorities thereof, will recognize and maintain the freedom of said persons.

And I hereby enjoin upon the people so declared to be free to abstain from all violence, unless in necessary self-defense; and I recommend to them that in all cases when allowed, they labor faithfully and for reasonable wages.

And I further declare and make known that such persons, of suitable condition, will be received into the armed service of the United States to garrison forts, positions, stations, and other places, and to man vessels of all sorts in said service.

And upon this act, sincerely believed to be an act of justice, warranted by the Constitution upon military necessity, I invoke the considerate judgment of mankind and the gracious favor of Almighty God. In witness whereof, I have hereunto set my hand and caused the seal of the United States to be affixed.

Done at the city of Washington this first day of January, in the year of our Lord one thousand eight hundred and sixty-three, and of the Independence of the United States of America the eighty-seventh.

Much was written in the mid–Victorian era in British journals of "morality and principle," and many writings claimed that President Lincoln's Emancipation Proclamation lacked these valiant criteria of British society. It not only lacked morality and principle but was "un-anti-slavery." This was the judgment of British journals representing a British governing class which condoned a British foreign policy that conducted some eighty colonial wars in some forty locations during the nineteenth century. These wars contrived to tyrannize, to dominate, and to enslave the indigenous populations of those countries.

The soul of the ruling ten thousand and the vitality of their pocket books were committed to the cause of the Confederacy. There was no lack of justification offered. The English were convinced that slavery was an abomination. With the expressed displeasure, however, there were conditions. The emancipation of the Negro should be gradual; emancipation would be the result of a Confederate victory; amelioration, not emancipation, was the solution; the North was not interested in freeing the slave, but only in empire; and, of course, a servile rebellion would ensue.

A decade before the war in America, on 3 January 1854, *The Times* set its standards for emancipation. In printing a letter by a "STATES-MAN" *The Times* proclaimed its position on slavery in America:

> Could instant emancipation be granted? As well might you yourselves let loose your beasts of burden and drought cattle to pasture in the fertile fields of England, while you took on your own shoulders the harness and the yoke. Or would gradual emancipation be preferred? Gradual emancipation and gradual amputation I reckon in the same category.

The importance of trade was not to be ignored in the same issue of *The Times*, or by its readership:

> After much reflection, I am happy to differ from those who are of the opinion that the institution of slavery will ever prove the occasion or the means of riving asunder the American Union. I can never be persuaded that the undefined and equivocal rights of three million, or of three times three

millions of blacks, who have in every war gained by the transplantations of their ancestors, will upset the definite interests of 25 millions of whites, which in 25 years will become the interests of 50 millions.

Although *The Times* often referred to morality and virtue, it was obvious that neither of these fine attributes would replace the need for free trade, as *The Times* suggested on 21 October 1861:

> If the North does not emancipate the slaves, why should it forbid the transmission of the produce which slavery gives to mankind? No principle is involved in the contest, and so Englishmen, they think, may with a safe conscience take which side they like.

We are again reminded of the power of trade in *The Times,* 21 January 1862: "Although the North, no doubt, will try to emancipate the slaves, slavery will exist as long as the welfare of so many nations depends on its existence."

Trade and Commerce must be respected, not only for the profits provided for the English ruling class, but because it would lead to emancipation in the Confederacy. So claimed *Blackwood's Edinburgh Magazine* (December 1861) 757:

> We all pray for universal emancipation. We have made enormous sacrifices in the cause ourselves. We think that the condition of the negro in the Southern States will remain long what it now is, but that, if European intercourse be established with the Confederacy, and she be admitted into the family of nations, commerce, always favourable to freedom, will then generally but surely effect far more humane results than those which the most sincere Abolitionist can ever attain.

The principal objection to emancipation voiced by the British press was the imminent danger of a servile rebellion, an event for which *The Economist* (6 July 1861) 732 issued warning:

> In such a condition of national affairs as America has reached, there is one thing which is even more clearly and more monstrously a crime than Slavery — and that is the fomenting of a general insurrection of the Slaves. Civil war is bad enough, but servile war is incomparably worse. And a servile war on a scale and with elements never before dreamed of in history, created for their own purposes by one of the parties in an internal political dispute, would be about the most enormous sin ever laid upon a human conscience.

Of course, the London press rose to the defense of the women and children to be murdered by the rampaging Negro. There was no mention of the plight of the Negro women as there was no mention of the treatment of Irish women by the virtuous English in *The Examiner,* 11 October 1862:

From the first we predicted that in this detestable quarrel, abolition would be the last arm of vengeance; that it would be made a pretense of till the game should appear desperate, and then resorted to as a sure stroke of mischief, — sure to carry the war of the knife to private homes where women and children are left undefended, their natural protectors being in the field, — sure to instigate some malcontent black blood to acts of ferocity like those which disturbed St. Domingo, though not sure of any important general result. A firebrand is thrown into a powder magazine, on the calculation that though it may fail of a general explosion, it will fire the loose powder.

The Glasgow Herald, 7 October 1861:

We are convinced that Slavery is a gigantic evil, and that measures ought at once to be taken, and ought long ago to have been taken, for having it removed. But we are no less convinced that these measures ought not to be rash and precipitate. It is perfectly true that the negro, by the law of nature, has as much right to freedom as other men; and that the 4,000,000 slaves in the Southern States of America have been unjustly deprived of that right. But those who argue on these grounds that the right ought at once to be restored, forget that these poor creatures have been deprived not only of their right, but of their ability to use the right.

The Glasgow Herald, 26 March 1862:

Slavery is an iniquity, and a gigantic iniquity, in spite of all that its advocates can say in its favour. There is no law in heaven nor earth that can justify the stealing of human beings from their own country, and making slaves of them and their posterity to all generations — to be bought, sold, flogged, and forced to labour by, and for the pecuniary advantage of other men. The negro has as much natural inherent right to freedom as the white man has; and so long as this freedom is denied him so long is the relation iniquitous, and slavery an outrage on human nature.

The British press had great difficulty with emancipation, and in differentiating between the actions of the North in not accepting the Negro socially, and those of the South in holding the negro in slavery. Asked *The Saturday Review* (18 January 1862) 62:

can 4,000,000 uneducated slaves be emancipated at once without danger to the lives, families, and properties of their former masters? Or could 4,000,000 new free negroes be received into the bosom of the New York and Philadelphia communities without intensifying the keen disgust which the citizens of the Northern States already regard the "Nigger" and all his belongings to the remotest degree?

There remained great faith among the press that the Confederacy would free the negro slave upon independence, a faith expressed in *The London Examiner*, 26 September 1863:

> We utterly detest and loathe slavery as the greatest crime that can be committed between man and man. It is better to kill than to enslave; and never was a palliation more preposterous than the pretense that a weak race could be strengthened by filling the pockets of the strong out of fruits of its forced labour. That slavery is too false to co-exist anywhere eternally with the free and wholesome growth of civilization, we do not for an instant doubt. Uninfluenced by selfish battle cries of trading politicians, left to provide for its own welfare in a distinct Confederacy with the old slave system confined within its borders, the South must either fall back into a mean rank among the nations, or push freely forward with the rest. As a separate state it would, in the course of nature, live not only to feel the need but find the way of clearing from its soil the baneful growth, of which the roots have struck so deep, and to which, baneful as it is, no man, slave and free, look for the moment as their only source of bread.

The Standard represented all that was odious and loathsome in the English press, as the following passage from *The Standard*, 20 July 1864, suggests:

> Through some mysterious fatality the Negro has been a huge affliction to the human race. For a hundred years past, wherever the civilized nations have interfered, either to enslave or to emancipate him, misery, rancour, and interminable carnage have ensued. His black skin is now held up in the New World, as a banner around which frantic myriads are fighting and perishing. He has established horrible traditions in the western Island of the Atlantic. He lures Christian travellers to die amid the equatorial depths of his own fervid and feverish continent, the coasts of which are dark with the records of European mortality, and a melancholy squadron designed to protect him pays its annual sacrifice on his behalf. Without touching the question whether all this is right or necessary, or what our duties are to the rest of mankind, we must admit the broad, patent, historical fact. The negro has been the MOLACH of our century. To him the world has offered up awful human sacrifices. He has kept the earth in a state of perpetual commotion, whether as a labourer in the cotton plantations of the West Indies, a slave on the fields of Carolina, a coolie in a French merchantman ... in all directions where his footprints remain we may be sure that strife, slaughter, dissension, and squabbling have followed them.

The conceit and self-aggrandizement of the British press was conspicuous in all discussions of slavery, as evidenced in *The Daily Telegraph*, 21 March 1861:

> The emancipation of the negro slaves in the colonies of the West Indies belonging to the Crown of England was one of the most hazardous, the

costliest, and the least satisfactory experiments ever undertaken from motives of pure philanthropy and a deference to public opinion. The philanthropy has been denied over and over again by our enemies; but time has manifested the truth, and shown that the abolition of West Indian slavery was well nigh quixotic in its self-sacrificing benevolence.

The Saturday Review (18 January 1862) 62:

> Could the mulatto—whom equality of condition, the admission into the honourable careers, and the protecting favour of the British Government in British colonies have not invariably conciliated, or made a contented and docile citizen — could he bear to submit to the Pariah life which society and government in America would impose on him? Could he bear an existence embittered by all the contempt which is lavished on the negro, with the addition of hatred and reviling, from which the negro is saved by his comparative innocuousness? When we look at these various points, we may well congratulate ourselves on having long ago turned the corner of Emancipation, and surmounted its worst dangers. The people of colour, too, in our tropical colonies, may well congratulate themselves on the good fortune which has placed them under the mild and benevolent sway of Great Britain.

Pamphlets printed during the American Civil War took a different view of the conflict and of slavery than the majority of the British press. By far the greatest number favored Lincoln's Emancipation Proclamation, the cause of the free states, and were disappointed at the crude and heedless manner in which their fellow Englishmen treated the attempts of the North to combat the insurgency of the Confederacy and emancipation of the Negro.

> Are there not some who are weary of palliating its enormities [emancipation] and eulogizing its champions? Are there not people amongst us who, two years ago, were shocked that the North should have gone to war for any cause less holy than emancipation, but who now, when emancipation is the policy of the North, are shocked that emancipation should be accomplished by means so unholy as war?— people who, while the Republican policy of limiting slavery, and thus providing for its eventual termination through gradual extinction, was possible and acted on, slighted it as half-hearted and temporizing, but who now, when, through the obstinacy of the slave holders, that policy is no longer practical — now, when the alternative lies between immediate emancipation and a triumphant slave power — exclaim that they only approve of emancipation which is gradual?— people who, in their jealousy for the honour of the negro, have so little patience with the American prejudice against colour, that the social slights passed upon the coloured race in the Free States are in their eyes more heinous sins than the selling and flogging and branding and burning, which are the incidents of their position in the South, yet these are the jealous sticklers for the negro's honour![20]

There were Englishmen who were astonished and perplexed at the reaction of their fellow Britishers to Mr. Lincoln's Emancipation Proclamation. Instead of encouraging those who were fighting the battle of freedom, the message of deliverance had been received coldly and callously.

> One would have thought that when Abraham Lincoln's proclamation was published, declaring that the slaves of every Rebel State would on the 1st of January next be thenceforth and forever free, that every English heart would have thrilled with joy, and sent forth one voice, loud as the ocean, from one end of the kingdom to the other, to encourage the hearts and nerve the arms of those who are now fighting the battles of freedom. But no: the message of deliverance for the captive has been received coldly and unmoved; while all "hell is stirred from beneath." Hear how the Confederates rant and rave, and clamour for blood. It has been proposed to hoist the black flag, and show no quarter to man, woman, or child. The Virginian legislature has declared that no man shall be considered to have committed a crime against that State who shall put to death any one found trying to give in any way effect to the Proclamation of Emancipation; and the demoniacal cry has been taken up by the ghouls of the English press. The proclamation "means nothing else than an inciting to assassination," bellows *The Times*. "This cowardly resort of a desperate cause — this message of midnight murder," screams *The Standard*; and the fiendish yell is echoed by the whole pack of anti-slavery hounds, that is bringing disgrace to the English name…. There we see a rebellion, began in the interests of Slavery, in order "to extend and perpetuate it," resulting in its utter overthrow and annihilation.[21]

To fellow citizens who have upbraided the Lincoln government and the free states for their lack of movement in the manumission of the Negro:

> What has the North DONE for abolition? Government measures are the only authorized exponents in answer to this question. Facts are better than words: — Slavery has been formally forbidden in all the territories of the Union. Slavery has been abolished in (the District of) Columbia, over which Congress has power by the Constitution. Compensation has also been offered from the treasury of the United States to any separate State which shall emancipate its slaves. A treaty has been entered into with Great Britain for the more effectual suppression of the slave trade. And wherever the Northern armies go, fugitive slaves are received in large numbers. As many as 60,000 have escaped from Missouri alone, and 80,000 from Virginia. At Port Royal 10,000 are protected by the Federal flag within a few miles of Charleston. Above all the President has proclaimed that after the first of January the slaves in all States continuing in rebellion shall be declared free, and that the power of the United States' government shall be employed in accomplishing such emancipation.
> Many people in England object to this proclamation. They say — "Why

was it not issued at first, on the ground of principle, and not after a period of ineffectual conflict, as a mere exigency of war? And why proclaim liberty only to the slaves of rebels, thus compelling to do right to the negro, those who do wrong to the government; and rewarding those who do right to the government, with the power of continuing to do wrong to their slaves?" It must still be remembered that President Lincoln was restrained by the laws he was sworn to administer, from interfering in the domestic institutions of the several States. The most he can do is to offer compensation. He cannot himself emancipate. But what he cannot do at all in any loyal State, nor by ordinary law in any rebel State, he can do in his military capacity, when required by the exigencies of war. He is restrained by the Constitution from abolishing slavery because he thinks it impolitic or wicked. This is a question for each State to decide. But in quelling a rebellion he may use whatever means become necessary for sustaining the government.

With the slaves as labourers, the white population of the South are disengaged for war. Proclaim freedom to those slaves, and they will either escape, or the Southern army will be crippled by the large numbers needed to guard them. It is on this ground that the President justifies his proclamation as being in accordance with law. He is blamed for doing that which alone he considers within his powers; while that which he is censured for not doing was impossible without breaking his oath and violating the Constitution. Feeling strongly, but not too strongly, of the monstrous wickedness of slavery, and not experiencing the difficulties of Mr. Lincoln's position, it is natural we should think that had we his power, we would at the first have declared slavery to be sinful, and fought against it on the highest and holiest grounds.[22]

Where were the Britons who for decades bathed in the self-glory of the emancipation of the slave in the British West Indies, and did not hesitate to cast abuses on the North for its complicity in slavery when Mr. Lincoln announced that slavery should go no further?

For thirty years, we have not ceased to reproach the North for its complicity with the South; yet, on the day when it repudiates it, on the day when, at the price of prodigious sacrifices, it utters the decisive speech, "Slavery shall go no further," on the day when it rejects that violent and gross policy which may be defined in a single sentence, the policy of slavery — on that day, we have for it only disdain, coldness, and distrust — on that day, we seem to have but one thought, to discover the weak sides of its conduct, to demonstrate that it does a generous deed without generosity, that its cause is not its cause, and the election of Mr. Lincoln was wrought by men not in the least affected by the question of slavery.[23]

The Republican government acted cautiously as the Constitution gave it no power to abolish slavery in the States:

We are fighting for human freedom. Obscure as this may be to foreigners, it is patent enough to us. It is true that the administration did not proclaim universal emancipation, and that it has interfered cautiously with slavery. Nor should it be condemned for this, since it acted under a Constitution which gave it no more power to abolish it directly in the States than in Turkey. But he is blind to the affairs of the United States who does not know these two things: — 1st, The South arose in rebellion for the sake of slavery; 2nd, The North put the present administration into power with a determination to do what it could, prudently and constitutionally, to check its progress. The South clearly saw that the system, if restricted, must sooner or later perish, and with it the ill-gotten wealth, the legal power, the political importance, and the feudal nobility which rested upon it. In anticipation of the crisis, it sought for slavery access to the territories, the possession of California, and then of Kansas, and the right of ingress, egress, regress, and progress for slave property in free States.[24]

As with the mainstream of the British press there were pamphleteers who regarded slavery as beneficial for the Negro, and hardly as iniquitous for denying the Negro slave the very fruits of his labor:

Had no civil war existed, had the South been in a state of peace and prosperity, the sudden emancipation of the slaves meant this, — A black population of four millions, accustomed to be plentifully fed and sufficiently clad, without any forethought or care on their part, with exemption from the care of providing for their old age, or providing for their children during infancy, or at all; on the other hand, a subjection to compulsory (and it may be assumed sometimes excessive) labour. The source of their maintenance, and the exemption from many of the cares that fall on the rest of mankind, was their labour; the fruits of which were received, husbanded, managed, and so applied by their owners. In the eye of the slave, labour is necessarily the evil of life, and the first use to which freedom will be applied by him, will be the enjoyment of rest. But his appetite for those things which his labour had procured is undiminished, while the source from which his appetites were to be satisfied is dried up; he cannot rest and also be fed, but he will rest and risk starvation. The slightest consideration would have convinced any man that it would be so; and that voluntary contracts for labour, and the fulfillment thereof, by the freed man, would be a rare exception. It was easy to foresee that a sudden emancipation, under the most favourable circumstances, would result in the waste of estates for want of labour, and the inundation of the impoverished country with hordes of lazy, starving paupers.

The attempted emancipation of the four millions of slaves by Mr. Lincoln's proclamation, on the score of statesmanship, was the greatest blunder, and on the score of morality, the greatest public crime of modern times. According to the authors of the proclamation, the slaves were uninstructed, oppressed, and smarting under their wrongs. The whole male white population of the South was in the field; the helpless old men, the women, and the children only were at home; the intention of the proclamation could only be to let loose an irresistible number of oppressed savages to wreak their vengeance on their helpless white victims.[25]

Arguing for English recognition of the Confederacy, one observer wrote:

The capacities and prospects of the negro race are very difficult questions. Aide toi, et Dieu t'aidera is a great rule in human affairs. But, neither in Africa, where they have been left to themselves, nor, transplanted to the midst of other races, have the Ethiopians been able to help themselves, and advance in civilization and happiness as the Mongols and Caucasians have done; while such is the repugnance towards them of the white races that know them best, that the people of the free states of North America, professing to be friendly, keep them in a position of painful and insulting degradation, and are planning to get rid of them entirely. "I repeat the assertion," says a southern senator, "that four millions of the negro race in this union are to-day under better circumstances, morally, socially, and religiously, than four millions of the same race anywhere upon the habitable globe. I submit that proposition to the Senate; and if there be four millions of the negro race so happy, well contented, well provided for, so moral, religious, and occupying so high a social position, tell me where they are to be found." There is, unfortunately, a good deal of truth in this. Not that we are thereby to conclude that slavery is justifiable, still less to look without reprobation on the harshness and cruelty which too often accompany it in the United States. Yet all these considerations should impress strongly on us the difficulty of the subject, and lead us to be very cautious about dogmatizing on complex practical questions, on such uncertain bases as abstract ideas of equality of races and equality of rights, in opposition to those who know and have to deal with the practical difficulties. We have been cured of the assumptions that all nations are adapted for the representative system, and that a Constitution such as the British would be a panacea for all political evils. Is it not equally an assumption that, because personal freedom is good for men in general, immediate or speedy emancipation is the best thing for those of the negro race now in slavery in America? Is it necessary for us to profess to understand and see our way clearly to the settlement of all the difficult questions in the affairs of all the nations of the earth? We have had somewhat too much of this self-sufficient dogmatism; and it might be well for us to refrain from positive judgments on matters we have not the means of judging of, and from meddling with what does not concern us.[26]

3. Democracy

As to the Civil War in America, the British press reported, as did all members of the Fourth Estate, what their readership demanded. The conflict in America became the rallying call for all Englishmen fearing an extended franchise, and the resulting democracy. The disingenuous claim that the victory of the Confederacy would lead to the amelioration and emancipation of the Negro because of "the moral pressure of Europe" would not survive careful scrutiny.

In the nineteenth century the British press developed an interest in the Founding Fathers based on what the press regarded as a commitment of the founders of the Republic to restrain democracy. *The Glasgow Herald*, 5 November 1864, illustrated this:

> When the political institutions of the Federal States of America are contrasted with those of Great Britain, one cannot help being struck, not so much by the wide differences between the two, as with the harmonious workings of the one in comparison with the rude jolting of the other. The contrast shows the superiority of that form of government which has grown through the centuries with the growth of the nation, which has adapted itself to the changing thoughts, habits, and feelings of the people, and which has fitted itself to every condition of national life, as the bark fits itself to the development of the tree. There can be no doubt that the eminent men who framed the American Constitution produced a very able piece of State workmanship ... but though it is not yet a century old time has already worn holes in it, nay, we may almost say rent it asunder.

The Economist (1 June 1861) 591 agreed:

> The moral is a plain one. The Constitution of the United States was framed

upon a vicious principle. The framers were anxious to resist the force of democracy — to control its fury and restrain its outbursts. They either could not or did not take the one effectual means of so doing; they did not place the substantial power in the hands of men of education and property. They hoped to control the democracy by paper checks and constitutional devices. The history we have sketched evinces the result; it shows that these checks have produced unanticipated, incalculable, and fatal evil but have not attained the beneficial end for which they were selected. They may have ruined the Union, but they have not controlled democracy.

The Quarterly Review 110 (1861) 249, pondered a return to democracy:

The United States were the first modern instance of the application of the democratic theory to the government of a large state. Even then it was not done without hesitation. A return to monarchy was at one time agitated, and the movement attained sufficient importance to alarm the democracy considerably. Washington appears to have sanctioned the new system without any strong abstract opinion in its favour, simply on the ground that in the exasperated condition of public feeling against the only monarch of whom they had any practical experience, it would have been impossible to bend the Puritan neck to a monarch's rule without certainly provoking a civil war. The American democracy was destined for no such noble end as the Romans. Its institutions have not fallen battling with the common enemies of all institutions — the mobs who form a standing menace to law and order and a standing excuse to tyranny. It has sunk from the decrepitude of premature old age. But the institution which should have held that nation together and guarded its sanity as a state perished from the same maladies that have marked the extinction of the most corrupt and most effete of the monarchies of Europe. The same disease which sapped the strength and ensured the fall of the monarchy of France in the last century, and the monarchy of Naples in this, has proved fatal to the scarcely-fledged powers of the American Republic. The same deadly symptoms have shown themselves in all three cases: the discontent of not merely the ruder masses, but of whole sections of its subjects, and the utter lack in the hour of need of rulers who could perform the commonest duties of government.

The Electoral College was established to contain democracy, *The Quarterly Review* 110 (1861) 263 notes:

The indirect elections have become an empty form, and the President is practically chosen by the direct vote of the whole population. The independent judiciary was another effective check, wisely devised if it could have been upheld, but which the encroaching spirit of democracy could ill brook.... The omnipotence of the majority has not been contented with a mere victory over constitutional restraints. It is not only supreme in the making and the administering of laws, but it exercised a despotic control over the life and actions of private individuals more minute and more penetrating than it would be physically in the power of an absolute monarch to carry out....

The Saturday Review gave vent to all the frustrations of the ruling class press. The failings of democracy, real or imagined, are exploited. Britain will not surrender to the will of the people.

American democracy and the extended franchise stuck hard in the throats of the ten thousand. Men like John Bright, the "Birmingham demagogue" were ridiculed for suggesting that England might look favorably on American institutions, as in the following item from *The Saturday Review* (1 February 1862) 118:

The Birmingham demagogue, in a series of elaborate and effective harangues, prepared his countrymen to bestow a particular close attention on the moral and political results of democracy precisely at the time when it was on the point of signally falsifying all his theories, and destroying his authority as a public teacher. Democracy, we were assured, is essentially pacific. It is only aristocracy and monarchy that love to play at soldiers, and keep up enormous armaments, and set quiet nations by the ears for the gratification of the insensate pride and sordid greed of the ruling few. While the dogma thus thundered in our ears from a score of platforms was still fresh in all minds, democracy was seen to plunge into one of the most aimless, hopeless, and ferocious wars known to history, and to raise armies large beyond all modern precedent in proportion to the population from which they are drawn. Democracy, we were also told, is essentially a cheap form of government. It secures the maximum of efficiency at the minimum cost. Where the will of the "intelligent working-man" is the sole and supreme law of the State, industry is safe against having its earnings squandered by an unprincipled and incapable Executive. Economy is guaranteed by the vigilance which the enlightened self-interest of the sovereign multitude naturally exercises over the acts of responsible trustees of its own selection. A Government created by, and dependent upon, the universal suffrage of a labouring class every man of which can read cheap newspapers and write his name at the foot of a voting ticket, has no choice but to disburse conscientiously supplies which are voted with an almost niggardly frugality. Under such a Government the tax-payer is sure of getting the fullest value for his money; and waste, jobbery, peculation, and corruption would be unknown. Democracy eschews national debt. Democracy has no "out-door relief" for privileged and titled idlers. It is only the wicked Old World oligarchies that job, and bribe, and squander, and run up debt, and saddle unborn generations with the liabilities incurred by their criminal prodigality. Such was the political philosophy inculcated by the Radical agitator immediately before the outbreak in his own model Republic, of one of the very hottest fits of reckless extravagance that ever took possession of any Government of people from the beginning of time.

The Times was in full agreement with *The Saturday Review* on 12 August 1861:

> The theories attributing immeasurable superiority to Republican forms of government have all been falsified in the plainest and most striking manner, and the last six months have proved beyond all question that the preponderance of popular will without check or limit is at least as likely to hurry a nation into war and debt as the caprice of the most absolute despot or the intrigues of the most selfish of aristocracies. The old French cry of "Fraternity or Death" was interpreted to mean "Be my brother or I will kill you," and that after the capture of Fort Sumter was the sentiment of the North. The people would listen to nothing but plans for an immediate campaign. Their statesmen seized the opportunity of establishing a "gigantic system of outdoor relief" for themselves. In this manner a dictator will deal with universal suffrage and other popular institutions. For the last ten years we have been told, with every circumstance of emphasis and adjuration, of American institutions on which every friend of economy, peace, and good government should fix his eyes. War was distinctly represented as the work of an interested aristocracy, anxious only for its own advancement. We were assured that with an unrestricted suffrage, and with electoral laws under which plain working citizens could make their voices heard, the old extravagance of a class Government would rapidly disappear. Debts were contracted and wars were fought to gratify an aristocracy subsisting on the taxation of the people. America was the model of a better system. There the wisdom and moderation of citizens managing their own affairs showed itself in peace, thrift, and contentment. Such were the points kept obtrusively before us. If the reader will refer to any speech of the Manchester orator he will find the Government of the United States extravagantly eulogized for the very qualities of which it is now proved to be utterly destitute, and the Americans exalted beyond all other people on account of gifts which it is plain they never possessed.... Our criticisms are suggested not by any joy over American troubles, but by feelings of the deepest and most immediate self-interest. When we see that unlimited democracy conveys not the slightest security against the worst of wars and the most reckless extravagance, we may apply the moral at home, and congratulate ourselves that the old British Constitution has not been precipitately remodeled after a Manchester design.

It was the "sovereignty of the people" which disturbed *The Times* on 18 October 1861:

> There is, we think, reason to believe that the more educated Americans see the real causes of their misfortune. Far be it from us to dogmatize about democracy, or to attribute the civil war to Republican institutions. The secession of the South was certainly not the necessary result of any form of Government. Yet it is not too much to say that the form which

democracy has taken during the last 30 years, or since the Presidency of General Jackson, was not unlikely to lead to such consequences. The doctrine of sovereignty of the people came to mean the sovereignty of any section of them, and half-a-dozen ruffians thought themselves entitled to hang a man on the ground that supreme power was vested in themselves. Amid all the turmoil of this war there is, we think, a change in the morals of the community to be descried. Where things had become so bad any alteration might seem an improvement, and it would be that those who hope for better things are doomed to disappointment.

The Times faulted democracy for the threat of war during the Trent Affair on 10 December 1861:

> If we are dragged into a war, it is now clear that it will be democracy who will force us into it. It will not be the rich or the educated, but the ignorant and penniless who will make a war in which they have nothing to lose, and of the events of which they have no power of perception.

A.J.B. Beresford-Hope and Charles Mackay represented the true spirit of the ruling class of England. Neither Beresford-Hope nor Mackay was as truly interested in the emancipation of the Negro as in the fear of democracy. For Beresford-Hope it was the dread of "universal suffrage." For Mackay it was "ultra democracy."

Beresford-Hope could not remain tranquil with the fear of encroaching democracy. Clearly, his support of the Confederacy was not without concern of an extended franchise, not to the slave, but to the Englishman who might challenge the ruling class of Britain.

> The slave trade is utterly unjustifiable, and the middle passage is damnable, although we must own that the Negroes of America, descended as they are from the kidnapped victims of that horrible system, are not only christianized, but also educated and civilized, as those in Africa cannot be; but yet their civilization is not one which should entitle them to place their feet upon the white man's neck, as they would do if the "abolitionists" permit a reign of universal suffrage.[27]

A.J.B. Beresford-Hope deplored universal suffrage: "the practical workings of the American Constitution are overruled and trampled down by that miserable, levelling democracy and universal suffrage which is so rapidly landing the Northern States in a perfectly Assyrian despotism."[28]

Charles Mackay wrote twenty years after his career as war correspondent ended, much as he had corresponded in the employ of *The Times*. His distaste and fear of "ultra-democracy" was a constant in his writings:

The government of the people, by the people and for the people, has been for ages considered by sanguine believers in the innate goodness and wisdom of mankind to be the best of all possible forms of government; but neither poets nor philosophers have ever strictly defined what they meant by the "people" who were to form the ideal democracy. A democracy is really an aristocracy in the occult and unavowed estimate of those who constitute it, inasmuch as the males of full age, and in adequate possession of their mental faculties, consider themselves to the best for the purposes of governing the greater portion of their fellow-citizens. Whether the form of government be free and constitutional, or autocratic and despotic — the mass of mankind cannot justly be accredited with political wisdom or unselfish virtue. The hard and engrossing toil which is their inevitable lot; the desperate competition for the means of bare subsistence which, as their numbers increase, is forced upon them by natural causes, against which it is in vain to struggle; and the ignorance of high State policy, which the conditions of their daily existence prevent them from conquering by intelligent study and enlarged experience, — all these causes combine to render them unfit for the government of their wiser fellow-citizens. The greatest worshippers of the people, in the widest sense of the word, cannot claim for the vast majority — counted by heads, and man for man — the purity of motive and the high intelligence that should rule a great nation. The will of a bigoted and cruel majority led, in Europe and America, to the burning of witches, and to the relentless persecution of dissentients from established doctrine; and to a tyranny, a self-seeking, and a corruption, on the part of the arrogant, the needy, and the greedy, that form the majority — the imperium in imperio — in all countries, and more especially in countries that are supposed to be free, and whose opinions find expression in newspapers, caucuses, and in public meetings, where fluent oratory, rather than sound common-sense and cogent reasoning, sways the passions and flatters the prejudice of the multitude. In all widely extended or ultra-democracies — such as the United States are, and as Great Britain threatens to become at no distant period — the power of popular speakers, endowed with what is vulgarly but emphatically called "the gift of gab," is on the increase, and bids fair to supersede wise, silent, or ineloquent statesmanship, both in legislative assemblies and in the caucuses that strive to override them. To the mob of voters — who are ever flattered and carried away by the ornate and bewildering eloquence of professional talkers — the man who is known to be rich, and the manufacturer who employs hundreds, or perhaps thousands, of workpeople, has a chance infinitely greater of securing their votes than fall to the lot of the purist saint or the greatest intellectual giant who might solicit their suffrage. The wealth which an ultra-democracy greatly reverences, the members of an ultra-democracy will do their best to acquire — honestly if they can; but if honesty is difficult, inopportune, and slow or uncertain of fructification, they will acquire it by the contrary method, and at the expense, if occasion offers, for the country which their suffrages help to govern, and of which they are virtually the masters. Popular elections in all free countries, Great Britain not excepted, are commonly, if not inevitably, attended by practices more or less corrupt — especially when the constituencies, whether large or small, are composed, for the most part, of men condemned to daily manual labour and sordid engrossing pursuits, without leisure, taste, or opportunity for the acquisition of political knowledge. The great and fundamental error of ultra-democracy in all countries — and especially in the United States — is, that it teaches and allows the power of voting to be a right with which man is born, and not a privilege to be acquired by him, or conceded to him, not for his own benefit, but for that of the community. In Great Britain — though, under the influence of Radical doctrinaires and unscrupulous and ignorant demagogues, we are rapidly approaching to manhood suffrage, with an extension to womanhood suffrage in due time — the inherent right of any one to vote is now acknowledged. To teach the people — whether white or black — that the suffrage is a right which it is unjust and tyrannical to withhold from them, is to instill into the minds of the ignorant and instill needy among them that it is a right which they may turn to pecuniary and other personal advantage at the expense of the men of a superior class in society who are so eager in asking for its exercise in their favour. One of the foremost dangers to the stability of the American Union, and to the perpetuation of the public liberties, springs from the acknowledgement of the rights of millions of black men to the suffrage. Before the close of the great Civil War in 1865, when Abraham Lincoln, as a measure of expediency, or, as he deemed it, of military necessity, abolished slavery by a stroke of his pen, the negro population of the Southern States amounted to less than four million, and of the Northern and Western States at less than a half million. In 1884, the negroes in the Southern States numbered upwards of seven millions. The negro population all over the United States is calculated to increase at the rate of thirty-five per cent. in ten years, and the white population inclusive of the European immigration, at the rate of less than twenty-eight per cent. during the same period.... The desire is for ascendancy and dominion rather than for liberty — a passion which is the vice of all democracies. Great Britain is the first power in the world, and the United States desires to become so — vice the mother-country relegated into the second rank. This, disguise it as they may, is the leading passion in American hearts — a passion which cannot be gratified until the Republic becomes "one and indivisible." It was more to indulge this passion for unity of dominion, as we think has been made apparent in these pages, than for any innate love of the negro, or any real abhorrence of the immoral and cruel system which enslaved him, that they ignored State Rights — the real corner-stone of their liberty, if they would but know and confess it — that they waged war upon and ultimately conquered the South, by dint of superior wealth and numbers.[29]

The Times became interested in democracy. Not the lack of it in Britain, for democracy was virtually non-existent on that island, but what it considered the loss of it in America. It wrote of "the consent of the governed" of "the right of out-voted minorities," and that the anti-slavery segment of the Republican party did not represent one half of the American people. All of which was another effort of *The Times* to convince its readers, if they were not already of the opinion, that the cause of the Confederacy was meritorious and virtuous.[30] *The Times*, 30 September 1861, furnishes an example:

> That the institution of Slavery is abominable in the eyes of Englishmen, and that the doctrine of emancipation, if always and sincerely professed by the Northern States, would have strongly commended to their cause the sympathies of this country, is not for a moment to be doubted. But the North was never generally possessed by any such feeling. The Republican party did, indeed, oppose the extension of slavery into new territories, but it was only a section of this party which advocated abolition; and the Democratic party, which was very strong, was not disposed to interfere with the slaveholders even to this limited extent.
>
> Even if we should assume — which would not be correct — that the whole of the Republican party desired the abolition of Slavery, that party would not represent one half of the American people — perhaps not much more than one half of the people of the North. The Democratic party, which, if it had been everywhere united, could have carried even the last Presidential election against Mr. Lincoln, is willing and anxious to concede to the Slave States all the guarantees they can demand for the security of their institutions, on condition only of their returning to the body of the Union. Any policy, therefore, which would extinguish this chance of reconciliation would be viewed by this numerous and influential party with unqualified hostility, and President Lincoln would find himself confronted in his prosecution of the war by a strong constitutional Opposition, so that his enemies would be exasperated and his own supporters weakened at one and the same moment.

PART TWO

The War

4. Gettysburg

The Battle of Gettysburg shall remain timeless in the annals of the Civil War and of America. It was the turning of the tide; no longer would Washington be threatened; no longer would Confederate forces have the ability to invade the Northern territories at will; and at the dedication of that battlefield the significance of America was so vividly rendered by President Lincoln.

The Battle of Gettysburg extended over three days and was one of the bloodiest of the war. On July 1, Wednesday, losses were heavy on both sides, but the Federals suffered more and victory on the first day went to the South. On July 2, Thursday, neither army had made any appreciable gain. On July 3, Friday, the Battle of Gettysburg ended with Pickett's charge. An eyewitness wrote:

> Men fired into each other's faces, not five feet apart. There were bayonet-thrusts, sabre-strokes, pistol-shots; men going down on their hands and knees, spinning round like tops, throwing out their arms, gulping up blood, falling; legless, armless, headless. There are ghastly heaps of dead men.... The Confederates moved smartly ahead through the artillery fire; muskets opened, and the infantry charged the dug-in Federals. General officers fell — Armistead reached the stone fence, crossed it, and shouting "Follow me!" he fell. Artillery and Federal infantry closed in mercilessly. Units were broken, battle flags falling with men.[31]

At the end the Confederates retreated across the trampled fields to a sorrowing commander. All General Lee could say was, "All this has been my fault." The Battle of Gettysburg was over. The casualty figures for the three day battle were staggering. For the Federals, out of a total engaged of over 85,000 men, 3,155 died, 14,529 were wounded, and 5,365 missing, for a total of 23,049. For the Confederates, whose strength was near 65,000, official losses were 2,592 killed, 12,709 wounded, and 5,150 missing for a total 20,451.[32]

The Examiner, 25 July 1863, among other anti–American writings, advised readers that the last battle of Gettysburg was a minor setback for the Southern forces:

> It turns out that the Federal accounts of the battle of Gettysburg were nearer the truth than we were disposed to think, previous exaggerations having caused us to take American boasts, even when apparently the most moderate, at a considerable discount. But we were right in our calculation that if the success would be on the Federal side, it would not be of the decisive nature of a Southern triumph almost at the gates of Washington. The event of the 3rd amounted to no more than a repulse.

The Examiner, 1 August 1863, followed the above assessment with the claim that the battle was a draw. Again one sees the theme that all goes well with the Confederacy; Lee withdrew his forces as if under little duress: "The North has to boast of a drawn battle at Gettysburg. General Lee was, however, strong enough to withdraw his forces from Pennsylvania without any material loss; and as regards Virginia, things remain in pretty nearly the former state." *The Manchester Guardian,* 20 July 1863, was less certain of the results of the Southern invasion into the North. It admitted of Confederate failure:

> If for the moment we assume the campaign (Gettysburg) to have been practically terminated at this point, the moral to be drawn from it is the same which has been taught by many previous passages of the war. Neither of the two main armies can manage to make way in the country of the antagonist, and in almost every great battle the assailants are the unsuccessful party. Could we suppose the Confederate invasion to have had no more serious object than that of getting access to the rich fields and storehouses of Pennsylvania, it might well be thought to have had its reward in the vast quantities of supplies which have unquestionably been transmitted to Virginia. But we cannot attempt to persuade ourselves that the Confederate leaders did not aim at a much greater result, in which they have certainly failed.... It remains to be seen whether the unsuccessful Confederates are made to pay the ruinous forfeit which according to all the ordinary rules of warfare ought to be the consequence of their temerity.

The Daily News, 21 July 1863, would have none of the inventions and half-lies of their fellow journalists in England and the Confederacy:

> A GLEAM of success, we are told by a Confederate contemporary, has fallen on the Federal arms in the surrender of Vicksburg and the incidents of the second Maryland campaign. The philosophical calmness of this generous and dignified admission will perhaps be envied by both parties who are

actively engaged in the great struggle on the other side of the Atlantic. These trivial incidents, which are insufficient to disturb the serenity of Southern sympathisers at a safe distance from the scenes of action, have filled the Federal North with the profoundest gratitude and exultation, while the South has never attempted to disguise its settled conviction that the fall of Vicksburg, by cutting the Confederacy hopelessly in two, would be a fatal blow to their cause. But the Southern journalist on this side of the water affects to see in the permanent command of the Mississippi and the possession of the Western States by the North only a transient gleam of success to Federal arms.... They [the English partisan press] have been as one-sided and intemperate as the most unphilosophical partisan could possibly be. They have been just as eager to prove that the South was about to succeed at all points as though victory had been really an important object. In fact, so intense and unscrupulous is this feeling, that it leads not only to the serious distortion but to the actual suppression of notorious facts. *The Times,* for example, in its comments last Thursday on the three days fighting at Gettysburg, made no reference whatever to the third and most important day of all — that terrible engagement of Friday, which lasted from dawn to sunset, and was the decisive battle of the invasion. Accordingly, it very naturally concluded that the principal struggle was yet to come.

The Daily News, 10 August 1863, challenged the continuous claims of *The Times* that all that appeared in the Northern press was malicious untruth, and all that originated in the Confederate press was pure, honest, and wholesome.

Amidst the accumulated commercial and military disasters that have recently befallen the South, many of its friends in this country profess to find a peculiar source of pride and consolation in the superior moral attitude of the Confederacy, as reflected in the reserved and dignified tone of the Southern press. *The Times* during the last few days has told its readers that if we interpret American affairs as we do those of Europe, there can be "no hesitation in drawing the most gloomy auguries for the Federal cause from a comparison of the tone of the New York and Confederate press." The Richmond press, we are assured, have no trace of false boasting, while the New York press indulges in a tone of more than usual bluster.... The Confederates, we are told, never indulge in the exaggeration which habitually marks the Northern press.... But the journals we have quoted (*The Times & Index*) while carefully extracting the worst specimens of insolence and malignity from the New York rowdy journals like the *Herald,* are very sparing indeed in their extracts from the Southern press....

The place of honour belongs to the journals of the (Southern) capital, and we will first, therefore, give some specimens of the comments made by the most reputable members of the Richmond press on the Battle of Gettysburg.... On the first rumour of a battle having been fought the editor of the *Richmond Enquirer* declared himself as sure that Lee had whipped the enemy as he was a living, moving, sentient being. The editor

of the *Richmond Dispatch* promptly gave form and substance to this imag-
ination in a detailed narrative, showing that "by skilled movement Lee had
induced the Yankees to follow him outside their position, and, outflank-
ing them, had captured 40,000 prisoners, and destroyed the whole Yankee
army." Only a week before the fall of Vicksburg the *Chattanooga Rebel*,
very successfully emulated the tone of the Richmond press, as the following choice extract will show: "For Vicksburg, Virginia, and Middle Tennessee the harbinger rays of peace seem to burst in harmonious lustre
from the long night of war. To drive Grant out of Mississippi; To invest
the Yankee capital; And to defeat Rosecrans; Are our present objects.
Never were the prospects brighter for the consummation of these legitimate and possible contingencies!"

Perhaps as important as the reporting of the Battle of Gettysburg was the
manner in which the British press related the happenings at the dedication of
the battle. *The Times,* 16 July 1863, had this short comment on the news from
Gettysburg and on Lincoln's address:

The few sentences he addresses to the country on this Fourth of July must
have read but sadly, compared with the fervid orations that were wont to
fill the public ear on the same anniversary. The "promise of a great success" has been so often made before, and been so often belied by events,
that the bloodshed, which is a certainty, must have cast a lurid shadow on
the day. Surely, never was the overweening pride of a nation so awfully
rebuked. Well may the President claim the "condolence of all for the many
gallant fallen," and prepare the public for the worst by a sentence that
breathes much more despondency than triumph.

On 4 December 1863, *The Times* had a more detailed account of the dedication at Gettysburg. President Lincoln continued to be the scapegoat:

The inauguration of the cemetery at Gettysburg was an imposing cere-
mony, only rendered somewhat flat by the nature of Mr. Everett's lecture,
and ludicrous by some of the luckless sallies of that poor President Lincoln,
who seems determined to play in this great American Union the part of
the famous Governor of the Isle of Barataris. Honest old Abe arrived at
Gettysburg on Wednesday evening, and after supper was serenaded by the
band of the 5th New York Artillery. There was a loud call for the President.
He appeared, and was loudly cheered, when he opened his mouth and
said: — "I appear before you, fellow-citizens, merely to thank you for this
compliment. The inference is a very fair one that you would hear me for a
little while at least were I to commence to make a speech. I do not appear
before you for the purpose of doing so, and for several substantial reasons.
The most substantial of these is that I have no speech to make. [Laughter]
In my position it is somewhat important that I should not say any foolish
things. [A Voice, — "If you can help it"] It very often happens that the only

way to help it is to say nothing at all. [Laughter] Believing that it is my present condition this evening, I must beg of you to excuse me from addressing you any further."

A Gettysburg attorney, David Wills, conceived the idea of dedicating a portion of the battlefield as a National Soldiers' Cemetery. Edward Everett of Boston, a well-known orator and former president of Harvard, governor of Massachusetts, U.S. Senator, diplomat and secretary of state, considered by many to be the greatest American orator of his day, was invited to give the main address at the dedication of the Gettysburg National Cemetery. Lincoln, though invited to be present, was not asked to speak, partly because, despite his acknowledged distinction as a political orator, it was felt that he was not adequate to this solemn commemorative occasion. Two weeks before the dedication, however, almost as an afterthought, those in charge of the ceremonies asked Lincoln to follow Everett with "a few appropriate remarks." About the occasion itself, Lincoln's Secretary, John Hay, wrote in his diary: "Mr. Everett spoke as he always does, perfectly — and the President, in a fine, free way, with more grace than was his wont, said his half-dozen words of consecration.[33]

On 19 November a crowd of between 15,000 and 20,000 listened to Everett speak for two hours before Lincoln rose and in his high-pitched voice delivered his imperishable statement on the meaning of the war, which was at the time still far from won. Witnesses record that he received a sustained ovation following these words:

> Four score and seven years ago our fathers brought forth on this continent, a new nation, conceived in Liberty, and dedicated to the proposition that all men are created equal. Now we are engaged in a great civil war, testing whether that nation, or any nation so conceived and so dedicated, can long endure. We are met on a great battle-field of that war. We have come to dedicate a portion of that field, as a final resting place for those who here gave their lives that that nation might live. It is altogether fitting and proper that we should do this. But, in a larger sense, we cannot dedicate — we cannot consecrate — we cannot hallow — this ground. The brave men, living and dead, who struggled here, have consecrated it, far above our poor power to add or detract. The world will little note, nor long remember what we say here, but it can never forget what they did here. It is for us the living, rather, to be dedicated here to the unfinished work which they who fought here have thus far so nobly advanced. It is rather for us to be here dedicated to the great task remaining before us — that from these honored dead we take increased devotion to that cause for which they gave the last full measure of devotion — that we here highly resolve that these dead shall not have died in vain — that this nation, under God, shall have a new birth of freedom — and that government of the people, by the people, for the people, shall not perish from the earth.

It was unfortunate that the English press, for the main, lacked the vision to appreciate Lincoln's Gettysburg address. *The Times* offered its botched version and *The Daily News* was guilty of confining its reporting to the following on 2 December 1863: "Mr. Lincoln, Mr. Seward, and the corps diplomatique, were present at the dedication of the Gettysburg cemetery. Edward Everett made an oration."

5. Sherman and Grant

For the most part the British press and the ruling class of Britain made sport with the talents of the Union military as well as with those of generals Sherman and Grant. Despite the late date of their comments, most originated in the middle of 1863, when the Federal armies had already stamped their mastery over the Confederate forces.

Charles Francis Adams, American minister to the Court of St. James, appraised the situation in Britain in a letter to his son, London, June 10, 1863:

> Our good friends in this country are always provided with a little later than the last news from America, which is equally sure to be very bad for us. We have just survived a complete capitulation of the whole army of General Grant. A few weeks since we went through the same process with all of you on the Rappahannock. Last year we had the same luck with General McClellan and all his force. The wonder is that anybody is left in the free states. Washington has been taken several times. I am not sure whether Boston has been considered in great peril or not.[34]

Grant had taken Vicksburg and Lee had been defeated at Gettysburg. No longer was there a threat of Confederate forces returning to the territories of the North. The Mississippi was cleared of Confederate forces, and Washington was free of menace from the Confederate armies. Desertions and the consequence of state rights had ravaged the army of the South. Nonetheless, *The Economist* (26 December 1863) 1444, made the argument for the ability of the Confederacy to continue the conflict. It was a theme fully exploited by the British press:

> Granting to the Federals the full extent of all the territory they claim to have wrested from their antagonists — and nearly the whole of which is still held

53

with difficulty, and only under the severe pressure of military occupation —
they, the Confederate states, still retain the two Carolinas, Georgia,
Alabama, all Florida, except a strip on the sea-coast, all Texas, a large part
of Mississippi and Louisiana, and the whole of that division of Virginia in
which the war has been chiefly carried on. The area of the States still admitted by the Federals to be held by Jefferson Davis (according to a coloured
map just issued in their interest) exceeds 512,000 square miles, — or ten
times that of England, nearly three times that of France, and twice that of
the Austrian Empire. The very extent of this vast territory, its hot climate,
its fatal swamps, its impassable forests, the very scantiness of its population, render it peculiarly dangerous and difficult for an invading army, and
almost impossible actually to subdue, if only its defenders are true to themselves and to each other. Now, up to this point, there has been no sign of
flinching; animosity has grown more intense, and resistance more obsti-
nate with each month of continued conflict; the army and the people have
borne their hardships and privations with marvellous gallantry and
patience; the superiority in military skill has been steadily and remarkably
on the side of the Confederates; and of the munitions of war, at least they
have shown no lack. Moreover, if they are, as we assume and believe,
absolutely determined never to yield, they are as yet only in the first stage
of defensive civil war.

The Saturday Review (26 March 1864) 372, found it troublesome to report
a Federal victory without some qualifications. So the report of a Sherman victory carried with it the baggage of future trouble for his troops:

> The report of a great pitched battle in which Sherman is said to have been
> defeated with enormous loss is perhaps altogether untrue.... Nevertheless,
> the loss of men and material in an unsuccessful advance and retreat through
> the entire State of Mississippi will probably disable Sherman for months
> from renewing any offensive movement.

At this late period of the conflict, The Saturday Review (1 April 1865)
365, continued to find it difficult to admit the hopelessness of the Confederate
cause.

> Although the prospects of the North appear almost unclouded, it is worth
> while to remember that a reverse is yet possible, and that the Confederate
> leaders still exhibit the heroic pertinacity which has hitherto defied supe-
> rior force. If General Lee were to succeed in crushing Sherman, without
> sacrificing his position at Richmond and Petersburg, the Federal opera-
> tions would be paralyzed during the present campaign. In this, or in some
> other way, the Southern Commander-in-Chief still thinks it not impossi-
> ble to redeem the fortunes of the Confederacy. It is presumptuous in dis-
> tant critics to condemn too positively the conclusions of a great and pru-
> dent soldier.

The Examiner, 15 March 1862, could find little praise for the Union army and General Grant after his splendid victory at Fort Donelson:

> The success, it appears, was achieved without generalship, at a great sacrifice of life that generalship would have saved. Here again one Northern regiment fired into another, or rather into two others; of fellow combatants who ran for miles in panic; and the captured rebel officers laugh at the stupidity of General Grant, who, they say, with a single field-piece, planted in a particular spot, could have prevented the escape of Floyd and Pillow.

Lloyd's Weekly Newspaper, one of the few newspapers that was not outrageously anti–Union, published the following article from *The Index* on 25 December 1864 (*The Index,* published by the agents of the Confederacy, made no attempt to treat the war without prejudice, and found ample readership among the denizens of England. *Lloyd's* noted that *The Index* found the item "a thoroughly reliable account" which would help illuminate the news of the day regarding Sherman's march):

> I think that the government will be perfectly satisfied if Sherman manages to reach a point of safety with but half his army. Finding that Grant intends to keep quiet, every energy of the Confederacy has been concentrated for Sherman's defeat. The remarkable skill with which they have managed is just showing itself. Sherman's raid is already defeated, and now the only question is whether he will get off in safety. Hood and Breckinridge have no little part in the great campaign of the south-west. Breckinridge has shown great ability. He defeated Gillem, and all the Federal troops in East Tennessee, so badly that they could neither invade South-western Virginia during his absence, nor leave Knoxville to help the garrison at Nashville.... Equally skillful were the Confederate movements in opposition to Sherman's other column.... Fatigued, and to a certain extent broken up by long marches, Sherman's army would then have had but a poor chance of doing anything. Beauregard and Forrest from Macon, Bragg and Ewell from Augusta, would follow him down to the seacoast, and you, as easily as I, can tell his plight upon reaching it. Sherman's raid had done its worst, and now the only question is whether Sherman can save himself.

The Manchester Guardian, 29 March 1864, situated in the center of the textile industry of England and subject to the pressures of the mill-owners, was decidedly partisan for the Confederacy. Its reporting of generals Sherman and Grant was guided more by desire than objectivity:

> It does not require the triumphant order of the day by the Confederate Commander in Mississippi to convince us General Sherman has been defeated in an elaborate plan to penetrate the South; nor does the boast on his part that he would have reached Mobile if he had received the

co-operation which he relied on from the Federal fleet, amount to more
than that he failed in his purpose.

The Manchester Guardian, 20 June 1864, offered more than mere hope for
its partisan readers, including a possible Confederate victory, and a vision of
Sherman defeated in Kentucky and Tennessee.

> There appears to be neither confirmation nor denial from Northern sources
> of the partial victory which had been claimed by the Confederates in Geor-
> gia. The accounts received from General Sherman to the 6th instant are,
> however, in forcible contrast to the easy and triumphant progress which
> appeared to mark the earlier stages of his operations. He now reports him-
> self at Acworth, having possession of the road for a few miles in the direc-
> tion of Mariettas, which place we were many days ago told that he had cap-
> tured. From nothing else but the new caution with which he seems to be
> inspired can we form any opinion respecting the extent of the force by
> which he is likely to be opposed. It will not be very surprising, however, if
> while he avails himself temporarily of the absence of any formidable enemy
> in Georgia, General Sherman should find himself effectually defeated in
> Tennessee and Kentucky.

The Manchester Guardian, 6 December 1864, again invoked the theme of
the patriotism and resolve of the Confederacy. The South is a solid block of
homogeneity and patriotism:

> If General Sherman cannot reach speedily the friendly arm which will
> doubtless be stretched out to meet him at any point on the coast at which
> he may aim, it is probable that a military disaster unprecedented in the war
> will be the punishment of temerity. The operation which he is conducting
> will also be an even better test than anything which has yet occurred, of
> the political feeling of the Southern Confederacy, inasmuch as the efforts
> of the Richmond Government to defeat it must largely depend on the tem-
> per and resolution of the population through which the invasion is intended
> to pass. On that point we do not see that any Southerner will admit any
> considerable apprehension.

If one would suspect Confederate partisanship of the English press to this
point, *The Standard,* conservative and biased, did much to confirm that suspicion on 16 July 1864:

> Now the insanity and the diabolical wickedness form the consistent policy
> of the Federal Government — The South is to be subjugated by the exter-
> mination of her people. But the idea has not become less insane or less
> fiendish than it would at first appear. The superiority of Southern troops
> has been manifested on a score of bloody battlefields. The Northern armies

have been repulsed with horrible slaughter. The South has endured the worst and overcome it; and now in the midst of war she finds the resources to support the war, and increases them from year to year. The question is not now when Richmond and Atlanta will fall, but what will become of Grant and Sherman. The war has become one merely of vengeance, in which New England preachers and orators purchase the delight of torturing Southern women and children with the blood of tens of thousands of rowdies from New York, ruffians from the West, and mercenaries from Ireland and Germany, but in which the original purpose has not merely been forgotten but rendered utterly and for ever unattainable....

The Standard, 8 August 1864, reported that the Confederacy remained supreme:

Atlanta has not been captured. Grant remains inactive in his entrenchments before Petersburg. So far the news ... is favourable to the Confederates. It is a part of the strategic system of the able Southern leaders to draw on the invading armies into position whereby they are tantalised with the near prospect of victory, but where they are farther from ever any tangible success.

The Standard, 12 August 1864:

The last advices from America, confused and somewhat contradictory as they are, are of such a nature as to be very reassuring to the friends of the Confederate cause. It is now admitted that Sherman was defeated before Atlanta in the battle of July 20, and that he received another severe if not fatal check on July 22. Instead of taking Atlanta General Sherman has taken the spade, and is busy with his entrenchments.

The Standard, 9 September 1864, continued with the difficulties of Grant and Sherman.

Grant has met with two more defeats, and lost 12,000 men. Sherman was retreating before Early. The pioneers of the Confederate army were already across the Potomac.... In Georgia, Sherman was hard pressed and trembling before Atlanta, unable to move forward or retreat backward.... There is no more a question of the extension of Federal conquests. Every foothold obtained by the North on Southern soil is now boldly challenged by the enemy, and beleagured by the men who are determined to claim their own. The occasion is not propitious for the election of a war President or the adoption of a war policy for four years more.

At the end of 1864, as the Confederate forces were in full retreat, *The Standard*, 9 December 1864, continued to write of the trouble facing Union forces:

The difficulties of General Sherman seem insurmountable and his danger great as Generals Hood and Breckenridge are persisting in their Tennessee campaign without heeding him, we may be sure that help will be sent from other quarters to the Georgians. From what quarter time will show, and that very soon. When to the difficulties of the country, the hostility of the people, the absence of food, and, perhaps, the scarcity of ammunition, there is added the sudden appearance in the form of a veteran army under Beauregard or Longstreet, Sherman may wish he had never left Atlanta.

6. General Butler and the Southern Belles

The women of New Orleans had subjected the occupying Union forces to a campaign of insults, sly and bold, verbal and physical. "The spirit of impotent but impertinent hate in this population is astonishing," one soldier from New England wrote home. Women who met Union troops in the carriage ways ostentatiously held their skirts aside as if they feared they might be contaminated if they touched the soldier, and this act was accompanied with every possible gesture of contempt and abhorrence. Butler suffered a similar indignity himself, while his naval counterpart, David Farragut, had the even more distasteful experience of being showered with what appears to have been the contents of a bucket of slops. In an effort to revive his men's spirits the General issued the order, although he no doubt relished the controversy it was certain to stir. Unfortunately, in addition to amusing the Northern public and exciting the Confederates to impotent fury, it attracted international attention and became a source of acute embarrassment to Union sympathizers abroad, especially those in Britain who cared not to investigate.[35] General Butler issued the order on May 15, 1862, from departmental headquarters in New Orleans.

> As officers and soldiers of the United States have been subject to repeated insults from women calling themselves ladies of New Orleans, in return for the most scrupulous non-interference and courtesy on our part, it is ordered hereafter, when any female shall by mere gesture or movement insult, or show contempt for any officers or soldiers of the United States, she shall be regarded and held liable to be treated as a woman about town plying her avocation.

The British press indulged in a delirium of vicious writings about this decree. In British opinion Butler's order was an incitement to his soldiers to commit atrocities; Americans understood it as merely an authorization to return insult for insult. In fact, the order promptly put a stop to attacks on Northern soldiers, whether by act or word, and all disorder ceased.

The Manchester Guardian did not directly condemn General Butler in its own newspaper, but called upon an unnamed American journal to perform the deception for them — not an unusual maneuver for the British press. There was always a newspaper in America that could be quoted to satisfy English persuasions. *The Guardian* hid behind the anonymous journal on 18 June 1862.

> There is, fortunately for the American character, no doubt, that before the echo of opinion from Europe could be heard, a strong voice in the United States declared that General Butler had disgraced his service. One journal of New York had the honourable distinction of saying plainly that he ought to be recalled; and many declined to believe, without positive official evidence, that any officer of the Union could have forgotten himself so far.

The Times was not to be surpassed in its distaste for all things Federal. On 13 June 1862, the newspaper printed its article of hate via Charles Mackay, their New York correspondent. Mackay had already distinguished himself as an unreliable journalist in America. There was little question that he represented the doctrines of *The Times*. The enmity Mackay felt for the Northern cause became more and more evident in his writings. As with *The Manchester Guardian* he sought confirmation in a New York journal, perhaps the same one:

> one New York journal, bitterly hostile to the South, declared that if General Butler had really issued such a document, he was a disgrace to the army, and should immediately be dismissed. But the proclamation is now admitted to be true, and is likely to be more prejudicial to the Northern arms than a defeat in a pitched battle. The people of New Orleans are subdued by superior force, but they do not acknowledge the Northern Government. They offer it passive resistance in default of any other; and the women, high and low, rich and poor, not only wave Secession flags from their windows, and wear Secession ribbons in their bonnets, and teach their little children to revile the "Yankees," but when they pass a Federal soldier or officer in the streets they move out of his way with expressions of disgust in their faces, if not on their tongues, as if there was contamination in his touch or presence. They resort to all the manoeuvre of women's malice — and how great that can be if aroused, either in love or war, need not to be told — to prove to the Federal armies how odious they are to the South, and that the ultimate subjection of such a people is impossible. General Butler would have done well to treat this display of feminine spite with indifference, if he could not treat it with good humour. He might even have gone so far as to say that if women mixed themselves in public affairs like

men, they would be treated with the severity of the sex they assumed, and locked up for a night in the guard-house, to teach them the impropriety of playing with edged tools; but when he went so far as to say that women insulting the soldiers of the United States by word, or look, or gesture should be treated as "harlots plying their vocation in the streets," he outraged all decency and humanity, and committed an error as a General only exceeded in amount by his breach of good manners as a gentleman....

Marshall Haynau rendered his name infamous by flogging women for political offences; but General Butler has done worse. He has hurled by implication the foulest possible epithet that can be applied to women against all the women of New Orleans.... If he does not apologize for and withdraw the edict, the worse for his fame and for the credit of his Government.

Of Mackay's diatribe one might comment that General Butler did not use the word "harlot" and it is not difficult to imagine what Mackay would have to say if the Southern belles were jailed. But General Butler was not without his supporters in the English press. *The Daily News* published the following comment on 28 May 1862:

Those who regard the rebel oligarchy of the South as amiable martyrs, are terribly shocked to find that martial law has been proclaimed at New Orleans. That the victors should follow the ordinary usages of war, stirs the souls of these tender critics to a passion of virtuous indignation. In their view, apparently, the first duty of the victorious general was to cherish the rebellion and comfort the rebels. It must be confessed that General Butler did not take this rather peculiar view of his duty. He simply adopted the most prompt and effective measures for protecting the life and property of all peaceable citizens, and repressing the violence of the ill-disposed. This seems to be regarded as a cruel outrage against the sacred rights of rebellion and disorder, and the indignation of the rowdy sentimentalists of this country accordingly knows no bounds.

The Economist (11 June 1862) 741, voiced an opinion corresponding to that of the *Daily News.* It was not like *The Economist,* conservative and representing the commercial interests of Britain, to be a bedfellow to the likes of the *Daily News.* But it wrote in the defense of General Butler's actions regarding the Southern belles of New Orleans, and in understanding of General Butler's actions as commander of the Northern forces:

Everyone has heard of General Butler's "women order." It was an error, no doubt; but a knowledge of the circumstances tends to palliate it. In the first place, the insolence of Southern ladies was such as no troops could be expected to endure permanently. Colonels of regiments requested to be informed what orders they should give their men on the subject, and the younger staff officers often asked the General to save them from the indignities which they could neither resent nor endure. He had for some time been considering these things, but had been withheld from acting by the extreme difficulty of wise interference. But when a report was brought to him of a woman spitting in the face of two officers who were quietly walking along the street, he determined to act. The difficulty was, how to stop the women without arresting them. Nothing would have delighted them more than to be arrested for insulting the Union troops, and nothing could have so surely excited the populace as to witness such a collision. The weapon which Butler made use of was one, nevertheless, which even this difficulty does not excuse. It succeeded, however, in spite of the clamour which it raised. In no instance was the order ever misunderstood by the troops, who, we should remember, were not brutal mercenaries, but New England artisans and farmers, the last men in the world likely to insult women…. It is abundantly evident that no woman was ever outraged under Butler's rule, and we fear that the same could not be said of very few.

The Economist article ended with a note unusual for a journal of its persuasion:

Among Butler's other repressive acts, were the taxing of wealthy rebels to feed the poor whom the war had reduced to a starving condition, the confiscation of rebel property (clearly defensible measures of war), and his treatment of the foreign consuls who were secretly aiding the rebellion.

The British Ministry agreeably endorsed the position of the British press viewing the "atrocities" of the Butler proclamation. Lord Palmerston was quick to accept the British press's judgment, perhaps as a co-conspirator of *The Times*, in a letter to Charles F. Adams, 11 June 1862.

My Dear Sir:

I cannot refrain from taking the liberty of saying to you that it is difficult if not impossible to express adequately the disgust which must be excited in the mind of every honorable man by the general order of General Butler given in the enclosed extract from yesterday's *Times*. Even when a town is taken by assault it is the practice of the Commander of the conquering army to protect to his utmost the inhabitants and especially the female part of them, and I will venture to say that no example can be found in the history of civilized nations till the publication of this order, of a General guilty in cold blood of so infamous an act as deliberately to hand over the female inhabitants of a conquered city to the unbridled licence of an unrestrained soldiery. If the Federal Government chuses to be served by men capable of such revolting outrages, they must submit to abide by the deserved opinion which mankind will form of their conduct.[36]

Lord Russell suggested prudence to Lord Palmerston on 13 June:

> Adams has been here in a dreadful state about the letter you have written him about Butler. I declined to give him my opinion and asked him to do nothing more until I have seen or written to you. What you say is true enough, tho' he denies your interpretation of the order. But it is not clear that the President approves of the order, and I think if you could add something to the effect that you respect the Government of President Lincoln, and do not wish to impute to them the fault of Butler, it might soothe him. If you withdraw the letter altogether it would be the best. But this you may not like to do.[37]

The Saturday Review (2 April 1864) 404 associated the edict with all that is savage and uncivilized.

> Of the method of warfare which the Federals are now committed to: As the black races in Africa, all the Chinese and Japanese, all the natives of India, and probably the Russians and Turks — all practice warfare upon the uncivilized plan. They give full rein to their evil passions, and look upon murder and malicious mischief on a large scale. The more murder and the more mischief, therefore, that can be committed, the more successful the war has been. The result for which the combatants fight is not to arrive at a permanent and peaceful settlement, but merely to indulge them in large amounts of exquisite pain and misery upon their antagonists. The pangs of those whom they have killed and wounded, the privations of those whom they have made destitute, the mental agony of those whom they have dishonoured, these are the trophies their valour carries off and the prizes for which they risked their lives. The exploits which the Federals are performing on this system of warfare would not have attracted much notice if they had begun by being the sort of people from whom such things were to be expected. But they began upon the European, not upon the Red Indian principle, and they still use the language of civilized belligerents.

It was not necessary to go to foreign lands to view British atrocities. On 11 October 1865, there was a Negro uprising in Jamaica. Governor Edward John Eyre declared martial law and ordered troops to Morant Bay. Under the rule of martial law, the troops, aided by the Maroons, shot or executed 439 blacks, flogged about 600 others, and burned over 1,000 huts and houses belonging to the suspected rebels. Eyre claimed that the military had quelled all signs of rebellion by 26 October, yet the reprisals continued for the full 30 days of martial law. During this time, the troops met no resistance, and suffered no injuries apart from the discomfort of inclement weather and fatigue from their strenuous efforts. British regard for womanhood was clearly indicated by the fact that the females flogged had their sentence reduced from 100 lashes to 50.[38]

It would be shameful to leave the subject of Butler's atrocities without permitting Karl Marx to have his say on the episode and the British reaction:

Humanity in England, like liberty in France, has now become an export article for the traders in politics. We recollect the time when Tsar Nicholas had Polish ladies flogged by soldiers [Polish insurrection of 1831] and when Lord Palmerston found the moral indignation of some parliamentarians over the event "unpolitical." We recollect that about a decade ago a revolt took place on the Ionian Islands. [From 1815 to 1849, the Ionian Islands were under British control; in 1849, a Greek uprising occurred there which was suppressed with great cruelty by the English] which gave the English governor there occasion to have a not inconsiderable number of Grecian women flogged. Probatum est, [it is approved] said Palmerston and his Whig colleagues who at that time were in office. Only a few years ago proof was furnished to Parliament from official documents that the tax collectors in India employed means of coercion against the wives of the ryots [Indian peasant cultivators who hold land under the ryotwari system], the infamy of which forbids giving further details. Palmerston and his colleagues did not, it is true, dare to justify these atrocities, but what an outcry they would have raised, had a foreign government dared to proclaim publicly its indignation over these English infamies and to indicate, not indistinctly, that it would step in if Palmerston and colleagues did not at once disavow the Indian tax officials.

But Cato the Censor himself could not watch over the morals of the Roman citizens more anxiously than the English aristocrats and their ministers over the "humanity" of the war-waging Yankees! The ladies of New Orleans, yellow beauties, tastelessly bedecked with jewels and comparable, perhaps, to the women of the old Mexicans, save that they do not devour their slaves in natura, are this time — previously it was the harbors of Charleston [the stone blockade] — the occasions for the British aristocrats' display of humanity. The English women who are now starving in Lancashire (they are, however, not ladies, nor do they possess slaves), have inspired no parliamentary utterance hitherto; the cry of distress from the Irish women, who, with the progressive eviction of the small tenant farmers en masse in green Erin, are flung half naked on the street and hunted from house and home quite as if the Tartars had descended upon them, has hitherto called forth only an echo from Lords, Commons, and Her Majesty's government — homilies on the absolute right of landed property. But the ladies of New Orleans! That, to be sure, is another matter. These ladies were far too enlightened to participate in the tumult of war, like the goddesses of Olympus, or to cast themselves into the flames like the women of Sagunt. [During the Second Punic War, the inhabitants of the town of Sagunt, an ally of Rome, stoutly resisted the siege of Hannibal, the women fighting side by side with the men.] They have invented a new and safe mode of heroism, a mode that could have been invented only by female slaveholders in a land where the free part of the population consists of shopkeepers by vocation, trades men in cotton or sugar or tobacco, and does not keep slaves, like the citizens of the ancient world. After their men had run away from New Orleans or had crept into their back closets, these ladies rushed into the streets in order to spit in the faces of the victorious Union troops or to stick out their tongues at them or, like Mephistopheles, to make in general "an unseemly gesture," accompanied by insulting words. These Magaeras imagined they could be ill-mannered with "impunity." This was their heroism. General Butler issued a proclamation in which he notified them that they should be treated as street-walkers, if they continued to act as street-walkers. Butler has, indeed, the makings of a lawyer, but does not seem to have given the requisite study of English statute law. Otherwise, by analogy with the laws imposed on Ireland under Castlereagh, he would have prohibited them from setting foot on the streets at all. Butler's warning to the "ladies" of New Orleans has aroused such moral indignation in Earl Carnarvon, Sir J. Walsh and Mr. Gregory, who has already demanded recognition of the Confederacy a year ago, that the Earl in the Upper House, the knight and the man "without a handle to his name" in the Lower House, interrogated the Ministry with a view to learning what steps it thought of taking in the name of outraged "humanity." Russell and Palmerston both castigated Butler, both expected that the government at Washington would disavow him; and so very tender-hearted Palmerston who behind the back of the Queen and without the fore-knowledge of his colleagues recognized the coup d'état of December 1851 (on which occasion "ladies" were actually shot dead, whilst others were violated by French troops) merely out of "human admiration"—the same tender-hearted Viscount declared Butler's warning an "infamy." Ladies, indeed, who actually own slaves—such ladies were not even to be able to vent their anger and their malice on common Union troops, peasants, artisans, and other rabble with impunity! It is "infamous." Among the public here, no one is deceived by this humanity farce. It is meant in a measure to call forth, in a measure to fortify the feeling of favor of intervention.[39]

Britain was in a poor position before, during and after the American Civil War to belittle any country, or individual, for pillage or plunder. Its record in the nineteenth century for looting and raping was without peer. Britain supported 88 colonial wars in 43 different locales during that century. None was for the good of mankind; all of the wars in the following list were for the pocketbooks of English industrialists and commercial adventurers:

Abyssinia—1868	Buner (India)—1898
Aden—1838	Burma—1852; 1884
Afganistan—1838; 1841; 1878; 1879	Canada—1837; 1870
Ambela (India)—1863	Chilas (India)—1892
Ashanti—1874; 1900	China—1840; 1859-60; 1900-1
Australia—1854	Chitral (India)—1895
Bengal (India)—1857-9	Egypt—1882-5; 1896-8
Benin—1897	Gwalior (India)—1843
Bhutan (India)—1864	Hunza (India)—1891

India — North-West Frontier 1848;
  1849; 1850; 1852; 1853; 1854;
  1858; 1864; 1866; 1867; 1877;
  1878; 1879; 1880; 1881; 1884; 1888;
  1890; 1891; 1892; 1897
Japan — 1864
Jubaland — 1898
Levant — 1840
Lushai (India) — 1871
Malay — 1875
Malta — 1878
Manipur (India) — 1891
Mashonaland — 1896
Mombasa — 1896
Natal — 1879
New Zealand — 1861; 1863-4
Niger — 1898

Oudh (India) — 1857-9
Persia — 1838; 1856
Punjab — 1845-6; 1848
Siddim (India) — 1861; 1888
Sind (India) — 1843
Somaliland — 1890
South Africa — 1846; 1847; 1848;
  1851; 1852; 1877; 1879; 1881;
  1898-1902
Sudan — 1884; 1885; 1896-8
Tibet — 1888
Transvaal 1881; 1898-1902
Waziristan (India) 1894
Zanzibar — 1896[40]

7. The Trent Affair

On 8 November 1861 as the *USS San Jacinto* was cruising in the Old Bahama Channel, the British mail packet *Trent* bound for Britain steamed into view. The ensuing events became a cause célèbre of international relations, and threatened war between the United States and Great Britain.

The Confederate agents sent to Europe at the outbreak of the Civil War had accomplished little, and after seven months of waiting for a more favorable turn in foreign relations, President Davis determined to replace them with two "Special Commissioners of the Confederate States of America." These were James M. Mason of Virginia, to be minister for Great Britain, and John Slidell of Louisiana, for France. Their appointments indicated that the South had at last awakened to the need of a serious foreign policy. It was publicly and widely commented on by the Southern press, thereby arousing an excited apprehension in the North, almost as if the mere sending of two new men with instructions to secure recognition abroad were tantamount to actual accomplishment of their object.

Mason and Slidell succeeded in running the blockade at Charleston on the night of 12 October 1861, on the Confederate steamer *Theodora,* and arrived at New Providence, Nassau, on the 14th. They proceeded by the same vessel to Cardenas, Cuba, and from that point journeyed overland to Havana, arriving 22 October. In the party there were, besides the two envoys, their secretaries, McFarland and Eustis, and the family of Slidell. On 7 November they sailed for the Danish island of St. Thomas, expecting thence to take a British steamer from there to Southampton. The vessel on which they left Havana was the British contract mail-packet *Trent*, whose captain had full knowledge of the diplomatic character of his passengers. About noon on 8 November the *Trent* was stopped in the Bahama Channel by the United States sloop of war, *San Jacinto*, Captain Charles

Wilkes commanding, by a shot across the bow. A boarding party from the *Trent* transferred Mason and Slidell, with their secretaries, to the *San Jacinto*, and proceeded to an American port.

Protest was made both by the captain of the *Trent* and by Commander Williams, R.N., admiralty agent in charge of mails on board the ship. The two envoys also declared that they would yield only to personal compulsion, whereupon hands were laid upon shoulders and coat collars, and, accepting this as the application of force, they were transferred to the *San Jacinto's* boats.

The scene on the *Trent,* as described by all parties, both then and later, partakes of the nature of comic opera, yet was serious enough to the participants. In fact, the envoys, especially Slidell, were exultant in the conviction that the action of Wilkes would inevitably result in the early realization of the object of their journey, recognition of the South, at least by Great Britain. Once on board the *San Jacinto* they were treated more like guests on a private yacht, having "seats at the captain's table," than as enemy prisoners on an American warship. Wilkes did not act illegally in stopping the *Trent,* but he violated international laws in removing the Confederates. Instead, he should have brought the entire ship into port for adjudication, letting the courts decide whether or not Mason and Slidell were "contraband" and therefore subject to seizure. On 15 November the *USS San Jacinto* arrived at Fort Monroe, Virginia, with the captured Confederate commissioners. The prisoners were ordered sent to Fort Warren in Boston Harbor.

Captain Wilkes had acted without orders. His actions were without authority from the United States Navy Department, and solely upon his own responsibility. A challenge had been addressed to Britain, the "Mistress of the Seas," certain to be accepted by that nation as an insult to national prestige and national pride not quietly to be suffered.

In a few hours the news of the seizure of Mason and Slidell from the British packet *Trent* resounded through the North. When Captain Wilkes boarded the English vessel and carried off these two eminent men, whom the North considered traitors, a general jubilee arose; especially as the North remembered that England for six years had harassed the Union by boarding its ships to search for Englishmen (a major cause of the War of 1812), and had steadfastly refused to renounce the "right" when she made peace.

Within a few days, however, the bloom was off. Sober minds reconsidered and saw the danger of serious trouble, perhaps even war, with Britain and France. On 27 November, news of the seizure of the Confederate commissioners from the British packet *Trent* reached Great Britain. The word spread rapidly, igniting blazing indignation. "Outrage on the British Flag," placards announced. On 30 November, the British Foreign Secretary Lord John Russell wrote Lord Lyons, minister to the United States, that the seizure of Confederate commissioners Mason and Slidell was aggression against Britain and Her Majesty's Government, and trusted that the commissioners would be turned over to British protection with a suitable apology. If an answer was not forthcoming in seven days, Lyons was instructed to leave Washington with his legation and return to London. At the same time, Lord Russell directed the British Navy to take such measures as circumstances required, but to refrain from any act of hostility.

President Lincoln was not carried away. He and Secretary of State William Seward knew that Captain Wilkes' deed was indefensible on American principles, however justifiable by English practice. From Seward's dispatch of 30 November 1861, Ambassador Charles Francis Adams had already warned Lord Palmerston that the two nations were drifting into war, and had obtained from him far more satisfactory assurances than before. In a very friendly spirit it states that they have just heard of Captain Wilkes's exploit and that he acted without instructions. Seward guaranteed that his government would receive with the best dispositions anything that the British government had to say. Of course Seward desired to elicit from Earl Russell a condemnation of the practices which had so aggrieved America in 1812. Ambassador Adams read this letter to Earl Russell. Meanwhile the warlike excitement in England had become intense. Day and night without cessation preparation for war went on in the docks. Merchant shipowners could get no freights. American funds fell low in the market and great losses were sustained by sellers. Suddenly the news transpired that a friendly dispatch from America had been received, and for one day the funds were favorably affected by it. It was three weeks before Earl Russell was pleased to produce tranquillity by publishing it. Why was this? Was it thought polite to keep up the public exasperation, on the hypothesis of *The Times*, that the "mob" in America would overrule the President and force a war, or was someone in England trying to exasperate that "mob" and the mob of the English gentry too, in hopes that the exasperation must, somehow or other, at last lead to a war.

The British press and orators in and out of Parliament persisted in repeating that the seizure of the *Trent*, and the removal from it of the Southern commissioners, was a wanton and predetermined act of the government of the United States, and that the latter only made reparation for the act upon the threats of the British government. Seward's despatch to Adams, however, which declared that the U.S. government had not authorized that seizure, regretted it, and was willing to pay any suitable reparation for it, was dated on the same day as the British demand for restitution and satisfaction.

Led by *The Times*, the newspapers and periodicals of Great Britain seized upon the Trent affair to make war on America. On 28 November 1861 *The Times* reported to its readers the incident which was to become known as the Trent Affair. At this early date the language was deceitfully tranquil.

> It requires a strong effort of self-restraint to discuss with coolness the intelligence we publish today. An English Mail Steamer, sailing under the British flag, and carrying letters and passengers from a Spanish port to England, has been stopped on the high seas and overhauled. Four of the passengers

have been taken out and carried off as prisoners, claiming, and vainly claiming, as they were forced away from the protection of the flag of Great Britain. These are the naked facts. We put out of sight the accidents that the four gentlemen thus kidnapped were accredited with a diplomatic mission from the Confederate States of America, to the Courts of Europe, and also the peremptory manner in which the Federal frigate acted in making her seizure. The intention of the Federal Government evidently was to act upon their strict right, and do so in as little ceremonious a manner as might be. If they are justified by their rights as belligerents in what they have done the manner of doing it is a mere question of good or bad taste. If a rude fellow claims his rights coarsely we must yet give him his riches; and if we would not find ourselves in the wrong we must not quarrel with him on account of his ill manners.... We have recognized both Republics as belligerent States. We declare neutrality between them as between two warring Powers. We mete out a precise degree of equal consideration for the ships of each.

Unwelcome as the truth may be, it is nevertheless a truth, that we ourselves established a system of International Law which now tells against us. In high-handed, and almost despotic manner, we have in former days, claimed privileges over neutrals which have at different times banded all the maritime Powers of the world against us. We have insisted even upon stopping the ships of war of neutral nations and taking British subjects out of them; and an instance given by JEFFERSON out of his Memoirs in which two nephews of WASHINGTON were impressed by our cruisers as they were returning from Europe, and placed as common seamen under the discipline of ships of war.... So far as the authorities go the testimony of International Laws writers is all one way, that a belligerent cruiser has the right to stop and visit and search any merchant ship upon the high seas.

As if to prove that the previous article was not in error, *The Times*, 30 November 1861, continued its restrained stratagem.

All that now remains for us is to adjure the Government and the people of the Northern States to do us justice in this matter. They must by this time know us and our unwillingness to draw the sword against them, or to take any part in their unhappy quarrel. Indeed, our patience and long-suffering have not improbably led to the series of insults of which the outrage on the Trent is the last and most offensive. We have maintained the most rigid neutrality in their dispute; during the year which these troubles have lasted the Americans cannot complain of a single unfriendly act on our part.... We appeal to the moderate and enlightened of the Northern people.

On 4 December *The Times* was taking the high road of British diplomacy. All was to remain calm. All was to be articulated with eloquence and moderation:

The comments of the New York journals of the seizure of the Trent produce a feeling not so much of disappointment as of melancholy. We had hoped, and, in spite of every species of discouragement, we have clung to the hope, that beyond the Atlantic would arise a race not only speaking our language, but destined to give to the world a new type of civilization, and to take its place not only among the most powerful, but among the most respectable nations of the earth. With no motive for aggression, with every blessing of nature lavishly spread out before them, with the advantage of our dearly bought experience in every species of conjuncture, and with institutions to copy from those matured by the struggles and sacrifices of eight hundred years, we were not over sanguine in supposing that our former colonies were launched on a career as brilliant and glorious as could be wished for them.

But the "high road" was not to be maintained for long. *The Times* fell into her war-mongering mode.

Either America must stop short in the aggressive and overbearing course on which she has entered, must retrace her steps, and make such reparations as to leave even the New York Press no excuse for saying that she has gained anything by doing violence to men who sought protection under the British flag, or she must prepare to assert in another arena the claim to trample under her feet the plainest rules of International Law and the dearest rights of friendly Powers. Have her Statesmen and her Press, who think it is so safe and so profitable an amusement to insult the flag of Great Britain, really set themselves to consider the position they will occupy should the whole weight of this empire be thrown — perhaps not alone — into the vibrating scales of the Civil War? We recoil from such a conflict, for we well know what even we must suffer, with everything in our favour, before we bring it to a victorious issue.

As the chances of peace improved, *The Times* grew more blustering and offensive. The article of 9 December 1861 was a continuation of the war-mongering approach. *The Times* so intent on negotiation to settle the American Civil War, showed little desire for negotiation in the Trent Affair:

We hope it will be remembered by the Government in Washington that the four captives at Boston have been forcibly taken away from what we consider to have been a sacred asylum; that every moment of their captivity is an outrage to that sanctuary in defense of which we have always been ready to meet the world in arms; and that until these men stand once more under the flag which is pledged to protect them there can be no negotiation, either protracted or accelerated.

By 9 January *The Times* was busily engaged in self-congratulation. England and *The Times* had triumphed over the wantonness of America:

The Old World is no longer at enmity with the New.... With a clear conscience and a placid self-respect we can congratulate ourselves that in doing what is right we have done also what is expedient. The straightforward course of honour and of duty always has its compensations, but in this case it has had the unusual reward of a signal and immediate success.... We have manifested a deliberation and a tranquillity under insult which even we could not have shown towards a people for whom we thought it right to make fewer allowances, or whom we feared more. The Government of the Federal States had done more in wantonness what no nation of the Old World had ever dared to do. They had invaded the sanctuary which England extends to all political exiles who seek her protection; and to this wound, inflicted on her most sensitive pride, they had added an insult to her maritime flag and a menace to her security in traversing the seas. On all hands it is now admitted that the offense was at once insult and wrong, and it is no great triumph, therefore, that it should have been followed by reparation. If we had to deal with a friendly and courteous people, we should have had no occasion for preparation of war.

By 10 January *The Times* could not resist the temptation of bringing their favorite bugaboo into print. The villain, of course, was democracy:

If we are dragged into a war, it is now clear that it will be democracy who will force us into it. It will not be the rich or the educated, but the ignorant and penniless, who will make a war in which they have nothing to lose, and of the events of which they have no power of perception. It would be vain enough to reason with such a multitude as to the justice of the case at issue. The more obviously unjust the advantage gained, the greater would be their admiration of the dexterity which had acquired it, and the greater their triumph over the country which permitted it.

Lord Russell as well as Lord Palmerston was involved with *The Times*. On 11 December John Thadeus Delane wrote to Russell. The letter was clear evidence that in 1861 *The Times* was the spokesman for the "War Party" as it had been in 1812:

I send the enclosed which "just about expresses our sentiments" on the Trent affair. You will have heard all about it when this reaches you — if it ever does. The country took to the Crimean war because it was so long since we had enjoyed that luxury, it did not much care about the Pruth or about the Turks but it had paid so many millions a year so many years for its army and wanted the natural equivalent in glory.... But it is another affair here. It is real, downright, honest desire to avenge old scores; not the paltry disasters of Baltimore or New Orleans, but the foul and incessant abuse of the Americans, statesmen, orators and press, and if we are foiled by a surrender of the prisoners, there will be an universal feeling of disappointment. We expect, however, that they will show fight — and *hope* it, for we trust that we will give them such a dusting this time that even Everett, Bancroft and Co. won't be able to coin victories out of their defeats.[41]

Palmerston's attitude toward the United States had always been characteristically English, that is, in this context, offensive. His outlook was, no doubt, shaped by his having been a member of the government that had embarked on the war of 1812. He did little to avoid giving the impression that burning the White House only once was a mistake. The prospect of a government of radical ex-colonials being gravely weakened was highly attractive to him; and, to worsen matters, while Lincoln's secretary of state, Seward, was a confirmed Anglophobe, Palmerston convinced himself that the real aim of the North was to attack Canada.[42]

Palmerston disliked Americans and distrusted their Republic. As befitted a Tory, he had only contempt for American democracy. The only political lesson the Americans could teach the British, he asserted, was the foolishness of extending the franchise to the lower classes.[43]

8. Neutrality

Despite the recognition of the South as a belligerent and the construction of privateers for the Confederacy, the British press and journals continued to chime the carillion of neutrality throughout 1861 and 1862.

The Times, 15 May 1861, lost little time in enlightening its readers as to the neutrality proclamation of the government, and left little doubt that this edict would meet with universal compliance, as indicated in its publication of the following proclamation by Queen Victoria:

> Whereas we are happily at peace with all Sovereigns, Powers, and States: And whereas hostilities have unhappily commenced between the Governments of the United States of America and certain States styling themselves "the Confederate States of America": And whereas we, being at peace with the Government of the United States, have declared our Royal determination to maintain a strict and impartial neutrality in the contest between the said contending parties.

The British press, including the few newspapers and journals who gave credence to the North, whatever their differences, all gloried in professed British neutrality. As 1861 drew to a close, *The Times,* 30 November 1861, continued to advise its readers of the stance practiced by its countrymen: "We have maintained the most rigid neutrality in their dispute; during the year which these troubles have lasted the Americans cannot complain of a single unfriendly act on our part."

By 30 October 1862, however, *The Times* was writing of different forms of neutrality. There was now in the vocabulary of *The Times* an "absolute neutrality" and a "neutral theory." All of which was a clear sign that the neutrality of the British government was not clearly established:

> The truth is that it is practically impossible for any neutral to withhold from belligerents those particular supplies which an absolute neutrality

would be presumed to refuse. Directly or indirectly, munitions of war can be obtained from our markets; but of this breach of the neutral theory, such as it is, the Federals get almost the exclusive benefit.... It is but little that the Confederates have got from us. They have been too strictly watched to do much. Their trade this way is small, contraband, and precarious, while that of the Federals is carried on with little disguise and on an immense scale.

The remainder of the London press continued to sing of England's neutrality without the loss of a single note, but at *The Times,* their neutrality was not impartial and championed the Confederacy. *The Daily Telegraph,* 29 October 1862, wrote of the North being better supported by the English than the South. That support owed certainly not to reasons other than its ability to pay for more, and not for favour:

> Our neutrality has been scrupulous, and if it has been enforced so as to favour one side more than the other, it has been the North which has profited; for the North has unquestionably obtained through English ports supplies and munitions of war, including even men and money, to a far larger extent than the South.

The Examiner, 15 June 1861, stood on the principle of strict neutrality:

> It is one thing to be neutral, it is another thing to be indifferent. Neutrality is often the duty of a government, where indifference would be in the highest sense unworthy of a people. In the present case our Government, acting in unison with that of France, has resolved to show no active partiality to either party; to allow its subjects to enlist under the banners of neither; and to treat the ships of both as belonging to belligerents with whom it has no feud.

The Examiner, again, on 2 November 1861, wrote that "As for the policy of this country, our opinion remains unaltered that it should be a strict neutrality." *The Examiner,* 10 May 1862, and its readers were evidently more sensitive than the people of the North: "Our sensitive cousins in the Northern States are unable to comprehend or appreciate sincere neutrality."

The Manchester Guardian, 5 December 1861, called for justice from Washington — justice and an open pocketbook: "We have hitherto, inspite of endless provocations, preserved a strict neutrality in the present unhappy conflict; and, if the government at Washington only do us justice, we trust to continue neutral."

The Daily News, 18 May 1861, pro–North but English, looked to England as conforming to the Foreign Enlistment Act:

> England, therefore, occupies towards each of them the position of a neutral, and is bound to conduct herself with perfect impartiality to both

parties.... Upon the whole it must be admitted that the Proclamation which has just been issued with respect to the American civil war is a document well framed to define the position which this country occupies.

The *Daily News*, 4 June 1861, continued in the same vein: "But as the British Government has proclaimed the principle of strict neutrality, and has demonstrated by every one of its public acts its resolution to abide by that principle. The *Morning Post*, 30 April 1861, joined the neutrality brigade: "But great as is our interest, it behooves the Government of this country to maintain a position of strict and impartial neutrality."

As early as the spring of 1861 it was apparent that the British shipbuilders along the Clyde and Mersey were constructing privateers for the Confederacy. The British Ministry as well as the London press turned a blind eye, with the exception of the *Morning Post,* which published three articles in May of 1861, giving a lie to all talk of strict neutrality:

Morning Post, 10 May 1861:

> From a question which was put to the Foreign Secretary last night we infer that there are agents in this country who hope to engage British ships and British seamen in the service of the Southern Confederacy. Mr. W. Forster, who made the enquiry, desired to know whether it would not be a criminal offense for any subject of her Majesty to serve on board any privateer licensed by "the person assuming to act as President of the Southern Confederation." The hon. gentleman alluded to the provisions of the Foreign Enlistment Act, which, we all know, was passed in 1818 for the purpose of prohibiting the employment of British subjects in the service of the South American colonies, which at that time were engaged in rebellion against Spain. That act in substance followed the American statute on the same subject which had been passed in the previous year. No doubt it is a misdemeanour for any British subject to assist in the equipment or fitting out of any vessel to be employed in the service of a State, province, or colony, engaged in war or revolt against a nation with which the British Crown is in amity. We have a very confident belief that British shipowners, with a salutary dread of marine risks before their eyes, will consider well before they embark valuable property in adventures which certainly, after the Treaty of Paris, cannot receive the sanction or the protection of the Government, even should the claim of Mr. Davis to commission American privateers be conceded as a belligerent right ... on public as well as private grounds, it behooves the mercantile classes of the community studiously to abstain—either by fitting out privateers to be commissioned at Charleston or Savannah, or by consigning arms and other munitions of war to the Southern States—from endangering that position of strict neutrality on the part of this country which the forthcoming proclamation will certainly announce. The commercial and speculative public in England must wait to see not only a repetition of that warning against

foreign enlistment which was given last year when the Irish priests were beating up for Papal recruits, but a specification of the articles of ambiguous use, such as coal, iron, and steam machinery, which were for the first time deemed contraband of war during the late Russian contest.

The Morning Post 14 May 1861:

But the English law of neutrality is perhaps plain, straightforward, and intelligible, because it follows the American Act of 1818. By the Royal Proclamation, dated 9 March 1854, issued before the declaration of war with Russia, Her Majesty's subjects were warned against "fitting out or equipping vessels in Her Majesty's dominions, for warlike purposes, without Her Majesty's licence." The words of the Foreign Enlistment Act, which are incorporated in the Proclamation, are sufficiently stringent; they are that — "if any person within any part of the United Kingdom, or in any part of Her Majesty's dominions beyond the seas, should, without the leave or licence of Her Majesty under the sign manual, or signified by Order in Council, or by Proclamation, equip, furnish, fit out, or arm, any ship or vessel with intent or in order that such ship or vessel should be employed in the service of any foreign Prince, State, or Potentate, or of any foreign colony, province, or part of any province or people, or of any person or persons exercising or assuming to exercise any power of Government in or over any foreign State, colony, etc., as a transport or store-ship, or with intent to cruise or commit hostilities against any Prince, State, Potentate, etc., with whom Her Majesty shall not be at war, shall be guilty of a misdemeanour, and, on conviction, punishable by fine and imprisonment, at the discretion of the Court; and every such vessel shall be forfeited." We believe that the forthcoming Proclamation will simply contain a warning in the terms of the Foreign Enlistment Act, a warning which is highly necessary at a time when the agents of the Southern Confederation are busy in this country, not only in chartering vessels, but in purchasing arms and munitions of war. It is the policy and the duty of this country to keep out of the contest, to observe a position of strict and impartial neutrality, and to take its stand upon those great and fundamental principles of English justice and English fair play which neither belligerent can gainsay nor controvert. In adopting this course, in strictly and rigidly limiting the Order in Council to a simple warning, the government has acted wisely and well. It does not possess the power of adding new enactments to the legislation of public law, but it can enforce those provisions of English positive or municipal law which teach all subjects of the Crown not only their duties, but their liabilities, when commercial interests may be brought into antagonism with that principle of neutrality which it is the policy of this country to maintain and observe with respect to both belligerents.

The Morning Post 15 May 1861:

The Royal Proclamation which was issued yesterday, after noticing the fact that hostilities had unhappily commenced between the Government of the United States of America and certain States styling themselves the Confederate States of the South, strictly charges and commands "all the loving subjects of Her Majesty to observe a strict neutrality in and during the aforesaid hostilities, and to abstain from violating or contravening the laws and statutes of the realm in that behalf, or the law of nations in relation thereto, as they will answer to the contrary at their peril." The Proclamation next sets forth in extenso the provisions of the Foreign Enlistment Act of 1819, which prohibits British subjects from engaging in the naval or military service of any foreign prince, potentate, colony, etc., without the leave and licence of her Majesty; from equipping of fitting out vessels for the service of any such foreign prince, potentate, colony, etc., and adding to or increasing the warlike force of any ship or vessel of war, cruiser, or other armed vessel belonging to a foreign power which may enter the ports of this country. In order that none of Her Majesty's subjects may render themselves liable to the penalties imposed by the statute, the Proclamation strictly commands that no person or persons whatsoever shall commit any act, matter, or thing contrary to the provisions of the said statute upon pain of the several penalties imposed (fine and imprisonment and confiscation of the vessels and warlike stores) and of their Majesty's "high displeasure." The Proclamation, however, in several important particulars proceeds to define and lay down those rules of maritime war which exist independently of English positive law.

It warns British subjects that if in violation of their duty they enter into the service of either of the contending parties, on board a ship of war or transport, or serve aboard any privateer bearing letters of marque, or break, or endeavour to break, any blockade lawfully or actually established, they will do so at their own peril, "and that they will in nowise obtain any protection for or against any liabilities or penal consequences, but will, on the contrary, incur Her Majesty's high displeasure by such misconduct." There is also given the usual warning against carrying officers, soldiers, despatches, arms, military stores or materials or "any article or articles considered to be contraband of war according to the law or modern usage of nations." These words are studiously and perhaps purposely, ambiguous, because we all know that important articles which, in former contests, were of innocent use, have by the application of science become formidable implements of modern warfare…. It is well known that the Southern Confederacy has at the present time agents in this country who are chartering ships and purchasing munitions of war. Birmingham alone could easily supply all the small arms which both the North and the South require. The speculation would, no doubt, be lucrative; because a cargo of frills warned off from Charleston or Savannah could easily find as good, and possibly a better market in the Northern States via Canada. But it is the policy of this country, whilst acting upon the modern rules of Europe, which declare that privateering "is and remains abolished," and assert the great principle that blockades to be valid must be efficiently maintained, to observe a position of strict and impartial neutrality.... It is the duty as well as the inclination of the people of this country to be passive spectators of a contest which they lament and deplore equally on the grounds of humanity and personal interest. It is hardly to be expected that either American belligerency will recede from the assertion of that principle of "free ships free goods" which, from the date of the Treaty of Versailles, has been the constant contention of American statesmen and jurists. We in England must permit this unhappy contest to work itself out as best it may, even at the sacrifice of those commercial advantages which we are sure cannot be fostered and protected by proclamations respecting neutral rights, which, under present circumstances, are equally premature and unnecessary.

There now could be little doubt that the British Ministry and the British press were well aware of the responsibility of neutrality and the danger now being wielded by the construction of privateers for the Confederacy by the ship-builders of Britain.

The Economist (8 June 1861) 624 cited the letter of Lord John Russell, delivered before the House of Commons, which clearly proclaimed the intention of Britain to remain at the highest state of neutrality:

Her Majesty's Government is, as you are aware, desirous of observing the strictest neutrality in the contest which appears to be imminent between the United States and the so-styled Confederate States of America; and, with the view more effectually to carry out this principle, they propose to interdict armed ships, and also the privateers of both parties, from carrying prizes made by them into the ports, harbours, roadsteads, or waters of the United Kingdom, or of any of Her Majesty's colonies or possessions abroad.

The Economist (22 November 1862) 1292 continued to expand on English neutrality, a neutrality that would ignore the Foreign Enlistment Act. To excuse the obvious violation of that Act, *The Economist* alleged that "we have simply acted commercially." In truth, this assertion was valid: Britain acted, as usual, for profit, and for little else. The defense of England and the Foreign Enlistment Act on the matter of the Alabama was both puerile and insulting to the readers of *The Economist*. "We simply acted commercially" is a truism of English relations, and not to be confused with cries of neutrality:

England, as everyone knows, professes to be, and to have been from the outset, and to intend to remain till the end, perfectly neutral in the present unhappy contest between the two sections of the American Republic, both of whom she has acknowledged, and was obliged to acknowledge, as belligerents. England, as all except the Federals admit, has faithfully adhered to this professed neutrality — a neutrality, which, as even Federals cannot deny, has practically operated enormously to the advantage of the North. This neutrality requires us to act alike to both parties — to sell to both impartially, to execute orders for both impartially, or to refuse to sell to or work for either party impartially. We chose the former phase of impartiality; and the Northerners ought to be very glad we did so. Had we declined to deal with either party, we should have been guilty of a virtually hostile proceeding towards both. Had we dealt with one and not with the other, we should have made ourselves judges of and parties to the strife, and should have become belligerents ourselves. As it is, we have done nothing for the one party that we have not done for the other. We have simply acted commercially. We have sent out merchandise to the South at its request, just as we have sent our merchandise to the North at its request — though in infinitely smaller quantities, and of far less questionable articles. When the Federal cruisers have succeeded in capturing our ships with these goods for the South on board, in their own seas, or anywhere near the prohibited ground, or under circumstances of reasonable suspicion, we have made no remonstrances and no claims for damage or restoration. If Confederate cruisers made similar captures, we should have acted in the same way, and have accepted the misfortune and the violence with the same equanimity, as one of the ordinary risks attendant upon all dealing with belligerents. It is quite true that there exists a law called the "Foreign Enlistment Act," forbidding the Queen's subjects, without her sanction, enlisting in the service of any foreign Power, and prohibiting the "fitting out" or "equipping" of any ship for the purpose of being so employed. But this law and its reach are so well known that merchants and shipbuilders have been especially careful to avoid all violations of its provisions. In the case of the Alabama, so much cried out about, the vessel left the Mersey, a simple unfreighted ship, without a single gun or a single bag of powder on board. She cleared out for Nassau, but went off Terceira (we believe), where she was ordered to be delivered to the purchasers, and there, in the dominions of the King of Portugal and not of Queen Victoria, she took in her armament and her warlike stores.

Of the right of the Confederacy to send out privateers, *The Saturday Review* (11 May 1861) 462 fully concurred. *The Review* chose not to question the right in international law of England building those privateers for the Confederacy:

> Then, again, we can no longer have any hesitation about the right of the Southern Confederation to send out privateers. This is part of the rights which belong to every belligerent, and, apart from any special treaties that may exist, every Southern privateer bearing a proper commission from its Government may visit and search English vessels, and confiscate as good prize the property of Northerners found therein.

The Saturday Review (10 May 1862) 516, and *The Times* (16 August 1862), found it difficult to resist congratulating themselves and their readers on the long suffering but stoic Englishman. Neutrality must be preserved in spite of the suffering occasioned by the lack of cotton, at least until surplus stock of textiles were sold. Said *The Saturday Review*:

But Englishmen, notwithstanding the scandalous conduct of American politicians, still prefer a great sacrifice to any wrongful act, and they perceive that a practical protest against the annihilation of the cotton trade would at present be premature.

And *The Times*:

We are neutral, and neither the loss of the raw material of our manufacture nor the hard measures which have been dealt out to British subjects accused of intending to break the blockade will induce us to quit our present attitude of neutrality. There is nothing more to be said.

In the summer of 1861, Jefferson Davis tested the neutrality of the British. He sent a naval officer, one James D. Bulloch [Secret Service of the Confederate States], to England for the object of procuring warships and naval supplies in the ports of Great Britain. Bulloch procured eminent counsel, who submitted a series of propositions in interpretation of these laws.The law to be interpreted was the Act of Parliament of 59th George III, chapter 69, entitled, in common parlance, the Foreign Enlistment Act. Its exact title was "an Act to prevent the enlistment or engagement of His Majesty's subjects to serve in foreign service, and the fitting out or equipping in His Majesty's dominion of vessels for warlike purposes"; and its seventh section provided that "if any person within the United Kingdom should equip, furnish, fit out, or arm, or attempt or endeavour to equip, furnish etc. or procure to be equipped, etc, or should knowingly aid, assist, or be concerned with equipping, etc., with intent that such ship should be employed in the service of any foreign state, etc., as a transport or store ship, or with intent to cruise or commit hostilities against any state, etc. with whom His Majesty shall not then be at war, every person so offending should be guilty of a misdemeanour." These learned British lawyers advised him that it was no offence, under the act, for British subjects to fit out and equip a vessel outside of Her Majesty's dominions, even though it was intended for warlike purposes against a state friendly to Great Britain; that it was also no offence, under the act, for any person to fit out and equip a vessel within Her Majesty's dominions, if it were not with a warlike intent against a friendly state to Great Britain; that the mere building of a ship within Her Majesty's dominions by any person was no offence, under the act, no matter what might be the intent with which it was done. Furthermore, they drew the conclusion that "any shipbuilder may build any ship in Her Majesty's dominions, provided he does not equip her within Her Majesty's dominions, and he has nothing to do with the acts of the purchasers done within Her Majesty's dominions without his concurrence, or without Her Majesty's dominions even with his concurrence." Armed with this legal opinion from high authority, Mr. Bulloch found little difficulty in persuading the shipbuilders on the Mersey and the Clyde to undertake the construction of war-vessels for the Confederate navy. In truth, there would have been little problem in convincing the British shipbuilders to agree to the construction of privateers for the Confederacy without such eminent legal authority. The history of Britain and British industry was ample proof that profits would control their decisions.

The first ship built was the *Florida*. She was constructed during the latter part of the year 1861 and the first part of 1862, by Laird & Sons, at Birkenhead on the Mersey. It was pretended that she was being built for the Italian government. Her real destination was, however, suspected by the United States Consul at Liverpool, Mr. Dudley, who immediately imparted his suspicions to the United States Minister, Mr. Charles Francis Adams. Mr. Adams drew the attention of the British Government to the work being done at Birkenhead, but the Government did not see its way to interfere on the ground of mere suspicion. The *Florida* left Birkenhead during the latter part of March, 1862. She cleared for the Italian waters with a British crew on board. She had no guns or munitions on her. These were shipped from Hartlepool on the steamer *Bahama*. The two vessels met at Nassau according to agreement, and the *Florida* received her armament in the waters near that place. The British crew now clearly understanding the situation refused to serve longer, and her commander, after trying in vain to ship another crew in Cuba, ran her through the blockading squadron off Mobile into that port.

At the same time that these events were occurring Laird & Sons were building another ship of the same pattern as the *Florida*. This was the infamous *Alabama*. Although the builders kept her destination a strict secret, the United States Consul at Liverpool was on the watch, and he reported his well-grounded suspicions to Mr. Adams in regard to her ownership and purpose. Mr. Adams immediately requested the British Government to detain her. The ministers consulted the crown lawyers. After a considerable delay, caused by the illness of the chief advocate, a legal opinion was furnished the Government advising the detention of the vessel. Meanwhile, under pretext of a trial trip, she had slipped away in the latter part of July. She was not equipped with her armament and munitions when she left Birkenhead, but they were conveyed to her from the waters of the Mersey in two other ships. The three vessels met by arrangement in the water of the Azores. Here the *Alabama* was armed and equipped, and Semmes took command of her. A third ship, the *Georgia*, contracted by Mr. Bulloch, was, about the same time, being constructed on the Clyde. She too, escaped the watchful United States consuls on account of the slowness of the British officials, and sailed in the early part of 1863. She left the Clyde without her armament. But it was conveyed to her from Liverpool on the steamer *Alar*, and transferred to her near the French coast.[44]

The question of a belligerent's right to procure ships of war or to build them in the ports of neutral nations, a procedure which was to cause so great a difficulty between Britain and America, was, in 1860, still lacking definite application in international law. There were general principles already established that the neutral must not do, nor permit its subjects to do, anything directly in aid of belligerents. The British Foreign Enlistment Act, notification of which had been given in May 1861, forbade subjects to be concerned in the equipping, furnishing, fitting out, or arming of any ship or vessel, with intent or in order that such ship or vessel shall be employed in the service of a belligerent, and provided for punishment of individuals and forfeiture of vessels if this prohibition were disobeyed. But the Act also declared that such punishment, or seizure, would follow on due proof of the offence. Here was the weak point of the Act, for in effect if secrecy were maintained by offenders the proof was available only after the offence had been committed and one of the belligerents injured by the violation of the law.

Over twenty years earlier the American Government, seeking to prevent its subjects from committing unneutral acts in connection with the Canadian rebellion of 1837, had realized the weakness of its neutrality laws as they then stood, and by a new law of 10 March 1838, hastily passed and therefore limited to two years' duration, in the expectation of a more perfect law, but intended as a clearer exposition of neutral duty, had given federal officials power to act and seize on suspicion, leaving the proof of guilt or innocence to be determined later. But the British interpretation of her own neutrality laws was that proof was required in advance of seizure — an interpretation which some considered wholly in line with the basic principle that a man was innocent until proven guilty, but considered by others as not only fatal to the preservation of strict neutrality which Great Britain had so promptly asserted at the beginning of the Civil War, but as a means of deliberately avoiding the restrictions of neutrality to the profit incentive.

This question of belligerent ship-building and equipping in English ports was not a new experience for the British. As early as 1843, in the then existing Texan war of independence against Mexico, the British Foreign Secretary, Lord Aberdeen, had been a knowing conspirator. Mexico made a contract for two ships of war with the English firm of Lizardi and Company. The crews were to be recruited in England, the ships were to be commanded by British naval officers on leave, and the guns were to be purchased from firms customarily supplying the British Navy. Aberdeen advised the Admiralty to give the necessary authority to purchase guns. When Texas protested he at first seemed to think strict neutrality was secured if the same privileges were offered that country. Later he prohibited naval officers to command. One Mexican vessel, the *Guadaloupe*, left England with full equipment as originally planned; the other, the *Montezuma*, was forced to strip her equipment. But both vessels sailed under British naval officers for they were permitted to resign their commissions. They were later reinstated. In all this there was in part a temporary British policy to aid Mexico, but it is also clear that British governmental opinion was much in confusion as to neutrality responsibility.

There was little more confusion with the Palmerston government than with the Aberdeen Ministry. Neutrality to the British had as justification profits and little else. So long as there was scant concern of their actions resulting in injury to British industry, there would be nothing done to interfere with the building of ships for the Confederacy.[45]

By June 1862, there were plans already drawn, and contracts made with the Laird Brothers at Liverpool, for the building of two vessels far more dangerous than the *Alabama* to the Northern cause. These were the so-called Laird rams. They were to be two hundred and thirty feet long, have a beam of forty feet, be armoured with four and one-half inch iron plate and be provided with a "piercer" at the prow, about seven feet long and of great strength. This "piercer" would be three feet under the surface of the water. This was the distinguishing feature of the two ships; it was unusual construction, nearly impossible for use in an ordinary battle at sea, but highly dangerous to wooden ships maintaining a close blockade at Southern ports.

Lord Lyon, British minister at Washington, was convinced that an American issue of letters of marque would surely come if England did not stop Southern ship-building, and he wrote in such a way as to indicate his own opinion that effective steps must be taken to prevent their escape.

"At Washington anxiety was aroused by the court's decision in the *Alexandra* [ram] case, and shortly after the great Northern victories at Vicksburg and Gettysburg. Seward wrote a despatch to Adams, 11 July 1863, which has been interpreted as a definite threat of war. In substance Seward wrote that he still felt confident the Government of Great Britain would find a way to nullify the *Alexandra* decision, but renewed, in case this did not prove true, his assertion of Northern intention to issue letters of marque, adding a phrase about the right to 'pursue' Southern vessels into neutral ports."[46] On 5 September 1863 Adams advised Lord Russell that if the *Rams* escaped, "It would be superfluous in me to point out to your Lordship that this is war." On 1 September Russell had already given instructions to take steps for the detention of the rams and that on 3 September, positive instructions were given to that effect.

The year 1863 brought a fundamental change in the attitude of the English press. The construction of privateers by the English shipbuilders was now a matter of public record. No longer was it a secret of British neutrality. Was the change due to humanitarian reasons? Was the question of slavery to change their perspective? Hardly. Militarily the scene in America was changing. No longer could Britain depend on the victory of the Confederacy. Nor was there a likelihood of a mediated peace.

On 4 July 1863 Vicksburg surrendered to General Grant; on the 9th Port Hudson fell to the Federals and the Union had complete control of the Mississippi, splitting the Confederacy in two. On 3 July 1864 the three-day battle for Gettysburg ended with a Union victory. The change in the military situation in America brought changes in the reporting of the war among the newspapers and journals of England. For the first time since the beginning of the war there were questions concerning the building of Confederate privateers. The rams under construction at the Laird Yards had been detained and Britain was under the ominous threat of the Union issuing letters of marque.

The following articles offer a few examples of the flood of commentary that filled the newsprint on the Foreign Enlistment Act and the construction of privateers for the Confederacy: *The Saturday Review* (March 1863) 391 called for circumspection. No longer does the *Review* insist on the rights of building vessels to prey on the merchant marine of the Federals:

> The whole history of the *Alabama* is now before the public, and we are able to understand precisely how it is that the English Government is charged with neglect in permitting her to go to sea, and what is the answer to this charge which Earl Russell sets up. It is a case which ought to be discussed with the most jealous impartiality. The general conviction of the uselessness of the prosecution of the war by the North, and admiration of the skill and gallantry shown by the commander of the vessel since she left England, it is to be feared, engendered a slight wish that international law should somehow be made to show that it was quite legal to build the *Alabama* here, and to let her go out and try her luck. International law is not to be treated in this way; and if there was a duty imposed, under the circumstances, on the English Government to detain the ship, it would be a most lamentable thing if we were to refuse to acknowledge that we had done wrong, and were to trifle with the principles of law simply because there is something exciting in the adventures of the *Alabama*. England has every proper motive to do right in this matter. We cannot expect to be always neutral; and if a war arises to which we are parties and the Americans are not, the power to have our enemies to have ships of war built in American harbours would be a most serious danger to British commerce. If we can but clear away the passions and prejudices of the moment, we may easily see that prudence would bid us wish that the measures taken to prevent the building of ships of war in neutral ports should be as stringent as possible.

The position of the *The Saturday Review* (21 November 1863) 659 emphasized the elaborate investigation now being conducted by the British Ministry in order to procure justice, and a recognition that should England become, at some future date, a belligerent, her present conduct would be most detrimental to her well being:

> The Federal Government certainly cannot complain that we are now treating too lightly the question whether we ought to detain vessels intended for the service of the Confederates. We are trying to ascertain our duty and our powers by one of those elaborate investigations which give justice, although their length, the technicalities on which their issue frequently turns, and the tedium of hearing the same arguments hour after hour by

an array of counsel, are apt to perplex the mind. There is a general feeling of satisfaction in England at the exhaustive nature of the present inquiry. We wish that justice should be done in the particular case before the Court, and also that we should be helped to see what are the principles at stake, and what decision it most concerns England to uphold. The history of the original Act on which the power of detaining suspected vessels is based in America, and that of the judgments of American Courts, and of the course taken by the Government of the United States whenever the occasion rose, sufficiently prove that the United States have been sincerely anxious to do their duty as neutrals, and have taken means to ensure that nothing like a hostile armament shall leave their shore in time of peace. We ought to do our duty as neutrals equally well, and we ought to allow that those who have played their part fairly have a claim to be heard favourably when they ask us to be firm and equitable on the side of the law. Nor is it any longer doubted in England that, were the liberty accorded to neutrals of sending out ships of war to aid belligerents, England, as the country with the greatest commercial navy, would lose most. It is equally clear that there is a substantial difference between furnishing a belligerent with ships and furnishing them with guns — a difference rather of fact than of principle, but still a difference clear and indisputable. That an armed ship can commence hostilities at once, directly it gets into the open sea and falls in with a ship of the enemy's, while the guns must be taken to the country of the enemy to be of any use, is apparently an accidental distinction, and is practically not always true. But fact and common sense tell us that, in the case of the ship, we do generally make the neutral territory a basis for war by letting it go to prey on the merchantmen of the belligerent against whom it is directed; while, in the case of the guns, the neutral territory is generally nothing more than the seat of trade where the guns are bought. It is a great mistake to be too subtle and lawyer-like in dealing with questions of international law. We must look at general results, at the ordinary feelings of men, at the natural interpretation of our acts. If experience, and an induction from a tolerably large number of instances, prove to us that any particular thing or act tends naturally to cause neutral territory to be looked on as the basis of belligerent operations, it is wiser and safer to acknowledge the lesson, and profit by it. What we have to ask ourselves, therefore, is, what can belligerents reasonably complain of if permitted here or, in other words, what is our general duty about vessels of war intended for a belligerent? It is a further and a minor question whether violations of this duty are prohibited by the Foreign Enlistment Act; and a still smaller question whether, in the case of the *Alexandra*, the particular prohibitions of the Foreign Enlistment Act, whatever they may be, were violated?

By the autumn *The Daily Telegraph* was showing signs of recognizing the inevitable. On 10 October 1863 it printed the following passage on neutrality, as usual cloaked in sanctimonious bilge-water:

The sole motive that prompted the proceedings of yesterday (the seizure of the two steam-rams constructed by Messrs. Laird at Liverpool) was the resolute determination to abide by the most literal and unqualified neutrality, without favour to one side or the other, without hostility to either.

The Daily Telegraph, 3 November 1863, continued in the same vein:

We do not impute this apparent inconsistency of our side, as well as the other, to that leaning towards the North which our Foreign Secretary has avowed almost in terms, but we ascribe it to the obscurity and crudity of the international code, which makes such imperfect and conflicting provisions for contingencies like the present. It is, however, of the utmost importance that we should distinctly see the true origin of the embarrassment, in order that we may correct the imperfection at the earliest opportunity, but still more that the confusion may not be suffered to extend. Above all is it imperative that the controversy may not be regarded as entailing that departure from neutrality which the expression of Lord Russell's individual feeling might seem to imply, but which would certainly be inconsistent with the sentiments of the Government, and with the public opinion of the country.

The Times, 28 March 1863, remained steadfast in its support of the British Ministry and the management of the *Alabama* affair:

The Foreign Enlistment Act, it should be observed, is a statute, and to put it in force requires a prosecutor, who is bound to be provided with legal evidences of its infraction. In the case of the *Alabama* it appears that this evidence could not be obtained. All that has made her dangerous has been added to her since her escape. In the condition in which she left Liverpool she might have been captured by a single gunboat, for she was only armed when far out of British jurisdiction. For her feats on the sea we cannot be made responsible, as we certainly did not sell the South either Captain SEMMES or his skill. Just as little, in selling cannon or rifles to the North, did we furnish the more or less of efficiency with which they have been employed in the field.

It was not until 13 February 1864 that *The Examiner* felt the position of English neutrality needed some explanation:

We trust that no political misuse will be made of the wretched mischances that have attended this case of the *Alexandra*. Let our smart cousins on the other side of the ocean jeer and jibe as they please at the incoherent exposition of the Foreign Enlistment Act by Chief Baron Pollack, and the decrepit fumblings about rules and technicalities of procedure which have recently been witnessed; but let them not be misled into confounding these things with any desire or purpose on the part of the English Government or the

English people to elude the obligations of international justice, which the detention or liberation of the *Alexandra* is supposed to involve. On all hands it is admitted now that the language of the provisions restraining the clandestine equipment and fitting of vessels in our ports, meant to be employed for warlike purposes, are loosely drawn, and that they require to be amended. It would not have been possible for Ministers, perhaps, to have induced the Legislature to agree to a revision of the Act under existing circumstances until some attempt had been made to put the present statute into operation. Its inadequacy needed to be experimentally shown before clauses more stringent could with advantage be proposed. This implied, no doubt, the possibility of failure in the first instance; but this is habitually the Westminster rule of work, — never to think of rebuilding until some part of the old house is actually tumbling down. Commonwealths founded on philosophical principles may laugh if they will at our old-fashioned love of patch-work; but let them not mistake it for indifference or carelessness about decency. We are satisfied that on the main question involved in the days of the *Alabama*, the *Alexandra*, and Mr. Laird's steam rams, the mind of the country and of the Government is thoroughly generous as well as just. We did not like to be bullied into re-making a municipal law, by articles in the New York journals, or speeches in Congress, or despatches from Mr. Seward. But while remaining imperturbable and motionless so long as these were the only incentives to remedial legislation, we shall be perfectly open to entertain by-and-by any proposition that can be shown to be necessary for securing a genuine reciprocity to our neighbours on the subject of neutral obligations. We do not wish the few amongst us who may be capable of hazarding the peace of the seas for the sake of their own quasi practical gain, to find any shelter or protection for their lawless trade in British ports, which they or their fellows are denied in the ports of France or America. We admit that they had nothing to complain of when we were belligerents, and our transatlantic kinsmen were neutrals; and we should be ashamed to give them any just cause of complaint against us now that our positions are reversed. We must, however, be allowed to deal with these things in our own way. The arrest of the steam rams in September last, as soon as evidence was furnished to the Foreign Office on which it could act, coupled with the refusal of that department to interfere until it could do so legally, ought to dissipate unworthy suspicions regarding the policy of this country; and however disreputable to the character of our judicial system, and to that of our legislative handicraft the history of the *Alexandra* case may be, we believe that in the sequel it will be found to have served rather than dis-served the cause of permanent good understanding between America and England.

The Daily News, 30 March 1863, revealed the crucial part America played in the Crimean war by refusing to build warships for the Russians:

the most imposing fleet in the Baltic and Black Sea would have been powerless to protect our commerce if the fitting out of *Alabama* within the

territory of distant and nominally neutral Powers had been allowed to pro-
ceed with comparative impunity.... This disaster was averted during the
Crimean war not only by the prompt action of the American government
in stringently carrying out the provision of their Enlistment Act, but by
the unanimous decision of the most influential American merchants that
any attempt to evade its provisions would be a national dishonour, as well
as a flagrant offence against the comity of nations.

The Daily News, 25 July 1863, continued to review the evasion of the Foreign Enlistment Act by Laird and his fellow shipbuilders, with a caution for the
future:

Mr. Cobden was quite right to call the attention of Parliament and the
country to the memorial of the Liverpool shipowners as to the evasion of
the Foreign Enlistment Act. The sympathies of the majority of the upper
and middle classes in this country are so distinctly Southern, that it is vain
to expect that any proposal to increase the stringency of our neutrality code
will be adopted. The time may come when England shall occupy the position of belligerent and America that of a neutral. The remonstrances which
America now addresses to England, England will probably address to America. And Mr. Laird and his money seeking friends will then probably be as
indignant with the shipbuilders of New York for sending out *Alabamas* and
Floridas to ruin British merchantmen as they now are at the alleged insolence of Mr. Seward for attempting to interfere with their lawful gains.

Not all of the press was having second thoughts on the problem of ship-
building for the Confederacy. *The Glasgow Daily Herald* could not bring itself
to quarrel with the decision of the Chief Baron. Glasgow rests on the banks of
the Clyde, and shipbuilding was an important part of the economy of that area.
It was hardly surprising that the *Herald* should wish it to continue. *The Glasgow Daily Herald,* 27 June 1863, did not sustain the Ministry in the matter of
the *Alexandra.* There was enthusiastic support for the Chief Baron and the jury
in the Court of the Exchequer for the verdict in favor of the shipbuilders:

The case went on trial before Chief Baron Pollock and a jury in the Court
of Exchequer on Monday last, and on Wednesday it was decided by a unanimous verdict in favour of the defendants. The *Alexandra,* therefore, is not
a forfeited vessel, and her owners, we think, will have a very good claim
for damages against the Government or the parties who supplied the information. The Attorney-General, however, has tendered a bill of exceptions
against the ruling of the presiding Judge, but, so far as we can understand
the question, there is little chance of the decision being disturbed. Look-
ing at the nature of this decision, it is evident that considerable misconception has prevailed in the country regarding the provisions of the Foreign Enlistment Act. We have seen it repeatedly stated that warships are an

exceptional kind of merchandise, different altogether from arms and ammunition, and that they can neither be "built, furnished, equipped, armed, or fitted out" by private persons, without committing a breach of neutrality, and breaking the law of the land. It has been stated over and over again that it is perfectly legal to supply the Federal Government with arms and ammunition, while the Foreign Enlistment Act expressly forbids the manufacture or sale of war ships to the Confederates, or to any other belligerent Power at war with a friendly nation. It now appears, however, that all such opinions are simply nonsense. Ships, cannon, rifles, and gunpowder are all included in the same category; the traffic is legal, but the goods are liable to seizure on the high seas by any one of the belligerents, if it can be shown that they are on the way to the ports of the other ... it seems clear as noonday that the building of warships on speculation in this country is in every respect a lawful and legitimate occupation. It is only illegal when the builder knowingly and wilfully constructs a ship to be used against a friendly Power.

Writes Frank Owsley:

The shipping, the ocean-carrying establishment, of Britain had enjoyed unimagined success at the expense and distress of a similar enterprise in the Northern states. One of the profits treasured beyond all, one which was so enormous it cannot be measured in dollars and cents, was made possible in the complete destruction of the American merchant marine directly or indirectly by the Confederate privateers and cruisers. This destruction was done without England lifting her hand, except in a benediction upon the Confederacy for doing her work so thoroughly. In 1860 the United States was and had been for many years England's only serious rival in the world-carrying trade. So successful, in fact, had been the United States that she had largely driven England out of the direct trade between America and Great Britain — the most sensitive point of all. The United States had in this trade, in 1860, 2,245,000 tons of cargo, and Great Britain had only 946,000, while the total ocean-going tonnage of the American merchant marine was between 5,500,000 and 6,000,000 tons, practically as large as that of Great Britain and doubling every ten years. Its ships were magnificent. They could outsail anything afloat. The "Yankee Clipper" had been the despair and envy of the world. In 1861 England saw this magnificent fleet of seabirds begin to scatter and then disappear, until when the war ended only a little over a million tons of culls, mostly coasting vessels which could not be sold, were left. The American merchant marine was virtually extinct. The cruisers and privateers had sunk or captured above two hundred ships, destroying around thirty million dollars worth of property. But their greatest havoc was wrought by indirection. The hazard was so great that marine insurance rose higher than it was in the war with England in 1812 when England had the coast of America blockaded; shippers and merchants, American as well as European, were so fearful of the work of the *Alabama* and her sisters that they could not be induced to ship their merchandise on American ships. So the magnificent ships lay in dock swinging idly at their cables, their crews scattered, and their sails and hulls rotting, while less worthy craft plied the seas. Nothing was final except to sell them to neutrals whose flag would make them safe. England had bought over $42,000,000 worth out of a total sale of $64,799,750. The sale continued until little more than 1,000,000 tons of scraps were left. England's only rival had been destroyed for an indefinite span of years. England had fought wars for less than the destruction of a rival's merchant marine. Surely England could keep the peace for such a magnificent reward — especially since war would mean the destruction of her own merchant marine, in a similar fashion.[47]

By the summer of 1863, it became apparent to the shipping industry of Great Britain that its good fortune was in danger of evaporating. If the rams being built for the confederacy at Birkenhead compelled the relaxation of the close blockade, the only recourse of the North would be to establish a "cruising squadron" blockade remote from the shores of the enemy. If conducted by government warships, such a blockade was not in contravention of the British interpretation of international law. But the Northern navy, conducting a cruising squadron blockade, was far too small to interfere seriously with neutral vessels bringing supplies to the Confederacy or carrying cotton from Southern ports. A flood of privateers, scouring the ocean from pole to pole might, conceivably, still render effective that closing in of the South which was so important a weapon in the Northern war program. Nine-tenths of the actual blockade running still going on was by British ships, and this being so it was to be presumed that "privateers" searching for possible blockade runners would commit all sorts of indignities and interference with British merchant ships, whether on a blockade-running trip or engaged in ordinary trade between non-belligerent ports. The alteration of government policy as indicated by the arrest of the *Alexandra*, it might be hoped, would at least cause a suspension of the American plan, but assurances were strongly desired.

It would be unfair to leave the subject of English neutrality without noting that there were contemporary British authors who believed in the Union and did much to inform the reading public. The following represent just a few of the many articles that were available to the public in pamphlets and other short treatises:

> To render neutrality real, it seems to us plain that it will be necessary to go a step further than any scheme we have yet considered, and to place the distinction, neither in the quality of the transaction, nor in the destination of the enterprise, but in the kind of commodity. The line, in short, must be drawn between ships and other contraband goods; and for this we think it can be shown that there is solid ground in the nature of the case. We repudiate, indeed, the doctine which we have lately seen advanced, that a ship is a portion of the territory of the country to which it belongs — a doctine, in our judgment, at once artificial, questionable, and inadequate. We place the distinction for which we contend upon the plain fact, that an armed

ship, or ship prepared for armour, is a form of contraband, and the only form, which admits of being used directly from a neutral shore. That a ship admits of being so used affords a sufficient presumption that, when the temptation offers, it will be so used; and since, as we have shown, it is impossible in practice to distinguish a legitimate from an illegitimate destination, the one effectual remedy which remains is simply to proscribe this form of contraband from trading altogether.[48]

Goldwin Smith wrote on the case of the *Alabama* and English neutrality in a letter to the editor of *The Daily News* (March 1863):

> If there is anything at all analogous to the case of the Alabama, it is the permitting of troops to pass over your territory to the investion of a friendly power. Suppose Ireland, embracing the principles laid down by the Southern party in America and in this country, were to use the sacred right of secession. Suppose we had blockaded the Irish ports; and suppose Spain were to allow privateers commissioned by the rebel government of Ireland, with Spanish crews, to issue from the Spanish ports and prey on our commerce; what would the people of this country demand of their government? They must expect the American people to demand the same of theirs.... And what of the Confederate government? They are notoriously and systematically committing breaches of our neutrality, and tempting the subjects of this realm to violate its laws, at the risk of involving the people of this country in a terrible war.... The government of England may, I trust, on this and on all occasions, reckon on carrying the people with it into a just war, however great may be the dangers and suffering which the war may entail. But it cannot, on this occasion at least, reckon on carrying the people with it into an unjust war. The bond of nationality is strong, but it sometimes is inevitably superseded in the allegiance of the heart by the blood of a common cause. History does not blame the Protestant subjects of Catholic monarchies in the sixteenth century for having stood by Protestantism against their national governments. A case, similar in kind, though less extreme in degree, has occurred now. The cause of the aristocracy on both sides of the Atlantic is one; and according to our aristocracy, and the parliament which it predominates, have shown for the cause of the slaveowner an enthusiasm which they have never shown for any other cause in history. The cause of the people on both sides of the Atlantic is also one; and a large part of the English people now feel this to their hearts core.[49]

Count Agénor de Gasparin was elected a member of the French Chamber of Deputies in 1842. From then on, in and out of office, he travelled extensively and, as an influential writer and political figure, crusaded for the abolition of slavery. His book *America Before Europe*, a translation of which was published in New York in 1862, discloses his deeply felt revulsion toward slavery as well as his brilliantly perceptive analysis of Europe's role in the American war. Several of his observations follow:

First. The obligation of neutrality which Great Britain owes this nation (America) is based on international law, international comity, gratitude, the spirit of treaties, and, last and least, upon that compact with all the world, called the Act of 59 Geo. III. Second. That international law is the science of the external relations of nations, and that its sanctions are neither derived from nor independent upon things municipal, but bear equally upon democracies, aristocracies, and despotisms. Third. For this reason, no government can excuse itself from full performance of its international obligations by the suggestion of any lack of internal authority.... Fourth. That it was the duty of the British government to have seized and held the vessels, and thus preventing mischief, until a full investigation could have been had; and having failed in this, it was a duty all the more imperative, when the real purpose of these vessels was known ... to send British cruisers to prevent the consummation of a fraud, as well as to bring criminals to justice for their offence against the dignity and peace of England.[50]

We have until recently conceded everything to the South — fact and right. This is what we have called taking sides with no one! If I belonged to the South, I should ask nothing more, well knowing recognition and intervention to be the inevitable conclusion of these premises, which we must necessarily reach, if we go on in the same way. Who would have believed, — who would have said, that at the end of a few months we would come to admit all the premises of the South, excepting a single one — the legality of its secession, its immediate transformation between a rebel to a belligerent, our moral neutrality between the United States and the insurgents, the forgetfulness of the infamous cause defended by the latter, the conviction of their final success, the condemnation of the representative measures directed against them....[51]

To confer on the insurgents of the South the title of belligerents, and to claim for ourselves the position of neutrals, seems quite in conformity with the circumspect and unchivalrous wisdom which is sure of obtaining general approbation. What is better to be done, in the presence of such a crisis, than to stand aloof, to wait a little, to entertain neither opinions nor preferences? This is the first view of things, at which it is unusual to stop. It is only by scrutinizing more closely that we discover that the neutrality thus proclaimed is as little neutral as can be imagined; it settles the constitutional question discussed in the United States, and decides that the United States are a league; it bears so slight a resemblance to non-interference that not one of the first-class European powers would for an hour endure the application to its own affairs of the theory which they apply to the government at Washington.[52]

It seemed to us that England, which had not shown herself really prepared in the Crimea until ten or twelve months had elapsed, was ill placed to proclaim at the end of a few weeks the military powerlessness of the United

States. Their ministers had not yet reached the shores of Europe when this powerlessness was already admitted to the rank of proven facts; when it followed that the insurrectional government, sure of existence, deserved to be considered as a belligerent.... The South had a chance of success unique in history; its first gun passed for victory; its rebellion was immediately transformed into a revolution; it has no childhood, but was born full-grown. The rebellion of a day, behold it a government in fact, while waiting till it should make itself acknowledged as a government by right. This is not usually thus; before perceiving two States where there was lately but a single one, before placing on a footing of equality a regular government and those who are attacking it, we ordinarily wait until the latter have been victorious, have maintained their existence, and have shown some other sign of vitality than a first success, secured by treason![53]

The North ... instead of finding encouragement in England, has met there with nothing but distrust and hostility. In other cases, and with regard to other countries, England has found means of affording her powerful moral support — in journals, in parliamentary speeches, in public meetings. Here we find this moral support wanting. I know not what fatal misconception has kept down the generous sentiments of England in this crisis. But true it is, that the British journals, especially those which are reported to represent the views of Lord Palmerston, have unceasingly vindicated the right of secession, have declared the separation of the States to be not only complete and inevitable, but also good in itself, and acceptable to England. Nay, the recognition of the Southern Confederacy has again and again been presented to the public mind as an act for which only time and preparation are needed.[54]

9. The Blockade of Southern Ports

On 12 April 1861, Confederate forces fired upon Fort Sumter and on Sunday, 14 April, Fort Sumter formally surrendered and the most horrendous of civil wars began.

The Examiner reported the attack and surrender on 27 April 1861. Although there remained a hint in the article of serious consequences yet to develop, the newspaper treated the incident as a prologue to a comic opera:

> It is impossible to forsee any other than a deplorable immediate issue to the war begun between the United States in the North and South by the attack on Fort Sumter. Were the consequences less serious we might smile at the details of the act itself; a terrible outpouring of noise and smoke from forts and batteries; a large assembly of ladies seated before the spectacle with opera glasses in their hands; a few stones broken but no bones, and daring services performed under the lively fire of guns that poured anything but deadly shot.
>
> It is a civil war without a noble cause to sustain either side; more acting out upon a national scale, mandated as a national misery, of the old code, of a duellist, who fastens on his friend a challenge for a financial insult, and whose challenge must, as an affair of honour be accepted.

On 19 April 1861, Abraham Lincoln declared that he deemed it advisable to set on foot a blockade, and that when a "competent force" had been posted so as to prevent entrance and exit of vessels, warning would be given to any vessel attempting to enter or to leave a blockaded port, with endorsement on her register of such warning, followed by seizure if she again attempted to pass the blockade. The Proclamation named the original seven seceding states, and on 27 April Virginia was added. The blockade was actually begun at certain Virginia ports on 30 April, and by the end of May there were a few warships off all the more important Southern harbours.[55]

The blockade of the Southern ports presented a profusion of problems to the Ministry and to the press. England in the mid–Victorian era had emerged from a mercantile economy, and now its wealth and prosperity was dependent on free trade. It was an entrepreneurial England whose major industry, textile manufacturing, was in grave danger of losing its principal source of supply. Its cry was understandably to break the blockade. There was, however, a substantial group (today they might be perceived as nationalists) that understood that the breaking of the Blockade might endanger English ability to use its navy and continue as mistress of the seas. England, as a super-belligerent, had for decades used her fleet and blockaded ports with fewer warships to the mile of blockade than the North proposed.

In 1856, the major trading nations of the world participated in a conference at Paris in an effort to establish the rights of neutrals. England, at that time, renounced the great means of defense and attack that had grown up from her sea power and that she had maintained for 150 years against a world in arms. The British press attempted to explain a very complicated manifesto to their readers. In doing so they were not hesitant to note the inadequacies of the American blockade.

The Economist (25 May 1861) 561, 562:

> The rule laid down by the Congress of Paris was a compilation from the two opposed codes of naval war which divided the European world; from the one it selected the doctrine "that free ships make free goods," and from the other that only enemies' goods are to be seized on board any vessel of any country. Before the Declaration it had been held that the property of an enemy might be captured on the high seas in whatever ships it was conveyed. Thus the ships or goods of an enemy were in all cases and without qualification liable to capture at sea; and his trade with a neutral or with the hostile country was absolutely prevented, so far as it could be prevented by means of maritime capture. Since the Declaration, the rule may be considered to have been established as follows.
>
> The ships of any enemy are still liable to capture without qualification, on the high seas; but the goods of an enemy are liable to such capture only in one case, i.e. if they are conveyed in enemy's ships. A blockade to be binding ought not only (in the words of the Declaration of Paris) to be "effective," but established for military purposes. And it ought to be so, not in any vague or indirect manner, but directly and in the fullest sense part of a strategic plan. That no consideration as to its indirect effect in diminishing the enemy's military power by putting off from his people their sources of wealth, is sufficient to justify blockade, is implied in the very rule which allows neutrals to trade with him. A blockade, to constitute an

exception to this rule, should be clearly shown to have for its object direct military advantage to the blockading State. Thus a blockade forming part of a plan of siege or investment, or for the purpose of preventing supplies from reaching a hostile army, or intended to prevent the egress of, or to injure in any manner consistent with the laws of war, an enemy's fleet, would be entitled to observance by neutral States. As to what did or did not constitute a "military" blockade, within the meaning of the rule, diffculties would, of course arise, but there is no reason to suppose that they would be either greater or more numerous than those which attend the interpretation of many other rules of international law.

The assertion that the abolition of "commercial" blockades would be unfairly disadvantageous to Britain as a great maritime power, is open to much discussion. It is surely matter for doubt whether the profit which England would derive from it as a neutral State with the greatest commercial navy in the world, would not exceed any loss which it would inflict upon her as a belligerent State with the greatest military navy in the world; — for doubt, which the fearful calamity sustained by her in the former capacity on account of the present civil war in America may help to remove. But if the assertion were true, it would be a reason (so far as it went) not for maintaining in its present state the law of maritime capture and blockade, but for abolishing the rules of law with which the right of commercial blockade is irreconcilable. There is no need to insist on the suggestion that a code of international law which is inconsistent with itself requires alteration. A legal doctrine which declares that neutral trade with a belligerent is free, and at the same time declares that the whole coast of an enemy may be closed against neutral trade with the direct and ultimate object of excluding that trade is self-condemned. The only possible mode of rectifying the anomaly, except the abolition of "commercial" blockade, is one which is little likely to be adopted — a step backward to the principles and practice of a barbarous age. The American Government, however, never recognised the decisions of the Congress of Paris. It was invited to accede to those decisions, but it did not. The present American law is, therefore, exactly what the English old law was before the Congress of Paris; it exactly embodies what was called the rigid English theory. Its terms are concisely laid down by perhaps its greatest authority: "The two distinct propositions that enemy's goods found on board a neutral ship may be lawfully seized as prize of war, and that the goods of a neutral found on board an enemy's vessel were to be restored, have been explicitly incorporated into the jurisprudence of the United States, and declared by the Supreme Court to be founded in the law of nations."

The Times, 16 July 1857, shortly after the Congress of Paris, discussed the question of free trade, the history of neutral endeavor, and support of the Congress. Throughout the last half of the 19th century, The Times had great difficulty in deciding whether to pay homage to the ruling sovereign of the land or the captains of industry. In this instance it favored the captains of industry:

Within the last century several combinations of minor States have been
formed for the express purpose of extorting the surrender of the English
claim against neutrals. In every instance the attempt has been wholly unsuccessful. The Armed Neutrality of 1780, the Northern Confederation of 1801,
and the Allied Powers of 1814 were in turn compelled to acquiesce in the
maintenance of the ancient law. The present Government had the fullest
right to abide by the pretensions of former times, but it was their duty to
inquire whether this glorious inheritance had not become by a change in
circumstances a "damnos hereditas," as the negro in BWI [British West
Indies], a burdensome property, which it might be desirable to abandon,
and highly advantageous to dispose of for an adequate consideration. In
the days of Navigation Laws and of protective duties it was consistent with
the established policy of the country to discountenance neutral commerce.
Free Trade, on the other hand, welcomes buyers and sellers from every climate, and acquiesces, but unwillingly, in the necessity of refusing the
profitable visits of the enemy. Russian goods were in the height of the war
entitled to free circulation by land.

The moderation of *The Times* in 1857 was not duplicated by *The Daily Telegraph*, 22 September 1861. Now that the enterpreneurial class was faced with the
declaration of President Lincoln that the North intended to blockade the ports
of the South, *The Telegraph* rose to its defense:

In the midst of the conflagration, the head of the house sets an example of
convulsive alarm and lawless desperation; and a house thus managed is so
unsafe a neighbour, that all who live near must be prepared for something
still more terrible. If the rumour of the President's forthcoming proclamation be true, it is a crucial test of his utter recklessness. Recently we had
every reason to believe that Mr. Lincoln would not attempt to carry out
the new "law" of Congress, declaring the ports of the South no longer ports
of entry. Assurances were given that, although the blockade had not yet been
effective, it would be rendered so "soon." The Federal Government is computed to possess ample naval force for that purpose. Why, then, does it not
carry out the blockade? Is it — the question is momentous — because the
navy, its officers and men, are not to be trusted? Would they, sympathis-
ing with the merchant marine at New York, connive at any trading trans-
actions? Have they sympathies, as they have multiplied connections, with
the South? Are they infected with the distrust of the Washington Government which we see so rapidly spreading? We do not venture to assume the
answer; but it is certainly most strange that, while ostensibly possessing the
naval power to enforce a blockade, President Lincoln should deliberately
elect to attempt a closing of the ports by a paper proclamation, ridiculous
in idea, and in itself a violation of public law beyond all precedent. If the
act is to be perpetrated, it will amount to a declaration that the Seward-
Lincoln Goverment, impotent at home, has abandoned all hope of preserving the respect, if not the recognition, of foreign Powers.

The fear of *The Daily Telegraph* for the well being of its readership was manifest. The disregard for the truth was equally evident. In the fall of 1861 the Federal navy was not ready to attempt a full-scale blockade. And the English press was always on the alert to make the claim of a Union muddle. *The Telegraph* exercised a favorite tactic in accusing the forces of the Federals of corruption and deceit. Perhaps it was an omen of the performance of the great part of the English press during the entire war.

Sixty days later, 22 November 1861, *The Daily Telegraph* was selling similar malice. Then the sages of that newspaper concluded logically, but without verification, that the blockade was "inefficient" and therefore it was "non-existent":

> We believe that if the squadrons of commerce were to sail in any considerable numbers for the Southern ports, they could not be denied either entry or egress; and if so, technically the blockade must be regarded as nonexistent.... We have already supposed the ineffectiveness of the blockade as a proven fact; and, in that case, there cannot be the slightest doubt that any armed attack upon the merchant ships of a foreign Power, on any pretence whatsoever, would be an act of lawless aggression. Without a previous declaration of war against the State to which the vessel belonged, it would be an act coming close to piracy; and any European Government whose ships should be thus assailed would not simply be entitled to defend its subjects from wanton injury, but would be bound so to do.... Even in England, we are aware, there are commercial men who, knowing the blockade to be a fiction, have contemplated practical measures to bring the fiction to an experimental test.

Although both Lord Lyons as British Minister in Washington and Lord Russell as Foreign Secretary in England used language more ministerial and less accusatory than that of *The Daily Telegraph*, both were convinced that the blockade of Southern ports, creeks and bays, to the extent of 3,000 miles, was impossible. However, with a better knowledge of Southern ports they would have realized that if but seven harbors — Norfolk (Virginia), Wilmington (North Carolina), Charleston (South Carolina), Savannah (Georgia), Mobile (Alabama), New Orleans (Louisiana), and Galveston (Texas) — were effectively blockaded the remaining 2,550 miles of coastline would be useless for the export of cotton to any considerable amount. Although the bays and creeks of the South would provide access to small vessels, these were not adequate for the transport of a bulky export like cotton.[56]

As the American Civil War continued to develop, the British Ministry was attempting to resolve its own internal problems which resulted from the Declaration of Paris. The desire of *The Economist* (November 1862) 1205 to convert its readers to the support of the Declaration of Paris was unmistakable:

The interest of England now, if not formerly, is that the rules of maritime warfare should be relaxed as much as they can be. We are the nation which has the greatest imports and the greatest exports — which is most dependent upon foreign commerce. Both our consumers and our producers want foreign trade more than those of any other nation. We do not grow food enough for our own people; we import a most material part of the sustenance of our population. Our producers are even more dependent on foreign influence. We work up into useful articles the raw and coarse materials of ... distant countries. Our soil is limited, but our capital is great, our skill considerable, our industry inexhaustible. We therefore import from vast and distant territories, where capital is scarce and industry backward, innumerable materials in a state yet useless — in much the same shape as they are grown upon the soil — and we fashion them into useful shapes. Our people do not grow, but elaborate; they are secondary workers upon materials sent to them by preparatory workers. If you cut off the supply of the "preliminaries of industry," you starve our operatives and ruin our capitalists. So far from the permission of blockades being to the interest of England, a great blockade can scarcely be imagined which would not materially, perhaps vitally, affect an important part of our people. We are the receiving nation of the world; if you prevent any country from sending anything, the chances are that you prevent us from obtaining something which we are most in need of.

D.P. Crook writes:

Lord Russell was an historic British statesman, and, like others of his breed, saw in British policy not an improvisation to meet a particular crisis but a set of principles that were to endure for all time. He was thinking not only of the existing American war, but of future conflicts in which England itself might be engaged. And he accepted the rules of blockade introduced by the United States not for any other reason than they were the principles Britain had lived with and wished to see enshrined as international law. The Declaration of Paris, though accepted perforce by Great Britain, had always been exceedingly unpopular with gentlemen whose chief interest was the greatness of the British Empire. Britain's long term interest, a good many Englishmen felt, lay in affirming and expanding the blockade practice. Clearly, British acquiescence in a strong naval role by the north would set the Admiralty convenient precedents, superseding temporary inconveniences to British shipping and abrasions to national pride.[57]

Burton J. Hendrick writes:

That Declaration, they believed, had robbed Great Britain of the most powerful engine it possessed for protecting England's destiny — the British fleet. To weaken Britain in maritime warfare had indeed been the purpose of the Continental statesmen who had at length succeeded in foisting it upon their great rival.... The Paris rules of blockade would interfere with England's effective use of its fleet. Any blockade it would declare would necessarily be a loose one; the British fleet could no more blockade the whole coast of France — Atlantic and Mediterranean — than could the American Navy the 3000 miles of Confederate coastline.[58]

The Times, 1 March 1862, with an eye to Britain's future needs, confirmed the intent of the British Ministry on the Northern blockade of Southern ports. Lord Russell considered the blockade effective in the eyes of international law:

> In a Despatch dated the 15th of February, and which we published yesterday, Lord RUSSELL expounds the true policy of this country with regard to BLOCKADES. It is a policy which ought to be adopted for the sake of its magnanimity, if it were not for the sake of its wisdom. Although a sufficient blockading force is in station at the ports of Charleston and Wilmington, various ships have been successfully eluded in the Blockade; but Lord RUSSELL thinks that, the Blockade having been duly notified, and a sufficient number of ships having been stationed near the ports to prevent access to them, or to create an evident danger in entering or leaving them, while these ships do not voluntarily permit ingress or egress, the fact that the various ships have escaped will not of itself prevent the Blockade from being recognized as effective by International Law.

The Times, 16 August 1862, gathered all the true English grit and gloriously suffered all the torments of the American blockade in silence and with good resolve. The English textile merchant was reaping profits from the increase in the price of raw cotton and the sale of out-of-date inventory. Above all, neutrality is to be preserved:

> We are neutral, and neither the loss of the raw material of our manufacture nor the hard measures which have been dealt out to British subjects accused of intending to break the blockade will induce us to quit our present attitude of neutrality. There is nothing more to be said.... We will bear as patiently as we can those miseries which have fallen on a portion of our population.

The immediate problem facing the Ministry continued to be the need to deal with the Northern blockade which was denying cotton to the nation's most important industry. Without a continuous supply of that material thousands upon thousands of English workers would need private or governmental assistance.

There were powerful forces working to deter the Ministry from taking overt steps to break the blockade; some, however, in the early stages of the conflict were not so obvious. It was apparent to the Ministry that the Northern blockade of the Confederate coast was not sufficient in 1861 and early 1862 to deny the delivery of cotton to the textile mills of Britain. It was the decision of the Confederacy to place an embargo on the shipment of that precious raw material as a means of forcing Britain and France to come to their aid that resulted in the scarcity of cotton.

King Cotton had long been a boast with the South. Hostilities could not last long, for France and Great Britain must have what the Confederacy alone could supply, and therefore they could be forced to aid the South. This confidence was no new development. For ten years past whenever Southern threats of secession had been indulged in, the writers and politicians of the Confederacy had identified cotton as the one great product which would compel European acquiescence in American policy, whether of the Union, before 1860, or of the South if she should secede.

Adams writes: "In the financial depression that swept the Northern states in 1857, *De Bow's Review*, the leading financial journal of the South declared: 'The wealth of the South is permanent and real, that of the North fugitive and fictitious. Events now transpiring expose the fiction, as humbug after humbug explodes.... Cotton, rice, tobacco and naval stores command the world; and we have sense enough to know it, and are sufficiently Teutonic to carry it out successfully.' ... In 1861, *De Bow's Review* contained an article declaring that 'the first demonstration of blockade of the Southern ports would be swept away by the English fleets of observation hovering on the Southern coasts, to protect English commerce and especially the free flow of cotton to English and French factories.... The stoppage of the raw material ... would produce the most disastrous political results — if not a revolution in England.'"[59]

The Southern people did not propose to wait for the Federal blockade to become slowly effective, and by the same slow stages reduce the supply of Southern cotton going to British and French factories. They proposed to meet the blockade at the threshold with restrictive measures which would produce an immediate cotton famine: England and France should have no cotton with which to stave off this famine and postpone intervention. The first step to carry out this policy was the embargo of 1861-1862. Cotton planters, although heavily in debt, agreed that no cotton would be allowed to leave the plantations until the blockade had been lifted and Southern independence recognized. Newspapers, planters, factors, merchants, Congress, and state legislatures and executives all offered opposition to the export of cotton in the form of either advice or sterner means; but, backed by such strong sentiment in favor of an embargo, it was the citizens' organizations, usually taking the title of Committee of Public Safety, who had the final word. It was these local organizations, backed by public sentiment, which made it unnecessary, even superfluous, for Congress and the state legislatures to pass embargo acts. They saw that no cotton went through the blockade at the principal ports for many months, so long as the embargo policy was thought effective. "After the spring of 1862 the cotton embargo was slowly relaxed until it completely ceased. Some confidence had been lost in the power of cotton, but this was not so much the cause of the letting-up of the embargo as the absolute and immediate necessity the South labored under of obtaining supplies from abroad; and cotton was by the spring of 1862 the only medium of exchange left in the South which was acceptable abroad."[60]

The Times, 21 October 1861, gave evidence of its unhappiness with the Confederate Cotton Embargo:

Is the blockade everywhere effectual? It certainly is not. As might be expected, when a few frigates and corvettes undertake to seal up three thousand miles of coast there is in the great majority of places no blockade at all. Few only of the American vessels are steamers, and these are not of the fastest class.... We must remind our Lancashire friends that the event also shows that the cutting off of the Cotton supplies is the work of the South as much as of the North. If ships can get in, they can also get out; and, if the South desired to send us Cotton, it has not lacked the opportunity. But it seems to be forbidden by the Confederate Government in order that foreign nations may be forced to take a side in the quarrel. It would ill become England to make herself the tool of such machinations.

Neither the British Government nor *The Times* was unaware of the design of the Confederacy to embargo cotton. *The Times* appreciated the respite the Confederate embargo would entail for the textile industry. It also appreciated the difficulties in embargoing an entire crop, and seemed little worried. Certainly the newspaper harbored no concern for the workers who would be made redundant, but felt unqualified joy over the prospects that the industry would be able to sell its surplus inventory at considerable profits. *The Times* 24 October 1861:

> Cotton still rising in price; labour lacking employment, and manufacturers destitute of materials, — these, with the winter before us, are signs of no common trouble. It is true that we have some grounds for consolation and assurance. The state of the Cotton trade was such that it had become rather more desirable than otherwise that production should be slackened for a time. Markets were glutted with goods, and the stocks on hand were in excess of the rate of demand and consumption.
>
> It is also far from improbable that a portion of the American crop may reach us. We should look, indeed, upon this chance as considerable, were it not for the resolution taken by the planters themselves to withhold supplies. We know from our own experience on the coast of Africa, that a blockade on a large scale can never be absolutely effectual, and if the Southern States desired to send Cotton to sea, the weak squadrons of the Federal Government could intercept only a percentage of the cargoes. It is said, however, that the Confederates are purposely keeping the Cotton crop at home in order that the pressure thus put upon the European Governments may induce them to interfere for the termination of the blockade, if not of the war.

Adams writes: "In the generally accepted view of a short war, there was, at first, no anticipation of real danger. But beginning with December, 1861, there was almost a complete stoppage of supply from America. In the six months to the end of May, 1862, but 11,500 bales were received, less than one percent of the amount for the same six months of the previous year. The blockade was making itself felt and not merely in shipments from the South but in prospect of Southern production, for the news came that the negroes were being withdrawn by their masters from the rich sea islands along the coast in fear of their capture by the Northern blockading squadrons. Such a situation seemed bound in the end to result in pressure by the manufacturers for governmental action to secure cotton....

"The immediate result of the American war was, at this time, to relieve the English cotton trade, including the dealers in raw material and the producers and dealers in manufactures, from a serious and impending difficulty. They had in hand a stock of goods sufficient for the consumption of two-thirds of a year, therefore a rise in the price of raw material and the partial closing of their establishments, with a curtailment of their working expenses, was obviously to their advantage. But to make their success complete, this rise in the price of cotton was upon the largest stock ever collected in the country at this season. To the cotton trade there came in these days an unlooked-for accession of wealth, such as even it had never known before. In place of hard times which had been anticipated, and perhaps deserved, there came a shower of riches."[61]

Glasgow was the home of a substantial textile industry. *The Glasgow Herald*, 28 February 1862, could only rejoice at the cotton situation. It prized the comfort that the scarcity of cotton would give to the "glutted" markets:

> Since the war in America commenced and the blockade of the Southern ports was completed, we have been assured by authorities in the cotton trade that our stock of raw material would be exhausted by the close of last year, and the reasons annexed to these assurances seemed so indisputable that nobody had the courage to dispute them. Time passed, however, and circumstances exercised their accustomed influence on human affairs, and the result was that, notwithstanding the blockade and the prognostications of the cotton prophets, our stock of that material was larger at the beginning of the present year than it was at the corresponding period of 1861.... A deficient supply of cotton at the present time has also saved us from the accumulated evils of over-production, glutted markets, a monetary crisis, and prostration of trade. Our present suffering, great though it may be, has come upon us gradually; and while money was abundant, the over-production of past years is melting away and when this fratricidal war in America is finally settled down one way or another, we have every reason to expect a lengthened and prosperous run of trade as we have rarely or never experienced.

The Economist (4 January 1862) 45, supplied some additional information on the unexpected and undeserved profits of the English textile industry:

> The cotton which is worth 12d a lb today in Liverpool is worth 18d at New York, and despite closed mills, cotton was being shipped from Britain to

America. The profit chiefly pocketed by the British merchant. Only 16,000 bales had thus been sent up to the end of 1861; though larger lots are now in process of shipment.

The Economist (11 January 1862) 4 confirmed its fears of additional shipments of cotton from England to the United States continuing at a greater pace in spite of the textile mill closures and shortened work weeks:

> Up to the 31st December only about 16,000 bags had been shipped; but since then the quantity has greatly increased. Heavy purchases have been made, steamers have been engaged to take cotton to Boston and New York, and the freight asked and paid is unexampled, — being we understand, 2d per lb, and 5 per cent. primage. Up to Thursday there have been this year already shipped to New York 15,000 bales, and to Boston upwards of 5,000, and the shipment is still going on.

Writes Frank Lawrence Owsley: "It would be unfair to single out the good fortune and undeserved profits of the textile industry. The situation could be better computed by simply saying that the entrepreneurs of England made vast profits during the American Civil War. Besides her surplus stock of cotton and cotton fabrics selling at incredible profits, her linen and woolen industries reaped unexpected harvests of gold, her munitions and steel industries enriched themselves, her shipbuilding was enormously stimulated by the demands of the Confederate government and of the blockade business, and merchant houses made millions out of blockade-running. Finally, the American merchant marine was driven from the seas and largely transferred to England, without a loss of a single ship or bit of treasure. An examination of the volume of British imports and exports during the Civil War is rather eloquent of this profit, although much of the imports were the invisible earnings of the great enhanced merchant marine which do not appear on the books. The volume of foreign trade in 1864 was £509,000,000 as against £374,500,000 in1860, or 34 per cent greater than before the war."[62]

Owsley also says that "blockade running became, truly, the enormous profit maker of British industry. Between a million and a million and a half bales of cotton were run through the blockade at a net profit of seldom less than 300 per cent. Goods shipped into the Confederacy, exclusive of munitions which formed only a small portion of this trade, netted a profit frequently amounting to 500 per cent. One round trip through the blockade frequently paid for a vessel and its cargo and left a profit. Many of the vessels ran scores of times."[63]

Mary Ellison writes, "On the British side of the Atlantic, ships running the blockade eventually reached 588. They shipped 8,250 cargoes, worth $2,000,000, and 1,250,000 bales of cotton were run out from the South to pay for them. Despite the important subsidiary role of Glasgow, there is little doubt that the

majority of these ships sailed from Liverpool, and it was on her docks that
the valuable cargoes were loaded and unloaded. It was in Liverpool more
than any other British city that a flurry of indignation could be whipped
up against the smooth surface of official passivity at the same time that the
determined practical support given by Mersey shipping interests to the South
was undermining that inactivity…. So strong was the action taken by the
port of Liverpool in building ships for the Confederacy and defying the blockade that, in Charles Adams' view, it was 'virtually tantamount to a participa-
tion in the war by the people of Great Britain to a degree which, if not reasonably prevented, cannot fail to endanger the peace and welfare of both
countries.'"[64]

The pressure exerted on the English ministry to take measures to break the
blockade of the Southern coasts continued to mount. Nevertheless, English
profits from the blockade runners were enormous.

The Examiner, 15 February 1862, cautioned the British Ministry as to the
acceptance of the blockade. It was only fitting for the champion of free trade to
take this stance:

> As for the question of the effectiveness of the blockade, it is clear that our
> Government is not disposed to be very strictly critical, and it would wisely
> compound for some deficiencies; but it must be observed that indulgence
> in this direction cannot be carried far without trenching on what is due to
> the other belligerent….
>
> It is not without reason that the law of nations requires blockades to
> be effectual. An effectual blockade places all nations on the same footing of
> exclusion, and none of their merchants and shippers can obtain an advan-
> tage of intercourse at the expense of others. An ineffectual blockade, on the
> other hand, is a partial blockade, operating injuriously on those who
> observe international obligations, and giving advantages to the reckless and
> unscrupulous. It offers a large premium to the smuggler at the expense of
> the fair trader. And there is another reason of justice and policy why block-
> ades should be effectual. It is for the convenience of the whole civilised
> world that intercourse between nations should not be lightly interrupted,
> which would frequently happen if blockades could be declared without
> being maintained by adequate force. The naval force requisite to give effect
> and reality to the blockade is the tax on the belligerent, which forbids him
> to have recourse to the expedient lightly, or to continue it longer than the
> necessity of the case may require. While the one enemy suffers from a sort
> of national excommunication, the blockading power suffers too from the
> heavy cost of maintaining his fleets at sea, exposed to weather in all
> seasons. If we could see the expense of the American blockade we should
> thoroughly understand the international policy of requiring it to
> be effectual. And it is not till the wear and tear and loss of ships knocking
> about in all weathers begin to tell that the cost touches upon the maxi-
> mum….

Macmillan's Magazine (November, 1861–April 1862) 1149–1150, disagreed, and offered a warning to the Ministry and the people of England:

At the present crisis, when the question of "effective blockades" is once more before the world, it is well to see what is and what ought to be the recognised theory of nations in this respect. In 1780 the "armed neutralities" with France and Russia at their head, for their mutual benefit and the benefit of all neutrals, agreed by a number of conventions, — the language of all of which was virtually the same, — that the practice of this country with respect to blockade ought to be modified and limited.... The definition given by the convention of 1780 of a blockaded port was an attempt to put down for ever paper blockades, — a species of warfare designed rather to harass an enemy's trade than to occupy his ports.... According to the law of nations, as thus expounded by an ex parte declaration, the blockading vessels must be present and close to the blockaded port. No official notice would be sufficient to close a harbour until it was ipso facto closed by an investing fleet, nor could the sending of a few cruisers to a hostile coast give a colour of legality to a fictitious and illegal measure ... the definition required the absolute presence of the belligerent vessels in close proximity to the blockaded spot. Though the rules were laxer, yet the spirit was still the same as the spirit of the old treaties, which stipulated that ten, twenty, or half a dozen vessels, as the case might be, should be necessary to blockade the mouth of a harbour or a port. The history of the opposition offered by England to the above theory is well known. In the Anglo-Russian Convention of 1801, which was designed to abrogate the conventions of the "armed neutralities," both English statesmen and foreign jurisconsults have seen a triumph of reactionary principles of blockade.... There can be no reasonable doubt that, in respect of blockade "by cruisers," of diplomatic "notice," of "special notice," and of other details branching out of this part of the question, England may be broadly said to be at variance with the rest of the naval world. Having hitherto been the advocates of belligerent as well as neutral rights; — having — as we do not doubt, in the absence of evidence to the contrary — even so late as the Congress of 1856 refused to allow the difficulty to be settled in the interest of the neutral powers, England cannot now, with seemliness, insist on forcing down the throat of America an interpretation of the law of blockade against which we have always openly or tacitly protested.

We may take it for granted that the American blockade is nothing much better and nothing much worse than a blockade by "cruisers." For a blockade by cruisers it is tolerably effective. In estimating its efficiency allowance must indeed be made for the many ships which would break the blockade, were they not unwilling to run the risk, which for anything they knew may be a slight one. Yet, without doubt, the large ports along the coast, and most of the creeks that communicate with them, are closed virtually to general commerce; and if they are not hermetically sealed, it does not lie in our mouths to be too inquisitive or strict. America certainly ought to do more than cruise off the Southern coast if she wishes to be consistent

with herself. Her own official documents are in testimony against her....
But if America cannot properly defend her "blockade by cruisers," neither
can we demur to it, unless its defectiveness be more glaring than it has been
shown to be. Doubtless there are Admiralty decisions to the effect that an
occasional cruiser appearing off a port does not constitute a blockade, any
more than one swallow makes a summer. Still, we have contended too
stoutly against the views of the "armed neutrals" to permit of our forming
ourselves, in company with France, into that thing so hateful to us of old —
"an armed neutrality."

Lord Malmesbury and the Tory organs find themselves in a dilemma.
They are anxious to precipitate the separation of North and South, but they
are equally anxious that we should relax nothing of our old belligerent theories. We do not agree with them. For the present, we ought not to bear
ourselves impatiently towards an exaggerated doctrine which in other days
we refused distinctly to sacrifice, when it was to our benefit to retain it.
But, for the future, warned by this experience, let us accept a wider view
of blockades and the rights of neutrals in general. The true theory of blockade has not yet been advocated in England; but, it is one which is for the
interest to a besieged town. The neutral who gratuitously violates the cordon of blockade may be considered as having gratuitously interfered in the
hostilities to befriend the besieged. We have it that a blockading force takes
possession of the blockaded waters so far as the possession reaches. How
far over the jurisdictional waters does the blockading fleet extend the
dominion of its flag? The whole question of the effectiveness of blockades
seems to depend upon the answer....

Commerce is free to all, and on the belligerent who disturbs it lies the
onus of showing that he disturbs it lawfully. If blockade is a temporary
interference with the natural rights of neutrals, and rests on a de facto occupation, no unnecessary latitude can legally be allowed it. Beyond the
strictest limits of occupation the status ante revives, nor is the presumption in favour of blockade, but of liberty of commerce with the shore. If
this is so (and we submit that it is so), a ship is fully at liberty, even after
official notice of blockade, to visit the blockaded spot, and to assure herself that the official notice is not an idle menace.... A doctrine of blockade
more congenial to neutral commerce is chiefly to be advocated because the
change would be a benefit to the world, and in particular a benefit to ourselves. Our statesmen have remembered long enough that England, when
she is at war, is the greatest of belligerents. It is time they should remember also, that when she is at peace she is the greatest of neutrals. The interest of the most important trading nation of the age cannot really be at variance with the interests of neutral commerce.

The abolishing of privateers was a piece of international legislation
which the Congress of Paris carried out in the interests of universal trade;
but no country more benefited by the concessions than our own.... England's interest is, that each nation's power of inflicting damage on its
enemies' trade, should be in exact proportion to the regular force which it
can bring to bear in war time on a given spot. Irregular warfare, may be,

perhaps, for the benefit of those whose naval power is less overwhelming than ours. But England is chiefly concerned to see that the greatest possible advantage shall be reserved for the country that has the most considerable fleet. To limit as narrowly as possible the right of blockade; to put an end, if possible, to "blockade by cruisers"; and to insist upon the doctrine of blockade by investing force, is a policy which would increase rather than diminish our naval predominance. It is astonishing that this truth should not be more generally seen. If the Continent in its wisdom were to so state further, and to urge that no port should be held to be blockaded off where less than a dozen or even twenty ships were stationed, we should gain, not lose, by the proposition.

We can better spare twenty ships than anybody else for the purpose. We should be better off than other maritime powers in proportion to the facility with which we could detach the requisite number of vessels on such a service. The result would be that the privilege of blockading would virtually pass altogether into English, and into French hands. If the American civil war teaches us to examine the principles on which blockade should rest, and to abolish "blockade by cruisers," it will have taught us a valuable lesson. The day will perhaps come when all of us will acknowledge — what in our opinion is certain — that by enforcing strictness of blockade, and by admitting the inviolability of enemies' private property at sea, as we have admittted that of neutral property at sea, England and civilization will both be gainers. We are far from approving of intervention in favour of the South. Evidence is wanting to show that the blockade of the South coast is so completely a paper blockade as to justify us in protesting against it; and we are not the proper people, nor is this the proper time perhaps, to raise the question.

The Economist (19 October 1861) 1149 outlined the appropriate free trade policy of the English in treating with the blockade:

Now, as far as England is concerned, we believe we may confidently assert that her intervention will be strictly limited to insisting that the blockade of every port announced to be closed, shall be bona fide, efficient, and continuous. She must take care that the blockading squadron shall be ample and impartial, — shall be considerable enough really to prevent ingress and egress, and shall connive at the escape of no ships, and shall give papers to none. If these requirements are not fulfilled — and we are by no means satisfied on this head — then we are entitled, and are bound, to notify to the Government of the United States that the blockade of that port or that coast is not effective, is not therefore valid by the law of nations, cannot be recognised by us, and will not be respected by our ships. If we are vigilant enough in this respect, we apprehend that the blockade in several quarters will be found inadequate and will have to be renounced. But this is a very different matter from interfering to "prohibit the blockade" altogether, on the ground that it is very mischievous to us. The one proceeding is strictly in accordance with international law and justice. The other is a flagrant and manifest violation of both.

Count Agénor de Gasparin provided an historical background, and one that favoured the Federal attempts to interfere with commerce to the Confederacy. The blockade of the coasts of France and Italy by the British navy, which resulted in the War of 1812, put the British Ministry in a poor position to argue against the Federal restraints:

> On consulting the principal treaties and comparing their terms, we arrive at the conclusion that an effective blockade is that of ports which there is evident danger in entering. No one has ever dreamed of saying that, in order to be effective, the blockade must render the entrance impossible. The expression which I have just employed is precisely that which we read in the famous declaration published in 1780, by Catherine II, to guarantee the right of neutrals. Article 4 is couched as follows: "to determine what characterizes a blockaded port, this denomination shall be accorded to those only which, through the disposition by the assailing power of stationary vessels, placed sufficiently near each other, there is evident danger in entering." The second armed neutrality holds the same language as the first. I cite article 3: "A port can be regarded as blockaded only if its entrance be evidently dangerous in consequence of the disposition made by one of the belligerent powers, by means of vessels placed in its proximity." Let us leap over that long interval of violence when the rights of neutrals and the freedom of the seas were immolated without ceasing, when paper blockades were established, when England declared the whole coast of the Continent blockaded, while the decrees of Milan and Turin proclaimed all the shores of the British Isles in a state of blockade; let us arrive at the epoch when true principles were proclaimed anew by France and England. What do we find in the concerted instructions given by both governments to their navies at the outbreak of the Crimean war? I open those emanating from M. Duclos. Article 7 reads: "Every blockade to be respected must be effective, that is, maintained by sufficient force that there may be imminent danger in penetrating into the ports invested." The blockade does not cease to be effective solely because a number of vessels have succeeded in running it. The American cruisers are forced to contend with a terrible enemy — English commerce. Night and day, in the hundred openings of a coast pierced in every direction by natural inlets, behind innumerable islands formed from the union of rivers, lie a whole army of small craft, ready to profit by darkness or foul weather.... English commerce must know that there is evident danger in running the blockade, for the list of its vessels seized and confiscated is not small. The ports into which vessels of heavy draught can enter are all sufficiently guarded; which does not mean, I repeat, that one will ever be sure of preventing a steamboat like the *Bermuda* or *Nashville* from piercing the line of cruisers. It seems to me, on the whole, that the blockade is effective enough which results in interrupting communication and almost entirely suppressing the import and export trade. It would not occasion so much complaint if it were not effective.... But it is deceiving the European governments to maintain that it is easy to escape the

blockade, when not a vessel has entered the harbor of New Orleans by the river for the last five months, and when not a single foreign ship has arrived by the way of the Lakes.

... an "effective" blockade did not differ substantially from that put forward in the British Proclamation of Neutrality; a blockade to be effective must be "at least to the point where a vessel attempting to pass through was likely to be captured." It was not necessary for the blockading force to be 100 per cent successful to be considered as "effective."[65]

Early in the conflict in America, and to ensure the effectiveness of the blockade, the Northern forces contrived to sink ships laden with stones in the principal harbors of the Confederacy. Charleston was designated as the first port for the experiment. The reaction from England was instantaneous. Lord Russell immediately claimed that the Federals were conducting the war with "barbarity."

The sinking of obstructions in an enemy's harbor in order to render more effective a blockade was no novelty in maritime warfare, as Russell must have well known, and that there was no modern record of such obstructions having permanently destroyed a harbor. On the impossibility of an effective blockade, if conducted on customary lines, the British people and the Foreign Secretary had pinned their faith that there would be no serious interruption of trade.The very thought that the blockade might become effective, in which case all precedent would demand respect for it, caused considerable discomfiture in the English ministry.[66]

Lloyd's Weekly Newspaper, 19 January 1861, although sympathetic to the Northern cause was outraged at the "barbarous deeds" involved in the Federal employment of a stone fleet at the port of Charleston. British commerce, argued Lloyd's, must continue without interference of any kind:

> Our commerce is harmed; barbarous deeds are being committed; and we are looking on in anger. That which has been done in the harbour of Charleston [the stone blockade], has been condemned throughout Europe as a wanton outrage, in the reparation of which all civilised nations are interested. Are we lapsing into old, and barbarous, and unchristian days? Is this the act of one of the foremost nations in Christendom? Indignant men, roused by this outrage on the civilised world, ask — How long will Europe permit the North to commit acts which injure not only her enemy, the South, but all commercial nations on the face of the earth? Thus, under the ashes of one volcano, another rises. The Trent affair is past and gone; but how about the blockade? It is asserted, and in reliable quarters, that independent members of the House of Commons intend, early in the session, to press upon government the expediency of recognising the South, and of raising the blockade, since the fate of Charleston warrants the belief that the maintenance of the blockade will do permanent injury to all nations that are interested in the trade of the blockaded ports. There is a danger ahead that is to be avoided — as all dangers are best avoided — by being met manfully....

The Examiner, 15 February 1862, continued the attack on the setting of a stone fleet in the Charleston harbour.

> the Americans have certainly prejudiced their case very considerably by recourse to the detestable device of the stone fleet, which undoubtedly argues the want of power to effect the same object by more legitimate and civilised means. We may feel quite justified in imprisoning or hanging a traitor, but not by artificial means in giving him the cruel disease of the stone.... The American Government now finds it necessary to its pretensions to humanity and civilization, to protest that it does not propose nor contemplate the permanent obstruction of channels serving for communication and also refuge for distressed shipping. But unfortunately the scheme was ushered in with a boast that it was designed and thoroughly calculated to blot out of existence the cities which have grown up on the waterways, to be for ever choked by the sinking of the stone fleets. We do not believe it within the wicked will of man to effect so detestable a mischief as was proclaimed with glorification in the first instance; but for the opprobrium of such an intention the American Government has to thank the representation of its own New York press.

From *Macmillan's Magazine* (November 1861–April 1862) 432, came the denial of the catastrophic effects of the stone fleet. There were some in Britain who were not caught up in the yearning to destroy America:

> A great deal of denunciation has indeed been extended on the sinking of the stone fleet at the mouth of Charleston harbour. If the harbour was thereby destroyed or permanently injured, the measure would be a barbarous one, against which all Europe might consistently and properly protest. But engineers know that it is extremely difficult to block up a channel by sinking obstructions at its mouth. In all probability, the bottom of the Charleston harbour is composed of alluvial soil. The action of the outward current in such case will scoop out the bed of sand or mud from beneath the sunken ships. It is likely (judging from what is usually the case with wrecks) that they will in time disappear entirely, and even the very weight of stone which they carry will increase the rapidity of their disappearance.... If this view be correct, the sinking of the stones is not an outrage on the law of nations, though it is a severe and unusual measure. We are not of the number of those who think that America's difficulty is England's opportunity. It would be unjust and unwise to interfere unnecessarily with the naval operations of the North; and a cogent case for interference has not yet been established, either in respect of the stone fleet or of the blockade. But should the question of effective blockade be raised at all, we trust it will not be dismissed again until it has been more satisfactorily settled.

In the end, England made no attempt to interfere with the blockade. The nationalists and the entrepreneurs shared the victory. There was sufficient glory and riches for both.

The shipbuilding ports of Great Britain furnished the largest proportion of the blockade-runners which kept the South supplied for four years. One yard on the Mersey launched 5 blockade runners in a single day; Lairds built 7 or 8 such vessels. Over 1,200 vessels owned by, or carrying supplies for, the Confederates came into or left Liverpool during 1861.[67]

Writes Frank L. Owsley: "Altogether about 400 steamers, many of them iron, and eight hundred sail vessels were sold as blockade runners. Great numbers of these vessels were constructed during the war. In addition to this, six ironclads and two wooden cruisers were constructed by the shipbuilders of Liverpool and Glasgow for the Confederate government.... Between a million and a million and a half bales of cotton were run through the blockade at a net profit of seldom less than 300 per cent. Goods shipped into the Confederacy, exclusive of munitions which formed only a small portion of this trade, netted a profit often amounting to 500 per cent. One round trip through the blockade frequently paid for a vessel and its cargo and left a profit. Many of the vessels ran scores of times."[68]

Writes D. P. Crook:

> There were 2,960 runs attempted through the blockade of the Gulf ports, 2,054 at Carolina ports, 1,302 at Georgia and East Florida ports. Of the total of 6,316 runs attempted during the war, 5,389 were successful, an 85% success rate. Steam blockaders achieved a 92% success rate (2,525 out of 2,742 runs attempted). The ships best fitted for blockade running were light craft, preferably speedy, with necessarily limited tonnage; at night, by hugging the coastline, they could elude the vigilance of the heavier Union cruisers, which were usually forced by coastal shallows and other hazards to anchor four or five miles offshore. Small, fast paddle and crew steamers were popular, many being built especially for the trade on the Mersey or Clyde. Blockade-running became a highly organized and flourishing industry, paying high wages for skippers and crews (mostly foreigners, many British), and returning astronomic profits. Ports such as Nassau in British New Providence, St. George's in Bermuda, and Matamoros in Mexico became thriving entrepots for the illicit trade. Cotton and other southern exports made their way to these centers, and thence to Europe, while goods destined for the Confederacy were transshipped from large neutral traders to flotillas of small blockade-runners. These facts may also be construed as demonstrating the dislocative effects of the blockade. Modern naval opinion is inclined to the broad view that the blockade achieved its major objective by scaring off a potentially massive trade with the South. Risk of capture deterred huge numbers of regular merchantmen from making even a token attempt to enter the southern ports — the chances of heavy draft steamers or sailing vessels negotiating the major channels to the relatively few big ports such as Charleston, Wilmington, Savannah, or New Orleans were minimal.... The statistics of blockade-running are less impressive when

the light tonnages of runners are remembered, and also the fact that a substantial proportion of successful runs occurred in the first year of the war, when
Union blockaders were few and crews were unfamiliar with the demanding
routine of blockade duty. As an extreme indication, 1123 out of a total of 1302
runs attempted through the Georgia and East Florida ports occurred between
April 20 and December 31, 1861, before the cordon tightened. Furthermore,
most of these runs were made by coastwise traders, very few by ships engaged
in foreign trade ... blockade-running to these particular ports may be written off as an insignificant effort... insofar as its contribution to the war effort
of the South and the material needs of its far-flung civilian populace are concerned. More realistic would be an attempt to compare wartime clearances
with prewar figures. Projections based on clearance rates for Carolina ports
during May, 1861, while the blockade was still innocuous, would suggest a rate
of over 1400 attempted runs between May and the end of December, whereas
the actual figure is 733 attempts. Comparable figures for 1862-1865 fluctuate,
but never rise above 515, while a steady decrease is noticeable in the number
of vessels engaged in the trade as the war continued.[69]

Allan Nevins writes:

By the close of 1862, when the Union Navy had a strength of 427 ships, with
28,000 seamen and 3,268 guns, the entire Southern coast was held in an
increasingly effective grip. The Navy had captured 390 blockade-runners during the first eleven months of that year, 153 of them between late April and
early December 1861. It and the land forces had taken or closed one strategic
port after another: New Orleans, Norfolk, Roanoke Island, Savannah, (sealed
by the capture of Fort Pulaski) Fernandina, St. Augustine, and New Bern. In
addition, new Federal bases had been established, such as that at Hilton Head
north of Savannah, which enabled the blockaders to be coaled and supplied.
The only important ports still open — Wilmington, Charleston, Mobile, Galveston, and Brownsville — were patrolled with some success by blockaders. It
was boasted that in no previous war in history had the harbours of an enemy
been so largely closed by naval activity. Blockade had played a role in the Revolution, the Tripolitan War, the War of 1812, and finally the Mexican War,
when it had cut off from the Mexicans munitions and other supplies which
they vitally needed. Never, however, had it been half as important as now. Its
strength, moreover, was steadily growing. By December, 1864, the Navy had
671 vessels, mustering almost 5,000 guns, and about 471 of these ships were
in blockade-service.... When Appomattox came, a total of 1,500 blockade-
runners had been captured or destroyed.... But the fact that cotton exports
to Britain and European countries, which in 1861 has soared to about 3½ million bales out of a total production of 4½ million bales, dropped to a mere
132,000 bales exported in 1862, and 168,000 bales in 1863.... While the subject (blockade-running) must always be shrouded in doubt, our best evidence
suggests that in 1861 one blockade-runner in ten was captured; in 1862 one
in eight; in 1863 and 1864 one in three; and in 1865 one in two.[70]

The number of prizes brought in during the war was 1,149, of which 210 were steamers. There were also 355 vessels burned, sunk, driven ashore, or otherwise destroyed, of which 85 were steamers; making a total of 1,504 vessels of all classes. The value of these vessels and their cargoes, according to a low estimate, was thirty-one millions of dollars. In the War of 1812, which has always, and justly, been regarded as a successful naval war, the number of captures was 1,719. But the War of 1812 was waged against a commercial nation, and the number of vessels open to capture was therefore far greater. Of the property afloat, destroyed or captured during the Civil War, the larger part suffered in consequence of the blockade. Moreover, in the earlier war, out of the whole number of captures, 1,428 were made by privateers, which were fitted out chiefly as a commercial adventure. In the Civil War the work was done wholly by the navy; and it was done in the face of obstacles of which naval warfare before that time had presented no example nor conception. As a military measure, the blockade was of vital importance in the operations of the war; and it has been commonly said that without it, hostilities would have been protracted, and would have been far more bitter and bloody than they were. Its peculiar importance lay in the isolation of the Southern States and in their dependence upon the outside world for the necessaries of life. The only neutral frontier was along the Rio Grande; and the country for many miles on both sides of the boundary offered few facilities for trade and transportation. All supplies must come from the seaboard; and the purely agricultural character of Southern industry made supplies from abroad a necessity.[71]

PART THREE

The British Press—Speaker for the Confederacy

10. *The Times*

The Times remained without peer among British newspapers for all of the reign of Queen Victoria. Founded at the end of the eighteenth century, aided by a Stamp Act which permitted the newspaper to be circulated throughout the island at a minimum cost, it prospered for decades. Distribution of *The Times* in the mid-nineteenth century reached about 65,000.

During the American Civil War it was the principal spokesman for government and the governing class. It followed the prejudices of its readers, and while it claimed to speak for the British people it did little to enlighten them. Public opinion, as expressed in *The Times*, was the view of every law-abiding, money-making, church-going, beef-eating member of the gentry and aristocracy, i.e., the ruling class of England. It reflected the overwhelming self-conceit of Palmerston's England. Not even the debacle in the Crimea or the Indian Mutiny, to say nothing of the colonial wars of the nineteenth century, could restrain journalistic clouds of self-congratulation on English freedom, English wealth, and English might. *The Times* spewed anti–American and anti–Federal lies and half truths throughout the conflict. If not actively disparaging of America it lied by omission. It was relentless in its condemnation of American institutions, particularly American democracy. Its censure reflected a deep fear of a broadened franchise in Britain.

A survey of *The Times* establishment provided some insight on the prejudice so fervently expressed. John Walter III had succeeded his father as proprietor of *The Times* in 1847, and viewed the possible destruction of the American Republic without regret. Democracy was not to be trusted. The whole of the American conflict was looked upon in England as a breakdown of democracy, and that was one of the main causes of the lack of understanding.

John Thadeus Delane, editor of *The Times* from 1847 to 1877, was fond of spending his holidays killing stags and game birds in the company of dukes and lords. It is not surprising that he acquired the tone of the company he kept and came to gaze at the North Americans as if from across an abyss. He feared the menacing attitude of the Federal government, the audaciousness of the Northern press, and above all his middle class faith proved a barrier to his acceptance of democracy and universal manhood suffrage. All of his prejudices were futher fostered by his close association with the British Ministry, first Lord Aberdeen and then Lord Palmerston.[72]

As noted in *History of the Times,* "Mowbray Morris, manager of *The Times* from 1847 to 1873, was in sympathy with the South for its own sake. Born in the West Indies he had the background of a not dissimilar society. Morris was convinced that his family had been impoverished by emancipation in the Islands. At the end of 1856 he recalled his West Indian experience in writing to [Lewis] Filmore [former political editor of *The Illustrated London News* and former special correspondent of *The Times* in the United States], who was about to visit the Southern States: 'You will find much to interest you, but probably little ocular proof of the evils charged against their peculiar institution. As a rule the slave is well fed and housed, carefully attended in sickness & often cherished in old age: the exception is when the animal is not worth his hire'"[73]

Of the American correspondents of *The Times* during the Civil War, much can be said and inferred. Chosen by either Delane or Morris, or by both, they were rarely, if ever, impartial. Their letters from America were neither accurate nor objective. The English people received little factual information from correspondents Charles Maclay, Frank Lawley, or Antonio Gallenga.

W.H. Russell preceded the aforementioned and arrived in New York in March 1860. He was to replace Bancroft Davis, whose correspondence was too favorable to the Northern cause to conform to the partialities of *The Times.* Mr. Russell began his career by covering the general election of 1841 in Ireland for *The Times,* and became a famous war correspondent in the Crimea. He was summoned to London by Morris and, according to his own story, upon being given papers, clippings, and correspondence (largely articles from the *New York Herald* supporting the right of the South to secede), hastily took his departure to report upon the situation.

Russell's career in America came to an unfortunate end. In reporting the first battle of Bull Run, his narrative, although not inaccurate, was highly disparaging of the Union troops. It has been said that Russell was not actually at the scene of the conflict, and, therefore, his criticism not valid. Notwithstanding, he was persona non grata with Federal officials, and could not perform the duties to which he was entrusted, i.e., following the battles of the ensuing conflict. After Russell returned to England in 1862, he edited the *Army and Navy Gazette* which he had founded in 1860. Although *The Times* had granted him an annual pension of £300, Delane would not let him write on American affairs, as he was too pro–Northern.

The Times selected Frank Lawley to go out to the United States to replace

Russell. A gentleman by birth, well educated and well connected politically, Lawley had appeared set for a bright career. When as a very young man he entered Parliament and was appointed private secretary to William Ewart Gladstone, then Chancellor of the Exchequer in the Aberdeen coalition. Two years later, although still not thirty, he was named by another friend of the family, Newcastle, to fill the vacant post of governor of Australia. But his fair prospects suddenly became bleak when the suspicion grew that he had abused his confidential position close to Gladstone to speculate on the stock market, for it was well known that his addiction to the turf had left him saddled with debts. The upshot was that Lawley contrived at once to lose his place as private secretary, his position in South Australia, his seat in Parliament, and his money. Within two years of this humiliation he was obliged to flee Britain to escape his creditors. He went to the United States determined to labor as a journalist, in order to accumulate sufficient funds to settle his debts and perhaps retrieve something of his reputation in England. By 1861 he had done well enough to return briefly, if secretly, for some of his creditors remained on his trail. While on a second sub-rosa visit the following year he met Morris, and accepted his offer of the position of war correspondent. Lawley's view of the United States underwent a radical transformation in the six years that elapsed between his arrival as a refugee debtor and his return as correspondent of the most famous of newspapers. As an advanced liberal in English politics, he had worshipped the Republic from afar but closer inspection "wonderfully modified" his enthusiasm. Nevertheless, his conviction that the future lay with the United States weathered well, hence his advice to his close friend William Gregory to visit North America and read Tocqueville as part of a program of study that would equip him as a parliamentary expert on American affairs. Then came secession and the war to which initially he responded like a "great Northerner."

Living in the United States throughout the first year of the conflict, Lawley was profoundly impressed by the depth of Northern animosity toward his native land. He began to fear that if the Union ever subdued the South, domestic victory would be followed by a settling of scores with Britain for such humiliation as the Trent Affair. From this followed the true policy of British statesmen which was to place the Union in such a predicament that for a century to come it "should be of no more account in European affairs than the Sandwich Islands." The best way to guarantee this, Lawley believed, was to emasculate its military capacity and political influence by fostering an independent Confederacy. At the very least, it was necessary for England to recognize the South. Preferably she should do all that could be done for the Southern states and thus assist "as a man a midwife" at the new nation's birth. Subsequently, in reports well calculated to nourish British humanitarian dismay, Lawley repeatedly emphasized the bloodshed and horror of this "hopeless" struggle by the North. Nor did he stop short of a call for British intervention to halt it. After a few months he made his way into the Confederacy bearing instructions to the authorities, and to society in Richmond. Lawley promptly enlisted as an unofficial propagandist of the Southern cause. His accounts of the South's easy military position and its population's wonderful spirit made a most profound impression. They provided further evidence of the "impossibility of subduing such a people."[74]

Morris's approach to the Lawley chronicles was ambivalent. Encouraged and exhilarated by Lawley's pro–Southern correspondence, Morris retained a feeling of unease. Morris to Lawley, 31 January 1865: "The worse feature in Southern affairs is the growing discontent. We auger ill from this. I observe that you never notice the Opposition & always represent the Southern people as being unanimous. Are you sure you are right in this?" Morris, however, could not contain his pleasure and was congratulating Lawley on having "presented the public here with a continuous narrative which has served to correct the errors and exaggerations of the Federal Press, & has indeed been the only authentic record of the Southern side of the Civil War."[75]

Lawley remained in the South throughout the war, communicating with the paper through the French consulate and the Paris office. In the summer of 1863 he informed Morris that his health would not allow him to continue, but he seems to have withdrawn this intimation, and was certainly sending letters, though intermittently, down to the spring of 1865. *The Times* relied almost entirely for news of Confederate affairs on him, and he enjoyed in Southern society a position denied to Charles Mackay in the North.

Charles Mackay, a Scot who shared the anti–American views of Delane, crossed the Atlantic as American correspondent of *The Times* at about the same time as Russell withdrew. Mackay's chief function was to report from the most important trading city in America, forwarding political and commercial telegrams and sending what other reports he deemed appropriate. He rarely left New York, and when he did it was to confer with Copperheads or with downright rebels, whose cause he championed; worst of all, he never got near a battlefield. During the greater part of the war, *The Times* had no regular correspondent with the Northern armies and the Northern government, just as for the first eighteen months, neither had it one in the South.

Of Mackay and Lawley the *New York Herald*, 10 November 1862, soon concluded "writing stocks up or writing stocks down, as may suit their employers, and doing this country all the damage they can through their letters and through the editorials and speeches based on their letters, are the honorable, gentlemanly pursuits and the moral occupation of this pair of noble brothers."

Forty-eight years old when he took his post, Mackay brought with him a reputation as a literary dilettante. He was a poet of small critical acclaim but of large popularity, an author, and a journalist who claimed knowledge of the United States and friendship with prominent Americans. He had toured the Republic in the winter of 1857-58, giving a series of lectures, and later published his observations, first in the *Illustrated Evening News*, of which he was then managing editor, and subsequently in his book *Life and Liberty in America*. Like so many of his contemporaries he had concluded that the United States had grown too large to be successfully governed. It was his opinion, and his ardent hope, that the Republic was destined to break up into as many as four federations. The secession of the South had done nothing to prick the bubble of vanity which enveloped his judgements, nor did his association with leading Unionists such as Mr. Seward, for whom he had acted as a guide during the New Yorker's visit to London in 1859, dissuade him from publicly supporting the Southern cause.

Before leaving for Boston in February he chaired a public lecture by a rabid secessionist who, predictably enough, called upon the Union to halt the senseless war and permit the Southern states to separate. Although this indiscretion cost Mackay his Union friends, and earned him a frosty reception in Boston, it did not damage his position at Printing House Square. He was an ideal representative for *The Times*, embodying the principal social and political concepts of both Morris and Delane. Charles Mackay was anti-democratic, anti–Union; he was pro-slavery and pro-aristocracy.

Mackay had set forth his political and social philosophy in *Life and Liberty in America*. It was available to *The Times* and to all of Britain. Mackay was chosen to represent the newspaper because of, rather than in spite of, his beliefs. To Mackay, for example, the acceptance of Negro body odors and the abuse of Negro females by the Southern plantation owner were signs of a humane benevolence:

> whatever may be the fact as to the physical discomfort said to be produced by the odors of the black men on the olfactory nerves of the whites, it is evident in the South, where, if any where, this peculiar unpleasantness would be more likely to be offensively demonstrative than in colder climates, there is no such repugnance to the persons of the black population as there is in the North. In the South, the slave-owner not only cohabits with the more youthful and beautiful of his female slaves, but seems to have no objection whatever to the close proximity of any negro, young or old, male or female ... though Northern men, who talk so much of liberty, and of the political equality of all men, turn up their scornful noses at the slightest possibility of contact with an African.[76]

The slaveowner was not only a gentleman, but treated his slaves kindly:

> The slaveowners, who—as far as my observation has extended—appear to be very urbane, polished, gentlemanly, and estimable persons.... When they prove, as they may easily do, that they treat their slaves with kindness, and that, as a rule, slaves are better clad, fed, and cared for than the agricultural labourers of Europe.[77]

Mackay set forth the Southern excuse for slavery, affixed to the redundant comparison between the black slave and the white laborer:

> Slavery is no evil, so far from its being a wrong, or the curse of humanity, it is the proper condition of the masses of mankind, and better than the freedom for which they pine and starve, and — if they do not go to the grave before their time — in which they breed revolution and war. The black man is necessarily the first slave, because he is the stupidest, the least valuable, and most easily captured; but the white labourer with nothing to give to the world on whose bosom he was born but the unskilled labour of his brawny arms, is a slave de facto in every part of the earth, and were he a slave de jure, would be happier and more comfortable than he can ever hope to be under the system prevalent in Europe and in the Free States of America.[78]

Mackay set forth his bias of slave labour versus free labour. He was not unusual among the British in his sympathy for the plight of the white laborer. He remained in the mainstream of British thought in his decision to do nothing to aid either class:

> The profits made from free labour are the amount of the products of such labour, which the employer, by means of the command which capital or skill gives him, takes away, exacts, or exploits from the free labourer. The profits of slave labour are that portion of the products of such labour which the power of the master enables him to appropriate. These profits are less, because the master allows the slave to retain a larger share of the results of his own labour than do the employers of free labour. But we not only boast that the white slave trade is more exacting and fraudulent than black slavery, but that it is more cruel, in leaving the labourer to take care of himself and family out of the pittance which skill or capital have allowed him to retain. When his day's labour is ended he is free, but overburdened with the cares of his family and household, which makes his freedom an empty and delusive mockery....[79]

Neither the end of the Civil War in America nor the rupture of his relationship with *The Times* changed Mackay's social or political philosophy. *Forty Years' Recollections* and *The Founders of the American Republic* (1885) were used to further underscore his contempt for what he derisively termed "ultra democracy," and his attachment to the Confederacy and to the society it treasured. The following passage illustrates Mackay's basic beliefs:

> Law cannot say that the good and wise shall vote in the government of their fellows, because Law is utterly unable to distinguish and to declare who are the good and the wise, and to grant them privileges accordingly. But Law can take cognisance of physical if not intellectual facts, and can decree that, if a man occupies a house and pays annual rent for it, and contributes according to his means, directly or indirectly, to the necessary expenses of the Government which protects him in his life and liberty, he is, though

perhaps neither a very good nor a very wise man, entitled to the privilege of helping to elect a representative to act on his behalf in councils of the State. In giving him this privilege, the State makes him one of the trustees of the national interest. In so doing, it confers no inalienable right upon him but merely endows him with a privilege which he may forfeit if he becomes a pauper or a criminal or ceases to be a householder and a contributor to the national revenues. It is not so under the system of what is sometimes called Universal, but that ought to be called Manhood suffrage, which is established in America and France, and is gradually extending itself to Great Britain.[80]

Perhaps the most cogent criticism of the loathsomeness of Mackay's letters to *The Times* was written by a contemporary, Lord Leslie Stephens:

> Every patriotic action is explained to have really originated in corruption or selfishness. Scandal after scandal is raked together, and carefully exhibited as an average specimen of American affairs. If you put any faith in the writer, the whole political and social machinery is rotten at the core and is worked by the most degraded motives; America is peopled by an unprincipled mob, sprinkled with charlatans and hypocrites, and governed by pettifogging attorneys. They hire other men to fight because they have no loyalty, and abandon their liberty because they have no courage. We all know the process by which such a picture may be drawn of any people. If you test the waters of the purest stream, you may find places where it is as full of corruption as the Thames; if you send out your spies to those social depressions into which the viler part of the population of any country drains, he may honestly bring back a report that he has seen none but blackguards. I hope, for the sake of this correspondent's veracity, and I believe from internal evidence, that he mixed exclusively with a society justly out of favour with his countrymen. To New York flows a very large share of the foreign and disloyal element of America. Wall Street is not more likely to take exalted patriotic views than our Stock Exchange; to judge the American people by the gossip of a clique of Southern exiles, gold speculators, and refugee Irishmen in New York, is as absurd as it would have been to judge of the French Revolution exclusively from a Royalist emigré, or of English politics in the last century from a clique of Jacobists. *The Times* cannot evade the responsibility of having given him leave to vent in its pages some five or six weekly columns of unmixed abuse. It may be presumed to have considered them at least valuable contributions to our knowledge of the time, and tolerably fair pictures of what was taking place. It thought, that is, that a portrait of America, in which every virtue was scrupulously omitted, was not a gross caricature.[81]

When it became evident, belatedly, to *The Times*, that the conflict in America had drawn to a close, Mowbray Morris wrote to Mackay, 21 April 1865, dissolving his association with *The Times*:

The time is come which I have long anticipated when you can no longer retain the office with which we entrusted you three years ago, & it is my painful duty to inform you that a successor will shortly be despatched from England to take your place. This result which I greatly deplore has been brought about by your blind & unreasonable condemnation of all public men and measures on the Federal side, & your disregard of the remonstrances which I have frequently addressed to you against such a course. It is no slight charge about a public writer that his opinions have been proved to be wrong, but that might have excused him if he had given evidence of an honest desire to arrive at the truth. On the contrary it seems to us that you have persistently & wilfully shut your eyes to all facts & signs which did not tend to the support of your foregone conclusions. By dwelling exclusively upon the absurdities of the demagogues & fanatics who are to be found in every country which is prey to civil war, by exaggerating the errors of government & condemning its abuses of power without making allowances for its difficulties & temptations, you have presented the English public with a distorted picture of the Federal cause, & have, as I believe, contributed very largely to produce the exasperation which you allege to exist in the American mind against the English. Moreover your letters have been deficient in the qualities of a sound foreign correspondent. They have contained but few facts & a great deal of wild declamation. No one reading only what you have written could have derived sound information, such as could guide him in the conduct of his own affairs. Every statement was one-sided, & every remark spiteful. The end of all is that you have made yourself so unpopular that no government in the United States will tolerate you except under a sort of protest. Your usefulness as a correspondent is consequently much impaired, many sources of information are cut off from you, & your letters are almost unavoidably reduced to a mere empty bag of big words. We cannot commit the character of the paper any longer to one who so misconstrues his duties. Much as I appreciate your literary ability, your steadiness & punctuality, I cannot think these qualities so dearly purchased at the price you have made us pay for them. It was in your power, at any time, by giving due heed to the hints which I have given you, & to my open remonstrances, to have avoided the errors of which the measure now is full. You have preferred to take your own way, & you cannot complain of the direction in which it has led you.[82]

Three years is a long time to take in discovering so many defects in a correspondent, and Mackay might be entitled to a grievance about "the sudden cessation of my unfortunate connexion with *The Times*— in the favour of which journal I stood high as long as Fortune seemed to smile on the cause of the Southern Confederacy." Morris had, indeed, made no attempt to modify Mackay's one-sidedness, but the correspondent's case against the manager's injustice is complete, when the above indictment is set beside the glowing praise of two years before. After twelve months' experience of Mackay's quality, Morris wrote to him, 19 March 1863:

I assure you that your correspondence deserves in my opinion the most unqualified praise. Your views are entirely in accordance with those of the paper & I believe of the majority of this country, & you have the art of expressing them so that everybody must read.[83]

Mackay served *The Times* from February 1862 until the close of 1865, except during some months when he was replaced by Antonio Gallenga, the Anglicised Italian who was a zealous servant of *The Times* for nearly a quarter of a century. Gallenga was sent to America to report on the condition of the Federal, and particularly the Western states. Morris cautioned him not to "believe a word that appears in the American journals." Toward the end of 1863, however, Mackay was given a holiday, and Gallenga, who had received a pressing admonition from Morris to report nothing but facts — trebly underlined — took his place.

Mackay had more than a superficial patron in James Spence, the Confederate financial adviser in England, and the "S" correspondent of *The Times*. But even here Mackay was losing ground. When he was returning to America, Spence wrote to James Mason:

Public opinion has quite veered round to the belief that the South will be exhausted. *The Times* correspondents' letters do great harm — more especially Gallenga's — who replaced Chas. Mackay at New York. I have, however, taken a berth for Mackay by Saturday's boat, so he will soon be out again and he is dead for our side.[84]

There is little question but that *The Times* was badly served by its two principal correspondents in America. Both Mackay and Lawley invariably reported the circumstance from an extreme anti–Federal point of view. On 9 July 1863, *The Times* predicted editorially, and Mackay confirmed in a letter, that Lee was about to capture Washington and that this event would be met by a great cry of joy and relief from the North, now weary of the war and eager to escape from the despotism of Lincoln's administration.[85]

When Mackay returned to his post after a holiday in England in 1864, he sent glowing and thoroughly misleading accounts of the prospects of the South. On his authority, Delane passed on a rumour, at the beginning of April 1864 to the effect that a great Southern victory was imminent. On 24 May such a victory was announced as having been won by Lee over Grant before Richmond, on the banks of the Rapidan. It was stated that the Federals had suffered 40,000 casualties. The reality underlying this report was the opening of the long struggle known as the "Battles of the Wilderness," which ultimately led to the turning of the tide in favor of the North. But even when it became apparent that in the military sense the first reports had been too optimistic, *The Times* was more fixed than ever in its belief that the Union could not be restored by force.

From the summer of 1864 until the end of the conflict in America it had become evident that *The Times* had gone far astray in its military estimates. Letters from Mackay and from Lawley and editorials from their own editorial staff wilfully and maliciously misled their readers as to the exploits of the Federal armies, the strength and will of the Confederate forces, and above all the singular successes of General Sherman. Mackay did all within his power to delude the people of England. As 1863 drew to the end he gave an estimate of the future of the two armies. Gettysburg had been a disaster for the Confederacy, Vicksburg had been taken by the Federals, and, militarily, the prospects were dim for the armies of the South. But Mackay and *The Times* establishment continued without missing a step, on 12 November 1863:

> Everyone feels that now or never is the time for the Federal armies to be up and doing. But Meade's army of the Potomac has just been crippled by the destruction of the Alexandria and Orange Railroad, and that of the Cumberland, under Grant, has come into the hands of a new commander, who, however quick and far sighted, must yet require a few days to look about him, to take in the difficulties of the position into which his forces were thrown by the blind impetuosity of his predecessor, Rosecrans, and hit upon some plan by which he may extricate himself. General Meade is not expected to move forward for a month. General Grant is said to have to deal with a Confederate force of 80,000 men under Bragg; a force so aided by the natural and artificial strength of the position, that the Federals have but little chance of marching against it with success, and hardly more probability of marching away from it with safety. General Grant may condense a host of 150,000 combatants at Chattanooga, but the battlefield is not favourable for the manoeuvring of large masses. Cavalry is no great help in the narrow mountain defiles, and artillery little better than a positive encumbrance. Bragg, who occupies a ground of his own choice, a territory known to him inch by inch, need hardly shrink from a conflict in which the odds are no worse than two to one. On the other hand, although few here doubt that the object of General Lee in his last movement (Gettysburg) was merely to place a month's distance between himself and Meade, and that aim was signally attained — although he might now spare a division or two to strengthen Bragg....

Mackay, 27 June 1864, continued the fiction manufactured by *The Times* and its partners among the English press that the South was a "single patriotic and homogeneous segment" of America. "The strength of the Confederates lies in no city or locality," claimed *The Times*, "but in the hearts of a people, whom the prolongation of hostilities may exacerbate, but can never incline to peace."

Mackay reported of the failures of Sherman, and Grant, but more importantly, of General Lee's adventure into Pennsylvania, and the exalted expectations which ended in the failure of his armies at Gettysburg, in *The Times*, 22 July 1864:

Grant has been checkmated at Petersburg.... Sherman has gone round the Kenesaw Mountain, which he failed to capture, and approached a few miles nearer than before to the Chattahoochie and Atlanta, and General Lee has invaded Maryland, threatens Pennsylvania, and scared all Washington....

The Times, 24 September 1864:

The military situation no longer commends itself to the exultation of sensible people.... General Sherman admits that although he has taken Atlanta, he did not consider it prudent to attack the undefeated army of the Confederates in the new position which they have assumed at 30 miles south of the city....

The failure of the Union armies, Mackay reported to *The Times*, would have a major effect on the financial and political developments in the North, as he claimed in a report published 1 November 1864:

The failure of Grant's attempt to capture Richmond via Chapin's Farm, the absence of news from General Sherman, and the undoubted activity shown by General Hood in Georgia, and the renewed impetus given to his movements by the presence of General Beauregard in his camp, have had such effect upon the gold market as to alarm the Administration for the results of the Presidential election....

For Mackay "unimpeachable" was the sole province of the Southern press, as he suggested in *The Times* of 29 December 1864: "The public anxiety for news of General Sherman has been relieved by the announcement, on Confederate, and, therefore, unimpeachable authority...." Mackay was back in *The Times*, 3 April 1865, claiming Northern war crimes: "Sherman marches unopposed through South Carolina, and commits atrocities on the way which history will hereafter blush to record...."

Lawley, while admitting the success of Union armies, assured his readers that there would be little, if any, change. The rebellion remained intact as were the Confederate armies, according to Lawley's view in *The Times*, 18 November 1864:

Nearly one month has now elapsed since General Sherman took possession of Atlanta, a central town in the north-western portion of the State of Georgia.... On the other hand, the Confederates have borne their reverse with great fortitude; their army is perfectly intact, and undoubtedly ready to meet the enemy in his advance.

The Times, 6 January 1865:

But the rebellion lives and thrives, and gathers force and increasing resolution day after day, and year after year. It is possible that Richmond may fall in 12 or 24 months; it is possible that Sherman may carry fire and sword into Georgia, as many of his associates have carried it into Virginia and into every other State which they have entered. But that it is possible either to resuscitate the Union or to exterminate five millions of Anglo-Saxons and three millions of slaves (all as bitterly opposed to the Yankees as their masters) I emphatically deny....

The editorial writers of *The Times* could manage deceptions equal to those of their correspondents in America, as on 10 November 1864:

It is striking to remark the peculiar confidences and satisfaction with which the Southern President speaks of the Southern armies. If he finds despondency anywhere, it is never in the camp or in the field. The losses are great, the bereavements are awful, and the work of war is exhausting; but the armies and their Generals neither faint nor fail. Indeed, they have little reason to do so. Grant can make no impression on the lines of Petersburg or Richmond. Yesterday's telegrams bring no intelligence of Sherman, but they tell us, on the authority of Mr. Stanton, that Hood is threatening the invasion of Tennessee. In the Shenandoah Valley the Federal and Confederate armies still confront each other, while in Missouri it is at least certain that the Northern forces have been severly pressed, and not certain that they have escaped defeat....

Or on 7 December 1864:

It will be strange, indeed, if the army of General Sherman should arrive before Savannah, after such a march conducted under such difficulties, in condition to attack and storm a town so well fortified and so strenuously defended; and, if not, it is difficult to conceive a more embarrassing position than which General Sherman will occupy, with a wasted and weary army, a strong town at his front, and an army fighting on his own ground in his rear. We do not say that Sherman will not overcome all these obstacles. Any one of a hundred contingencies of which we have no knowledge may overthrow all our calculations, but arguing from the usual result of similar enterprises, from the well recognized principles of the military art, and from the spirit which the South has never failed to show, we cannot see the grounds for that tone of overweaning confidence with which the Northern press hails the commencement of an expedition so novel and so hazardous, in which a General abandons one base of communications without, so far as we can see, any very clear or definite idea where he is to find another....

And 20 December 1864:

Even the Northern press cannot persist in representing Sherman's desperate march as a deliberate and skillfully-calculated military operation. We believe it was not a calculation, but a necessity. Sherman had no choice, except of difficulties, long before he quitted Atlanta. His position was simply that of a commander who has advanced too far into an enemy's country, and discovers that his opponents have cut off his supplies and every line of retreat.... Sherman has undertaken a more desperate operation.... He must march to the sea, as no Federal flotilla can ascent the Savannah to aid him. His difficulty is one of frequent recurrence in military history, ancient and modern. An invading army must keep open a line of retreat in case of being outmaneuvered or overpowered, or run the risk of destruction or surrender, either fatal to the expedition. The ten thousand Greeks were led by Xenophon from the plains of the Euphrates to the shore of the Black Sea, but the enterprise was undertaken by the wreck of an army. The retreat itself is celebrated in history, but it told the world that the invasion of Persia was a ruinous failure. It is possible that Sherman may save as much of his army as he can march to the shore of the Atlantic; but none the less will the invasion of Georgia have been signally defeated.

Lord Leslie Stephen was little less than remorseless in his condemnation of the manner *The Times* reported the war as it drew to a close:

I have endeavoured to show that *The Times* gave a preposterous caricature of the origin of the war, of its effect upon the country, and of the means by which it was maintained. The prejudice, which denied the war to be in any way related to slavery, and which denied that it was leading to any result but a military despotism, led to an equal distortion of the facts of the war.... The fortunes of the Confederacy culminated in the spring of 1863.... The battle of Gettysburg and the taking of Vicksburg, which occured on the 4th of July, marked the turn of the tide.... At the close of 1863 the Northern side was distinctly in the ascendant.... At the close of 1864 Grant fought the deperate series of battles which resulted in the siege of Petersburg. Sherman forced his way to Atlanta and thence to the Atlantic coast. The series of victories under which the Confederacy collapsed are fresh in our memories. Let me now give *The Times'* account of these events.... In November, Mr. Lincoln had the bad taste to call for a public thanksgiving. *The Times* was astonished, "It is simply absurd to say that the condition of the South was worse, relatively to the North, than it was at the beginning of the war." *The Times*, however, in summing up results, observed (December 14) that the Federals had in this year "gained the one real victory of the war. We can hardly describe by that name the success of Grant against Bragg, but Gettysburg was a pitched battle fairly won." To explain this assertion about one of the most decided and skillfully planned victories of the war, I must remark that *The Times*, like its sporting contemporaries, kept a private prophet, one "S" (James Spence). This gentleman was always prophesying with signal want of success, as his prophesies were simply renewed applications of one single dogma, viz., that the more territory the North conquered the more they would have to keep and therefore the harder

it would be to keep it. At the commencement of 1864 the North was therefore in a bad way.... As the Confederates began the year with brighter
prospects than ever before, as Grant lost battle after battle at a fabulous
cost of life, as Sherman was retreating with little hope of safety, and Banks
had been all but crushed, it is not surprising that *The Times* continued to
think the Northern cause hopeless. Suddenly the ground it had thought so
solid gave way under its feet. Savannah surrendered, Wilmington was taken,
Charleston was taken, and Sherman pierced South Carolina as he had
pierced Georgia. The Confederacy seemed to be that hollow shell to which
Mr. Seward had compared it, much to the amazement of *The Times*. For a
time it made a feeble attempt at maintaining that, after all, the loss was not
so great. The "first act" of war was over. But that only had happened which
"all Europe" had expected to happen at once, and if the South stood firm
the end was no nearer. A guerilla warfare might be expected to succeed the
conflicts of regular armies. Suddenly Grant defeated Lee, and with the capture of Richmond the war practically expired.[86]

11. Midvictorian England: A Class-Based Society

The Reform Act of 1832 was not a democratic measure. In the crucial debates of 1830-32, it was agreed by both the Whigs and Tories that democracy was a dangerous form of government, that a "stake in the country" was an essential qualification in those who claimed political power, and that landed property had a special part to play in guaranteeing the stability of the political order. It was desirable that the respectable elements of the new centers of population should be given political weight. The national electorate was to be enlarged by the new elements, which were connected with property, had a valuable stake in the country, and a deep interest in its institutions. It was to be a question of balance and proportion. The influence of land and of numbers was to be so balanced in the election of the House of Commons that collision with the Crown and the House of Lords would be avoided. The privileged wealthy of the past admitted the new unprivileged wealth, created by the economic changes of a hundred years, to the closed circle of the ruling class. Property of certain kinds was to be accepted as a certificate of probity and good behavior. The purpose of the act was to win over the prosperous middle classes to the side of the governing order and so inoculate the constitution against the dangerous disease of government by the people. Writes Kingsley Smellie: "The Reform Act of 1832 was a complicated compromise. It managed to attach to the working constitution the bulk of the property, and education of the nation. The Whig supporters of the bill said that it represented the most that could be pushed through Parliament and the least that would satisfy the country. It was a practical remedy for four specific grievances: the nomination of members of Parliament by private individuals, the election of members by closed corporations, the expense of elections, and the inadequate representation of the large towns. The first grievance was met by the abolition of all boroughs with an electorate too small to preserve their independence and too isolated to be easily enlarged, the second by the £10 household franchise, the third by providing for the registration of voters and a reduction in the duration of elections, the fourth by giving seats to the industrial towns of the North and the Midlands: Manchester, Birmingham, Leeds, and Sheffield."[87]

In spite of the redistribution of seats the domination of the South of Britain over the North continued. A quarter of the population of Britain in the South had a third of the representation, while a quarter of the North had only an eighth. The unreformed franchise had been less than 500,000. The electorate immediately afterwards was 813,000. This was about one-thirtieth of the population. It was one in seven of adult males in England, in Scotland one in eight, in Ireland one in twenty.

The new qualification which was the most important—that of the £10 householder—was a most ambiguous category. It was an index neither of a class nor of a standard of living. In a few boroughs where rents were high it brought in the majority of householders. In some it excluded entirely the manual worker; in many it took in the skilled, while rejecting the unskilled laborer.

In truth, Britain had advanced little beyond the standards of George III. The Reform Bill of 1832 had abolished rotten boroughs and given populous regions representation in Parliament, but the British people, as before, remained without the vote. The ruling powers fought doggedly all movements intended to give city workmen or agricultural laborers any voice in electing members of Parliament. Until 1867, at least 20 million Britons had no representation in the House of Commons; of 7.5 million men twenty-one years old, less than a million could take part in elections.

Writes Adams in *Great Britain and the American Civil War* (28): "After 1832 the previous sympathy for America of one section of the British governing class vanished. More—it was replaced by a critical, if not openly hostile attitude. Soon with the rapid development of the power and wealth of the United States, the governing class of England, of all factions save the Radical, came to view America just as it would have viewed any other rising nation, that is, as a problem to be studied for its influence on British prosperity and power. The ruling class was not the British public, and to the great unenfranchised mass, finding voice through the writing of a few leaders, the prosperity of America made a powerful appeal. The ruling class was faced with the problem of the influence of a prosperous American democracy upon an unenfranchised public opinion at home...."

The propertied and aristocratic classes looked upon the American Republic as the greatest menace to their power. The "American example" was an ogre that haunted their dreams. The extraordinary success of the United States, its growth in population and territory, in wealth, in general happiness and enlightment, provided the reformers with a powerful argument for the spread of the same democratic system in England. John Bright, the leader of the rising masses, constantly pointed across the Atlantic: "Give Englishmen the vote, and they would correct existing abuses and march side by side with their American brothers in everything that made life worth living!" Bright and his associates were accused of desiring to discard the British Constitution and adopt the Philadelphia constitution of 1787 in its place. There was only one way of meeting these arguments, and that was by discrediting the American experiment. The travellers' literature published in the half century preceding the Civil War, picturing and exaggerating the faults of the United States and minimizing its virtues, was part of this campaign. From 1861 to the end of the War the newspaper and periodical press of Britain was actively engaged in disparaging America.[88]

And now at last, all these dire prophecies had been fulfilled; America had been destroyed by it own vices! No longer would it be heralded as a model for democracy in Britain. Now the British could see what fate had in store for them should they transform their nation into a republic or even give the unfranchised the ballot. Educated Britons cared nothing for the South; their true motive was the fear of the spread of democratic feelings at home in the event of a successful Union.

The real secret of the exultation which manifested itself in *The Times* and other newspapers and journals over the troubles and disasters of America, was their loathing not of America as much as of democracy in Britain. It was freely foretold at country houses that the success of the North would mean a republic in their own country.[89]

The Liberal party in control of the Government during the late 1850s and early 1860s, was, in the House of Commons, a predominantly aristocratic and landed gentry body. An analysis of the 358 Liberal MPs listed in *Dod's Parliamentary Companion* for 1859 produced the following table.

Social Background of Liberal MPs, 1859

Peerage connections	59 (16.5%)
Baronets	35 (9.8%)
Baronets' sons	14 (3.9%)
Landed gentry	71 (19.8%)
Heirs of gentry	14 (3.9%)
Gentlemen	35 (9.8%)
Merchants/Manufacturers	50 (14.0%)
Bankers	8 (2.2%)
Lawyers	41 (11.5%)
Miscellaneous	13 (3.6%)
No Information	18 (5.0%)

A total of 108 MPs, or slightly more than 30 percent of the parliamentary Liberal Party, were thus directly connected to the titled aristocracy of Britain and Ireland (in other words, they were the sons and brothers of peers, Irish peers, baronets or sons of baronets), and if to these were added the members listed in *Burke's Landed Gentry* (1858 and 1868 editions) and their heirs, 53.9 percent of the party can be classified as belonging to the aristocratic and landed classes. Another 35 MPs can be described as gentlemen, in the sense that they had more distant connections with the aristocracy and gentry, or else were retired members of the armed forces, and none had any other discernible occupation.[90]

"John Bright, MP and leader of the 'Radical' element, was selected by the London newspaper and journal press to be the focus of their anti–American and anti-democratic tirades. It was not democracy in America that was at the root of the anxiety of the media but any move that would bring an increased suffrage to Britain. Mr. Bright was considered the culprit who would deliver this foreign influence upon the face of Britain. He later declared his conviction that *The Times* had not published one fair, honorable, or friendly article toward the United States since Lincoln's accession to office."[91]

To promote their advocacy of limited suffrage and the status quo, the British press exercised every avenue to substantiate the failure of democracy in America. Nothing was to stay their condemnation of universal suffrage and the rights of the common man. Certainly not the truth.

Democracy, slavery, and the class structure of British society were cast as firmly in one as if by Siamese birth. The press sought resolutely to convince their readers and the world that the South had suffered from democracy and now was willing to endure all the pain of civil war to escape the domination of the common man. To the governing classes, democracy, or the prospect of sharing their power with those of a lesser caste, would lead to the destruction of efficient government and the end of freedom. The Confederacy was to be the showpiece of the upper class of Britain. The aristocratic and undemocratic South would be proof of the failure of democracy and the value of a limited suffrage.

The Southern states regarded with "genuine alarm" the workings of democracy, wrote the *The Quarterly Review* 110 (1861) 274:

> The really remarkable fact which is to be inferred from the conduct of the Southern States is the genuine alarm with which they regarded the workings of Democracy. Strictly speaking they were not Democracies themselves. The peculiar electoral law, by which each slaveowner enjoyed a plurality of votes in proportion to the number of his slaves, imported a strong oligarchic element into their institutions. But they were no mean judges of the working of a Democracy. They had acted in partnership with one for seventy years. They had watched it ripening year by year to the full development of mob supremacy, and they had enjoyed the fullest opportunity of judging of the temper and moderation with which it was likely to improve a triumph, or wield unfettered power over a conquered rival. We have seen what was the judgement they formed. They deliberately decided that civil war, with all its horrors, and with all its peculiar risks to themselves as slaveowners, was a lighter evil than to be surrendered to the justice or the clemency of a victorious Democracy.

The Manchester Guardian, 18 December 1861, divulged the problems of suffrage and of the value of slavery to avoid those difficulties:

> What chiefly concerns us now is the calm and deliberate condemnation passed upon mob-rule and all the contrivances by which it is maintained.... We have fewer opportunities of ascertaining what goes on in the Southern States; but we have not the slightest reason for supposing that they have yet witnessed anything approaching the systematic disregard of law and the arbitrary violence which now characterise the daily proceedings of the civil and military officials of the Federal executive....

There was a voice in the British press, however, that embraced the cause of democracy, that was anti-slavery, and represented the English worker. *Lloyd's Weekly London Newspaper* belonged to that small section of the press where circulation was limited, but the call was loud and clear. On 12 May 1861, *Lloyd's* was zealous in its defense of democracy and not of the Confederacy:

> "Democracy" — to adopt the un–English word with which the advocates of aristocracy seek to alarm quiet people — democracy, or the principle of the government of the whole, by the whole, having long sustained a disadvantageous war with the principle of oligarchy, is compelled to take arms against, if it would not be vanquished by, its most deadly enemy. All that is most virulent and repugnant in the vices of aristocratic governments is seized on and made the cornerstone of Southern policy. It was so before the disruption, and it is now.

If democracy does not work and the majority is not fit to govern, and an expanded franchise is a menace, who shall rule? To the majority of the British press the answer was fundamental — the "ten thousand." When the press spoke of "people," they did not have in mind the whole of British beings, male and female, but the one million males who possessed the franchise. *The Glasgow Herald,* 21 January 1865, defended the right of the one million to continue governing Britain:

> A great truth lies at the bottom of all Mr. Bright's reasoning on this subject [suffrage], but it is a truth which is more generally and more cordially accepted than Mr. Bright seems to think. That Parliament is the grand bulwark of our freedom — that Parliament ought to represent and protect the interests of all classes of the people — are propositions which we trust few persons in these days would be found to controvert; but how Parliament can best be made to serve this purpose is a very different question, and is the one upon which there is so much diversity of opinion. Mr. Bright thinks it could best be gained by ultimately admitting five millions more people to the electoral body. Now, the present electoral body consists of only about one million. The effect of Mr. Bright's measure would therefore be to throw

the present electors into a hopeless minority, and at once transfer the government of the country into new and untried hands. It is not unnatural that many should shrink from so tremendous and irrevocable a step. Here, too, arises the question of the fair representations of interest differing enormously in magnitude. The idea that a man should have some appreciable stake in the preservation of law and order before he was allowed to vote is not confined to monarchical Governments. It was strongly insisted upon by the founders of the American Republic. It is based on the very rational assumption that the man who has something to lose by a subversion of law and order is more likely to give these his support than the man who could lose nothing, and who may be said to carry his country in the sole of his shoe....

The *Saturday Review* (6 June 1863) 712, echoed the maxim of the antidemocratic British press:

The enormous extension of the suffrage does not seem to have made the American peasantry more sensitive about their political and personal rights than the peasantry of less advanced portions of the world. It would seem as though it were only at rare and exceptional epochs in the world's history, and under the pressure of great physical misery, that the masses will show any spontaneous jealousy for their freedom. The more educated middle and upper classes are the only guardians whose vigilance can be relied on. Their influence with their neighbours, in countries where wealth carries its due political weight, furnishes a ready-made organization; and it is only by such an organization, which can be called into play at a few days notice, that the sudden onset of an armed usurper can be repelled. Even in America, however, it can scarcely be conceived that the present patience can be permanent. The mass of people have been too long taught to believe that liberty consists in an abject submission to the will of the majority to have much sympathy left for freedom in the true sense.... But it is barely conceivable that even eighty years of unbridled democracy can have so rooted out the last instincts of freedom from the breasts of the Anglo-Saxon race.

The *Morning Post*, 2 March 1860, was wholly in favour of Lord John Russell's proposal for Reform:

The bill which Lord John Russell last night introduced "For the Amendment of the Representation of the People" may be regarded as the legitimate and natural consequence of the Reform Act of 1832. To stand upon the ancient ways of the Constitution is a duty which we are persuaded no English statesman would willingly venture to disregard. The theories of politicians who derive their experience and opinions from the United States of America have in reality no application to a country in which for nearly two hundered years civil liberty has been consolidated and enjoyed to an extent which the history of the rest of the world cannot parallel. The bill of the noble lord, therefore, wisely rejects all those empirical attempts — by means of fancy franchises and polling papers — to add to our representative system features borrowed from America, which would at no distant day lead to universal suffrage and the vote by ballot....

It was not democracy in America that raised the ire of the British press, but the thought of that democracy coming to Britain. How better to demonstrate the superiority of the English system of government than to parade the fabricated failures of the American democracy. *The Quarterly Review* 110 (1861) 283, warned its readers of the folly of John Bright and of democracy in America:

> But the thought of England, rather than the future of America, is the point to which our thoughts are naturally turned by the contemplation of these calamities (democracy). An Anglo-Saxon race, in the full light of modern civilization, free from all the aristocratic interests, which according to Mr. Bright, are the sole cause of war, has plunged into a deadly civil conflict of which no one can foresee the end. It is a spectacle full of warning to those in whose veins the same blood flows, and whose political constitution has sprung from the same stock. We naturally look about us to see whether any similar danger threatens ourselves. May it not be, that we have been sucked into the same current, and are insensibly gliding towards the same fatal shore? If we have thoughtlessly aped the extravagances of America in the heyday of her folly, it is time we should take warning from her ruin. What is England doing? How has she received the lesson which has been given to her in the history of her headstrong offspring?

The Quarterly Review 112 (1862) 538, had few honors for American democracy:

> If Mr. Bright or his friends had been formerly content to claim for their pet democracy nothing more than that it was no worse than some of the old European monarchies, few people would have cared to question their modest panegyric. But it is the background of their extravagant adulation which throws forward into so strong a relief the calamities under which the Americans are suffering. They never ceased to assure us that democracy was a cure for war, for revolution, for extravagance, for corruption, for nepotism, for class legislation, and, in short, for all the evils with which the states of Europe are familiar. It is too late for them, now that America is a prey to all these old-world maladies at once, to turn round and tell us that the model Republic is no worse than an average despotism, or no worse than England was four hundred years ago. For years they have been proclaiming to us that it is infinitely better....

In pondering the difficulties which America encountered, the British press experienced sheer rapture. *The Glasgow Herald* was convinced that universal suffrage was on its "last legs"; *The Quarterly Review* could only view democracy in America as an overbearing majority violating the rights of a minority; *The Economist* was certain that the Constitution of the United States was producing great evil. Opined *The Glasgow Herald*, 25 April 1861:

> It is not necessary to suppose that statesmanship in America has suddenly become a nonentity; but the universal practice of pandering to the prejudices of the multitude, induces men to conceal their embarrassment and indecision with a verbiage of high-sounding phrases signifying nothing.... In the first place, the head of the Government is elected by the mass of the people, and yet during the continuance of his four years' reign, he is almost independent of the people's representatives. The Executive Government was almost as little in direct contact with the people in Republican America as it is under a despotic monarchy; and in the one case the Government is supposed to be regulated by popular will, but ... the popular will is regulated by the Government.

The Quarterly Review 110 (1861) 249:

> The omnipotence of the majority has always been looked upon as the germ of future danger to the Republic by the most keen-sighted observers both of America and Europe. "The Federalist" contains very earnest warnings against the tendency of "the superior force of an interested and overbearing majority" to violate the rights of a minority. Both Madison and Jefferson have left their apprehensions upon record. Accordingly the first founders of the Republic took many precautions to moderate its action, and to curb its excesses. A restricted suffrage, an independent judiciary, a system of indirect election in the choice of the President, were all contrivances devised by the creators of democracy to fetter the Frankenstein they had raised. The checks were well intended, but they were utterly in vain. Washington and his contemporaries had never seen democracy at work. They could not know by experience its impatience of control and certain tendency towards despotism. They did not recognise, what with better warning too many among ourselves are apt to forget, that when once the balance of democracy and the other powers in the State is overset, it will never rest till it has swept them utterly away, and reigns not only supreme, but alone. It was idle to restrict the suffrage so slightly that the supremacy still remained with the class whose sympathies were democratic. That happened, which, if we lowered our suffrage, would happen among ourselves. Preponderance was converted into absolute rule. The lower classes, with whom the supremacy had been left, hastened to confirm and to extend their monopoly of power. It is useless to fence men about with limitations and restraints which at the same time you give them the means of pulling down. The low franchise was used to make the franchise lower still; and bit by bit every restriction that removed it from universal suffrage was abolished....

Steeped in its constitutional authority, *The Economist* advised its readers of the evil of the American instrument (1 June 1861) 251:

> Even now the Constitution of the United States is producing great evil. A President, especially a new, an untried, and comparatively untrained politi-cian like Mr Lincoln, ought to be able to call to his aid a popular assem-bly, animated by all the feeling which a great crisis calls forth in a great people, and containing all the wisdom which the whole nation can collect to meet the crisis. Mr Lincoln has no such power. He can, it is true, con-vene an extraordinary session of the existing Congress; but that Congress was elected years since, when no such crisis as the present was ever thought of, when any one who dreamed of it would have been considered to be mad, when other hopes, other fears, and other thoughts absorbed the pub-lic mind. Such a Congress would be worse than useless as a counsellor, and might even be very dangerous as a restraint or as an opponent. Mr Lincoln is doubtless right in naming a distant day for its session. But what a com-mentary is it on the working of a political Constitution, that it compels an inferior, unknown, untried, and tired man to decide upon national difficul-ties without aid and without control? The moral is a plain one. The Con-stitution of the United States was framed upon a vicious principle. The framers were anxious to resist the force of democracy — to control its fury and restrain its outbursts. They either could not or did not take the one effectual means of so doing; they did not place the substantial power in the hands of men of education and property. They hoped to control the democ-racy by paper checks and constitutional devices. The history we have sketched evinces the result; it shows that these checks have produced unan-ticipated, incalculable, and fatal evil, but have not attained the beneficial end for which they were selected. They may have ruined the Union, but they have not controlled democracy.

The Morning Post, 4 May 1861, gushed forth its fears of equal citizenship, sovereignty of the people, and the popular will. But first its readers would be forced to face the nauseating untruth of the editor's affection for America.

> The exciting news from America will be read with deep interest and sin-cere regret by all classes in this country. Sprung from ourselves, the Amer-icans have a high place in our affections. We have admired their enterprise, and witnessed without envy their commercial success and social improve-ment. We have even felt much sympathy with their political institutions, and have never fallen short of them in their ardent love of liberty.
>
> The Americans have prided themselves upon their equal citizenship, the sovereignty of the people, and the almightiness of the popular will. Late events have put all these to a powerful test. The result is not likely to encour-age other nations to imitate the transatlantic constitution. Equal citizen-ship has turned out to be only an equality amongst white skins, and that equality an abstraction. The sovereignty of the people has come to grief for

want of a popular sovereign, and the popular will is all to pieces for want of a centre of unity.

When a great social and political question of many years' silent growth came to maturity, the machinery was thrown out of gear, and neither equal citizenship nor popular will could stay the storm of popular passion.

If the American Union falls to pieces it will for lack of that blending of popular representation with responsible administration and monarchical supremacy which have grown up through many centuries in this favoured country, and which has always given the people a centre for their loyalty as well as directing power to their strength. Equal citizenship, popular supremacy, vote by ballot, and universal suffrage may do well for a while, but they invariably fail in the day of trial. Those who wish to change the Constitution of England would do well to ask why it is that the republics of Greece, Rome, Venice, France, and now America, have all suffered and died from intestine disorders.

In the Victorian era the ruling class of Britain felt more comfortable with the American leaders of the War for Independence than with Abraham Lincoln and his followers. The veneration of Washington, Jefferson, and Hamilton was founded on the belief that these leaders were not believers in democracy nor the rights of the common man. It was a great disappointment to the British press that the Electoral College, which to their minds was formed to defeat the electoral rights of the common man, had failed in that purpose. *The Saturday Review* (8 September 1860) 291, comments:

The miscarriage of certain sections to the Constitution of the United States forms a curious subject. One such failure is brought into very conspicuous prominence by the pending election. There is no doubt that the College of Presidential Electors provided for in the Constitution was intended by the founders of the Republic to be an active and substantial, and not a merely formal institution. The people, voting with such suffrage laws as each State allowed, were to select a number of persons possessing weight, station, and character; these gentlemen, after deliberating among themselves, were to choose the best man in the Union for President. Strange as it may seem, WASHINGTON, JEFFERSON, HAMILTON and ADAMS never contemplated the choice of a President by universal suffrage. Not only was universal suffrage, except in a few States, unknown in their day, but there was also a body interposed between the people and the ultimate election, which the statesmen of the last century considered to be a sufficient safeguard against the caprice and ignorance of a multitudinous constituency. There never was an institution, however, which more completely disappointed the expectations of its authors.

The Quarterly Review 110 (1861) 263:

The indirect elections have become an empty form, and the President is practically chosen by the direct vote of the whole population. The independent judiciary was another effective check, wisely devised if it could have been upheld, but which the encroaching spirit of democracy could ill brook.... The omnipotence of the majority has not been contented with a mere victory over constitutional restraints. It is not only supreme in the making and the administering of laws, but it exercised a despotic control over the life and actions of private individuals more minute and more penetrating than it would be physically in the power of an absolute monarch to carry out....

The Economist (1 June 1861) 291–293:

The framers were wisely and warmly attached to the principle of liberty, and, like all such persons, were extremely anxious to guard against momentary hurts of popular opinion. They were especially desirous that the President to whom they were entrusting vast power should be the representative, not of a small section of the community, but of a really predominant part of it. Accordingly, they not only established a system of double election, in the hope that the "electoral college" would exercise a real discretion in the choice of President, and be some check on popular ignorance. They likewise provided that an absolute majority of that electoral college must give their votes for the elected candidate. In any other event the election was to be void, and the right of choice lapsed in a peculiar and complicated way. The effect had been painfully different from the design. In reality, the electoral college exercises no choice: every member of it is selected by the primitive constituency because he will vote for a certain Presidential candidate, and he does nothing but vote accordingly. The provision requiring the consent of an absolute majority has had a still worse effect; it has not only been futile, but it has been pernicious....

The fear of the ruling class of a government subservient to the majority was reflected throughout the press. The growing pressure for a new Reform Act, which was mandated in 1867, obligated the press to express the concerns of their readership and the dangers of a widened suffrage, and to hold America as an example of the failure of popular government. *The Quarterly Review* 117 (1865) 284, castigates American "ultra-liberal" thought on freedom:

Freedom, in their definition, is the supreme, unchecked power of the majority. The doctrine has not been nakedly stated here — it would be too repulsive to the ears of Englishmen who have been brought up to value freedom of a different kind. But in America, the school of politicians with whom our Radicals so closely sympathise do not conceal it.... Again and again in almost every contemporary vindication of the Federal cause, the dogma is broadly laid down that the majority must rule....

When the hour of trial came, its institutions were found to be too feeble to bear the strain, until propped up by the perilous support of a military despotism. Now we see the government of the multitude under its
other aspect. It is animated by a passion as thoughtless and unreasonable
as its former security. All care for the prosperity, which formerly was its
first care, all thought of freedom, all scruples of humanity, have been swal-
lowed up in the one longing for a colossal empire.

The British press consistently expressed its love and eternal regard for America, an appreciation which was hardly supported by the evidence. The underlying deceit was manifest and did little to enhance its honor. *The Times,* 12 August
1861, hypocritically expressed its desire for America's future:

Though it is impossible to avoid reflecting that the division of the Union
into two great States may relieve us from many of the troubles with which
we were menaced by the overbearing policy of the old Federal Government,
we can safely assert that Englishmen desire nothing more than to see the
quarrel terminated and the strife appeased. We wish no harm to either
party, and would far rather see America strong, united, and prosperous,
than speculate on the advantages which its premature disruption might
possibly bring to its neighbours....

The class structure of England had greater ramifications than extended franchise. The very life of the working classes depended on breaking the control of
the governing act and bettering their existence. To those who live in the West,
the following chart from G.M. Young, *Victorian England,* on life expectancy in
mid–Victorian England must come as a shock:

	Gentle folk	Traders & Farmers	Laborers
Bath	55	37	25
Rutland	52	41	38
Wilts	50	48	33
Derby	49	38	21
Truro	40	33	28
Leeds	45	27	19
Manchester	38	20	17
Liverpool	35	22	15

In London the mortality rate was twice as great in the East End as in the
West End.[92]

12. Humanitarian or Mercantilist

In the end, for all the back-slapping and self-applause, the British parliament did not actually give the slaves full and unconditional freedom. It had given them — as it had always done — the name without the substance. It had talked for fifty years about humanity and justice for the blacks. It had prided itself on ending the slave trade and colonial slavery, ending them, it must be added, with considerable reluctance and ill-will. But to what extent did its legislation affect the real situation? During those fifty years the importation of blacks from Africa continued. During those fifty years the treatment of the slaves in the West Indies remained as brutal and unjust as it had always been.

Following their politicians' lead, the British public indulged itself for nearly one hundred years in paeans of self-praise, with the result that, instead of Britain coming out of this shameful period with some humility ... it emerged with even greater arrogance.

British pockets had been filled by the West Indian slave system it had created. Britain's pride was puffed up by the erroneous belief that it had destroyed the system; but it was slavery that destroyed slavery. The economics of the system forced it in the end to collapse, as Adam Smith had predicted sixty years before.[93]

The British West Indies were rapidly losing their leading position in the British overseas economy. Soil exhaustion in the smaller islands, the increasing severe competition from Saint Domingue (Haiti) and then from the nearly virgin lands of Cuba, left the British islands behind in the race. More important still, the new industrial economy of Britain had more serious interests to foster than those of the sugar colonies. The abolition of the slave trade, then the abolition of slavery, were not merely the results of a rising standard of political ethics in Britain but were a form of cutting losses. The West Indies sugar monopoly became intolerable to a booming industrial society, rightly confident in its invulnerable competitive position in the early days of the Industrial Revolution. So we had the paradox of the reversal of roles. It was all very well for the Abolitionists to deplore the use of slave-produced sugar in the West Indies, but no one proposed to stop the use of slave-produced cotton in the United States. Indeed, no one proposed seriously to stop the use of slave-produced sugar from Brazil or Cuba. Money, not passions, passions of wickedness or goodness, spurred the plot.[94]

The West Indian monopoly was not only unsound in theory, it was unprofitable in practice. In 1828 it was estimated that it cost the British people annually more than one and a half million pounds. In 1844 it was costing the country £70,000 a week and London £6,000. Britain was paying for its sugar five millions more a year than the Continent. Three and a half million pounds of British exports to the West Indies in 1838 purchased less than half as much sugar and coffee as they would have purchased if carried to Cuba and Brazil.... Two-fifths of the price of every pound of sugar consumed in Britain represented the cost of production; two-fifths went in revenue to the government; one-fifth in tribute to the West Indian planter. The capitalists, eager to lower wages, advocated the policy of "the free breakfast table." It was an injustice and a folly to impose protective duties on food. Time was when the leading statesmen were on the West Indian side. Now Palmerston lined up with the opponents of the planters — and with the new industrialists.[95]

There was a new capitalism in England. The Industrial Revolution was spreading through the British Island. The mercantile economy and the importance of colonies were giving way to a system of free trade. And the new order was mirrored in the House of Commons. The Reform Act of 1832 seated in the Commons the wealthy merchants of the industrial towns. Men who had little patience with the need for colonies; men who wanted "the free breakfast table" so that they could pay their workers less. It was little wonder that in the 1840s the Corn Laws were repealed with the import tax protecting West Indian sugar.

The mid–Victorians measured the success or failure of the emancipation policy in the West Indies by the standards of their own social background. Emancipated slaves failed to adjust to the established English pattern of wage-labour, therefore the blacks appeared not only slothful but also culpably neglectful of their duty to work. The black community failed to meet English expectations about the rise of a vigorous, self-reliant, industrious, and self-improving multitude which, in the abolitionist vision, would act as the salvation of the West Indies. As a consequence, English philanthropists became less sanguine about the ability of blacks to conform to the English model.[96]

The work-ethic, or lack of it, was very much the subject of discussion during the mid–Victorian era. Among the many pamphlets that appeared in

England during the mid–1800s on the question of slavery, the following, published in London in 1862, represented the English God-fearing interpretation of the work imperative:

> In this letter, which I will here resume in a few words, I establish the following truths: I. That men must work; since it is only by working that they can individually rise from ignorance to knowledge, and can advance collectively from barbarism to civilization. That to advance from one of these conditions to the other being the destiny of humanity on this earth, work is the paramount duty of man. II. That those who do work have the right to compel those to work who do not; for the earth, however it may have been divided among nations, is only a common domain given by God to all mankind; that all therefore have, as coparceners, the right of compelling those to work who neglect that duty. III. That this right, the right of man to compel man to work, has been from all time one of the means which God employs to make humanity advance in the path of progress; a fact which would now be universally acknowledged if our historians had been able to discover and make known the whole of the means employed for this end by Providence. IV. That in imposing work upon the black race, which has remained in total idleness, the white race only accomplishes its right and duty....[97]

The Daily Telegraph, 21 March 1861, quickly followed *The Times* in disapproval of the labor situation in the British West Indies, and a critique of the lack of the English work-ethic displayed by the ex-slaves. Like *The Times, The Daily Telegraph* was a supporter of the old economic regime; there was approval of the former era of the slave-holding, sugar-growing British West Indies. And a critique of the lack of work-ethic displayed by the Negro:

> We had more than half ruined the finest colonies in the world. Subsequently an impartially rigorous adherence to the doctrines of free trade forbade us to extend to the planters of the West Indies the slightest modicum of protection, and slave-grown sugar and slave-distilled rum were allowed to oust the products of our own colonies from the market. So tender were the emancipationists of this country of dark-skinned interests that they deprecated the slightest approach to forced labour; and, for a long time, Coolie immigration was discouraged and denounced as another form of slave trade. All this we did for concience sake.
>
> He awoke one morning, and found himself free; but, to the Imperial dismay, it was speedily discovered that we had created a new Frankenstein, in the shape of a lazy, worthless, saucy vagabond — a sable scamp, who would work no more and no longer than was necessary to provide him with a few rags and a few vegetables, and who tranquilly allowed the most fertile coffee and sugar plantations in the West Indies to run wild, while he basked in the sun, and satisfied himself with plaintains and pumpkins.

The Saturday Review (18 June 1864) 749, emulated its fellow English newspapers in disparaging the work-ethic of the Negro:

> What is English opinion — i.e. the opinion of Englishmen who have seen the negro as he exists in civilized communities? Englishmen have seen him in three qualities — as a slave in the Southern States; as a freeman without rights in the Northern States; as a freeman, with all and something more than all the ordinary rights of freedom, in the English colonies. In the first character, they have pitied him probably more than they have admired him. They have pitied the squalid savage whose sluggish drudgery brought as little profit to himself as to his master. But perhaps they have more deeply pitied the master whose property was left to the thriftless care of such a drudge. In the North, they have seen him gradually ousted from every decent trade and calling, partly by the superior skill and industry, partly also by the increasing jealousy, of the Teuton and the Celt. And here, again, their pity has been not wholly simple and unmixed. For, while they may not have seen much to choose between the untidy fussiness of the unkempt Irishman and the self-complacent half-work of the conceited negro, they cannot have failed to see that even if the latter had been less vain, less conceited, and less idle than he really is, he would have had a hard battle to fight, not only against the stern prejudices of his white rivals, but also against their superior energy, directness of purpose, and honesty of work....

It was not long before the British press unveiled active support of the Confederacy and the Southern treatment of the Negro as opposed to that of the North. It is truly amazing to read such rubbish, even by the English press. The black for all practical purposes, did not exist in England, and to suppose he existed in the never-never land of English colonies as painted by *The Quarterly Review* 114 (1863) 145, contradicted all documentary evidence. What did become clear was the untoward prejudice of the British press in their dealings with the Irish:

> he must be content to be regarded as an outcast and a pariah by the drab coloured philanthropists of Philadelphia and the Celtic aristocrats of New York. Not only is he not politically the equal of the white man, but he is socially far his inferior. He pays for his nominal freedom by an amount of hatred and contumely which is wholly unintelligible on this side of the Atlantic. His freedom bears a bitterer fruit than the slavery of his compatriots in the South; for the slave in the South is often the pet of his master, and is caressed with a fondness which would not be lavished on an equal or a rival race; while the negro in the North has to bear the whole pressure of the galling contempt with which men who have a certain position sneer down the attempts of those who vainly aspire to attain it. He is the victim alike of German rudeness and Irish brutality, and the practical aid which he obtains from his Abolitionist friends is of the slightest and coldest kind. His career is that of a poor devil born to be a waiter, a

barber, or a porter; to be shut out of omnibuses and churches, jostled in the streets, and sworn at as an unreasonable intrusion on the every day life of mankind. How different his condition and prospects in the British Colonies! There his freedom is as secure in fact as it is admitted in theory. He is free to choose his own line of life, and fix the remuneration of his own labours. Not only a professional but an official career is open to his ambition. American visitors to the West Indies start to find the public peace maintained by black policemen, public justice dispensed by black magistrates, criminal trials proceeding before black jurymen, and sometimes laws passed by black members of the Legislature....

13. Tariff and Secession

When South Carolina and other sections of the South were asserting their individuality and desire to secede from the Union in 1860, the economic interests of Britain and the United States were already diverging. It was true that the liberalization of the American tariff in 1833, 1846, and 1857, together with the extension to Americans of full trading privileges with the British West Indies, the repeal of the Corn Laws, and the dismantling of the Navigation Code, created a climate of relatively free trade as British manufactures were exchanged for American raw products. Indeed, for a time, it seemed that the two economies were complementary. There was a heavy British investment in the United States and these funds helped to finance the transportation revolution and to release domestic capital for industrial development. Thus the British assisted the growth of an industrial America and by so doing contributed to the emancipation of the American economy from its colonial status and to its elevation to the rank of competitor. Although the rivalry was not formalized until the enactment of the Morrill Tariff, the economic clouds had been gathering over the Atlantic for some time. Englishmen may not have realized in 1860 that the United States was an industrial nation second only to their own, but there was reason enough for uneasiness. As early as the 1840s British manufacturers were complaining of the exodus of valuable workmen to the United States, having seen their exports to that market more than halved since 1832. Mid-century found the two nations competing for commerce of the west coast of Africa and in Latin America, and brought evidence of superior American technology. The Americans' exhibits at the Crystal Palace in 1851 attracted much attention, and before long their sewing machines and reapers were being imported into Britain or manufactured there from patents. Finally, the 1850s witnessed Lancashire's loss to New England of the lucrative American market for coarse cottons. By 1860 American mills were consuming a third of the quantity of cotton needed to supply those in Britain.[98]

Although the London press made much of the cotton crisis in Lancashire, there was a far more important and permanent advantage to England from the separation of North and South than the momentary relief in the cotton trade, and it was this advantage which lay at the bottom of the attitude of the British governing class. A powerful and ill-mannered rival should be permanently weakened by disunion. England had, with the exception of a few radicals, always disliked the United States. This dislike was based upon maritime rivalry, commercial rivalry, and upon past bitter experiences with America. It could not be forgotten that America had once been an English possession which had successfully revolted and involved England in a series of humiliating defeats. Then there was the War of 1812 which rankled the British. After that were boundary and fishery disputes, the Oregon controversy, the Texas controversy, the clash in Central America, and, withal, the gigantic growth of the accompanying ill-concealed willingness of America to fight England on the most trivial pretext.[99]

The London press lost little time in enjoying the plight of Britain's former colonies across the Atlantic. Separation of the North and South was synonymous with prosperity for England and the appreciation of which was a constant thread in the press. Separation of the North and South was presented to the reading public in terms easily understood by those of trade. It was the cupidity of the North that led to the cold and callous tariffs which were so grossly unfair to the South.

The Quarterly Review 110 (1861) 271, supplied readers with the rationale of the secessionist South as seen through English eyes:

> They were suffering, and had long suffered, from the effects of the various Northern Tariffs; and they believed from past experience that as soon as the North had the power in its hands they should be exposed to some perilous dealing with their slaves.... Thirty years ago the question of the tariff had nearly taken South Carolina out of the Union. It was a grievance that had constantly grown, both in its actual burdens and in the severity with which it galled the feeling of the Southerners. Year after year the protective policy enacted by Massachusetts and Pennsylvania was stifling the industry of the South and draining its prosperity in order to fatten on the proceeds of what was in effect, a distant nation, antagonistic in its convictions and policy, alien in its traditions and habits of life. It had been forced at first by the sheer weight of a majority on the reluctant South. The protective system had been worn as a triumph by the North, and had been turned by them to the utmost possible profit, and for many a year it had left a wrankling sense of wrong in the Southern mind. The South felt the double sting of humiliation and of loss. They felt that they were wronged because they were beaten. And it did not seem likely that the evil would abate of itself in the course of time, and as those wants grew the tariff was likely to rise....

Lost to the London press was the simple reality that the tariff passed Congress only because of the departure of cotton representatives; it was the result, not the cause of secession. "The South had contolled the administration for sixty out of seventy-two years, and had made the tariff and government what they were. The tariff became useful as war propaganda mainly because it detracted world attention from the slavery issue and appealed to the free trade opinion...."[100]

John Bright, MP from the North of England and leader of the Radicals faction, could find nothing in the tariff, onerous as it might be, to vindicate secession. And did not England retain a loathsome tariff some twenty years earlier?

> Whatever might be the influence of the tariff upon the United States, it is as pernicious to the West as it is to the South; and further, that Louisiana, which is a Southern State and a seceded State, has always voted with Pennsylvania until last year in favor of protection, — protection for its sugar, whilst Pennsylvania wished protection for its coal and iron. But if the tariff was onerous and grievous, was that any reason for this great insurrection? Was there ever a country that had a tariff, especially in the article of food, more onerous and more cruel than we had in this country twenty years ago? We did not secede. We did not rebel. What we did was to raise money for the purpose of distributing among all the people perfect information upon the question; and many men, as you know, devoted all their labors, for several years, to teach the great and wise doctrine of free trade to the people of England.[101]

Perhaps the greatest preoccupation of the London press was to inform their readers of the immeasurable prosperity that would settle on England with the disintegration of the Union. *The Examiner,* 12 January 1861, however, objected to any implication that the English press would have such base considerations. The article was published before the fall of Fort Sumter, and perhaps *The Examiner* had not yet considered all possibilities:

> If the hackneyed charge against England were true, that her sympathies always take the direction of her commercial interest, we should now be rejoicing at the rupture of the American Union, and the prospect of a Southern Confederacy, with a liberal or Free Trade tariff. But the very opposite of this is the notoriously universal feeling, and indeed, our wishes have so much influenced our judgment that we have refused to believe in secession till the accomplishment of the act. And to this hour the fact has been discussed here with reference only to the welfare and importance of the great American community. It is, then, certain that our opinions are not made so exclusively of cotton, as our detractors pretend. The question now is, how far the rupture will extend, and whether it will be permanent, or only what the children call a make-believe, to extort terms from the North....

Eight months later *The Economist* (28 September 1861) 1065, was now well aware of the possibilities of the disintegration of the American Union and relished every morsel:

> We, of course, must condemn the Protective Tariff of the Union as oppressive and benighted folly—silly and suicidal in itself, iniquitous towards the West, and hostile as regards ourselves. Of course we reciprocate the wish of the South for low duties and unfettered trade. Of course we are anxious that the prosperity of the States which produce so much raw material and need so many manufactured goods should suffer no interruption or reverse. Most of us are of opinion also, that they were entitled to secede, if so it seemed good to them; and that the claim of ten millions of Republicans to frame their own Union and to select their own fellow citizens could not logically be resisted by brother Republicans, though numbering twenty million. We saw, therefore, no reason why they should be hindered from seceding if they chose....
>
> We sympathise with the South (so far as we sympathise with it at all), not because we are slaves to our necessity for cotton, or because we fear that emancipation would ultimately cut off the supply—but because we think that, politically, the Southern States had a right to leave the Federation without the hindrance and without coercion; because their behaviour towards England has been more decent and courteous than that of their antagonists; and because they were desirous to admit our goods at 10 per cent. duty, while their enemies imposed 40 percent ... and that even tacit approval is as far from our thoughts as the impertinence of open interference; that Lancashire is not England, and, for the honour and spirit of our manufacturing population be it said also, that even if it were, "Cotton would NOT be King." There are other sources of supply besides the Negro plantations of America; but even were there none, our sentiments in reference to Slavery would undergo no change. England and Lancashire are ready to purchase cotton, if need be, at a cost of a shilling a lb,—but never at the cost of one iota of consistency or principle. And now we must add a few words in answer to the charge of selfishness so thoughtlessly brought against the views and sentiments entertained by England in reference to the American crisis. We admit that we do regard the disruption of the Union as a matter rather for rejoicing than for regret; and we maintain that we do this without laying ourselves open to the just imputation of any one mean, narrow, or ungenerous feeling. We avow the sentiment, and we are prepared to justify it as at once natural, statesmanlike, and righteous ... we do not see why we should hesitate to declare our belief that the dissolution of the Union will prove good to the world, to Great Britain, and probably in the end to America herself....

The Saturday Review (9 March 1861) 23, agreed. Unlimited prosperity for England would be the result of the disunion. With unqualified ecstasy, *The Saturday Review* foresaw no loss of trade with the North:

neither City nor the State of New York have any interest in establishing Protectionism; and to the more westerly Free States it is the cruelest blow at their prosperity which could possibly be struck. They are almost as much dependent as the South on the English market for their produce, and the slackening of their trade with the Slave States will render freedom of commerce with England even more important to them than before.... For the only trade which a Southern Union would care to have would be, as nearly as possible, Free-trade. It is of course the object of the cotton planters to manufacture nothing but raw cotton, and to buy every luxury and necessary of life in the very market in which they sell their staple. English calico and English cutlery will, therefore, stream into New Orleans and Charleston as soon as the Northern Union ceases to claim jurisdiction over their ports. How are these goods to be prevented from entering the territory of the United States? No natural frontier separates the two halves of the existing Federation — the dividing line has been exclusively created by an artificial difference in social institutions....

The Times fell in line with the thinking of fellow journalists as early as 21 January 1861, and could savo3r the benefits of the demise of the Union. England would again reign supreme:

we see no reason for anticipating that a severance of the Union, once effected peaceably and without catastrophe, will be in any way injurious to Great Britain. On the contrary, we are not sure that it may not indirectly be rather beneficial than otherwise. In the first place, we may expect that America will be somewhat less aggressive, less insolent, and less irritable than she has been. Instead of one vast State, acting on every foreign question cum toto corpore regni, we shall have two, with different objects and interests, and by no means always disposed to act in concert or in cordiality. Instead of one, showing an encroaching and somewhat bullying front to the rest of the world, we shall have two, showing something of the same front to each other. Each will be more occupied with its immediate neighbour, and, therefore, less inclined to pick quarrels with more distant nations. Then, too, for some time at least, that inordinate, though most natural sense of unrivalled prosperity and power, which swelled so flatulently and disturbingly in the breast of every citizen of the great Transatlantic Republic, will receive a salutory check. Their demeanour is likely to become somewhat humbler and more rational, and it will, therefore, be easier to maintain amicable and tranquil relations with them than it has been. In place, too, of Europe being obliged to watch and thwart their annexing tendencies the two federations will probably exercise this sort of moral police over each other. Neither of them will look with much complacency on the annexation of States or territories which will add power and minion to the other, and so disturb their equilibrium. Unprincipled and reckless Southerners like Mr. Buchanan, may talk of seizing on Mexico, Nicaragua, and Cuba; unprincipled and inflated Northerners like

> Mr. Seward, may talk of seizing Canada; but there will be some hope that we may leave them to each others' mutual control, and smile at the villainous cupidities of both.

On 6 September 1862, *The Times* finally jettisoned good manners and probity, and informed readers that the tariff was a device for the destruction of Great Britain:

> While the Northern States of America have been working so steadily and so successfully at their own destruction, they have, as becomes men of large views and cosmopolitan sympathies, found time among such absorbing occupations to compass and imagine the destruction of England also.... The very first use that Congress made of the majority acquired by the Republican party through the Secession of the Southern members was to pass a prohibitory tariff levelled at the trade and commerce of Great Britain. We have always regarded this measure as an injury. In America it is believed to be not merely injurious to Great Britain, but absolute destruction. The way they reason is this: — if we prohibit the importation of British manufactures into America, England will be obliged to pay for the corn which she requires from the Western States in specie. She will by this process be gradually drained of her specie, and will by this process be ruined. Thus, if we escape the perils by land and sea which are in store for us, we finally are to fall by this splendid magnetic contrivance, which is to extract from us all our gold and silver — that is, according to the American creed, all our wealth.... No man and no country, not even the United States themselves, can truly boast of security from the possibility of ruin, but, if England is to fall, it will not fall by the agency of the Morrill Tariff.

14. Homogeneity and Patriotism in the Confederacy

By the summer of 1861, Britons, especially those of the governing class, viewed the Confederacy through a curtain of blind prejudice. The South, surveyed in a cloud of unenlightenment, was conceived as a homogeneous patriotic state. It was a never-never land of handsome men and pulchritudinous women.

Members of the British upper and governing class considered the Confederate leaders to be distinguished gentlemen. They dressed appropriately and conducted themselves in a manner fitting to their English ancestry. Their command of the English language in speech and writing was impeccable. Freedom, English freedom, not democracy, was deep-rooted in the people of the South and a central part of their community. Patriotism was a prime ingredient of Southern society.

William Russell emphasized the feeling of camaraderie between the aristocracy of England and the Confederacy. Russell quotes Edmund Rhett, a prominent Southern secessionist:

> We are an agricultural people, pursuing our own system, and working out our own destiny, breeding up women and men with some other purpose than to make them vulgar, fanatical, cheating Yankees — hypocritical, if as women they pretend to real virtue; and lying, if as men they pretend to be honest. We have gentlemen and gentlewomen in your sense of it. We have a system which enables us to reap the fruits of the earth by a race which we save from barbarism in restoring them to their real place in the world as labourers; whilst we are enabled to cultivate the arts, the graces, and accomplishments of life, to develop science, to apply ourselves to the duties of government, and to understand the affairs of the country.[102]

Mr. Russell continued — The Southerners also take pride to themselves for their wisdom in keeping in Congress those men who have proved themselves useful and capable. It was a comment that gave much pleasure to the governing class of Britain. Again Russell quotes Rhett:

> "We do not," they say, "cast men aside at the caprices of a mob or in obedience to some low party intrigue, and hence we are sure of the best men, and are served by gentlemen conversant with public affairs, far superior in every way to the ignorant clowns who are sent to Congress by the North...."[103]

Such were the dogmas of the Southern secessionist and the English partisan. But there were other opinions of both British and Americans not so favorable to the Confederacy. Robert Trimble, an English contemporary, wrote in 1863 of the purity of Southern women. His view differed from Rhett's impression:

> It is a boast of the Southern people that their women are the purest under heaven, and in this regard far surpass the women of the North. Far be it from me to cast any reproach, or intimate disbelief in the goodness of the female population. I have no doubt they are as good as the average of women elsewhere. But, when such an assertion as that referred to is made, and made with a special object in view, it is necessary to view the case somewhat closely. The Southern partisan will not hesitate to give as a reason of the purity of the white women, the impurity of the black, and that the former are kept out of temptation by the fact that the latter are the subjects of the unrestrained passions of their master. [Frederick Law] Olmstead and others relate how the license taken in the intercourse with slaves tends to brutalize the masters, and that from boyhood on, there is the rankest corruption. Wives, sisters, daughters, are all cognizant of the state of affairs. Can it be that the minds of the latter are forced to dwell upon these matters as wrongs done to them, and remain equable and uncontaminated? The better people (for there are noble and good men to leaven even the vilest lump), deplore, but can find no remedy for existing pollution. But beyond this, it is stated, on unquestionable authority, that the purity and goodness referred to characterize those only who in all countries are more especially removed from the influence of temptation — the middle and upper classes; and that amongst the mean whites who hang about the plantations of the wealthy, immorality of every kind abounds. So much is this the case, so universally is estimated of their masters, these mean whites are regarded as still more degraded. But surely it is a frightful thing to find it coolly used as an argument in favor of the perpetuation of slavery....[104]

Perhaps the leading contemporary authority on the South was Frederick Law Olmsted, who recorded his impressions of the South and slavery in the fateful decade between the Compromise of 1850, which sought to avert national disunion, and Lincoln's election as President, which precipitated it. *The Cotton Kingdom*, which abridges and synthesizes his observations, is the nearest thing posterity has to an exact transcription of a civilization which time has tinted with hues of romantic legend. Olmsted's account is an indispensable work in the process of recapturing the American past.[105] Here is Olmsted on education:

> In spite of the constant denunciations by the Southern newspapers, I never conversed with a cultivated Southerner on the effects of slavery, that he did not express a wish or intention to have his own children educated where they should be free from demoralizing association with slaves.[106]

Olmsted on Southern gentlemen:

> The South has a traditional reputation for qualities and habits in which I think the Southern people, as a whole, are today more deficient than any other in the world. The Southern gentleman, as we ordinarily conceive him to be, is as rare a phenomenon in the South at the present day as is the old squire of Geoffrey Crayon in modern England. But it is unnecessary to argue how great must be the influence upon the people of a higher origin, of habitual association with a race systematically kept at the lowest ebb of intellect and morals. It has been elaborately and convincingly described by Mr. Jefferson, from his personal experience and observation of his neighbours. What he testified to be the effect upon Virginians, in his day, of owning and associating with slaves, is now to be witnessed to a far greater and deplorable extent throughout the whole South, but most deplorably in districts where the slave population predominates, and where, consequently, the action of slavery has been most unimpeded.... How can men retain the most essential quality to true manhood who daily, without remonstrance or interference, see men beaten, whose position renders effective resistance totally impracticable — and not only men, but women, too! Is it not partially the result of this, that self-respect seldom seems to suggest he should be careful to secure fair play for his opponent in a quarrel?[107]

Olmstead on violence in the Confederacy:

> A gentleman of veracity, now living in the South, told me that among his friends he had once numbered two young men, who were themselves intimate friends, till one of them, taking offence at some foolish words uttered by the other, challenged him. A large crowd assembled to see the duel, which took place on a piece of prairie ground. The combatants came armed with rifles, and at first interchange of shots the challenged man fell disabled by a ball in his thigh. The other, throwing down his rifle, walked toward him, and kneeling by his side, drew a bowie knife, and deliberately

butchered him. The crowd of bystanders not only permitted this, but the execrable assassin still lives in the community, has since married, and, as far as my informant could judge, his social position has been rather advanced than otherwise, from thus dealing with his enemy. In what other English — in what other civilized or half-civilized community would such cowardly atrocity have been endured?[108]

Commencing in mid–1862, *The Times* carried out an unending vilification of the North. Whether it was the Conscription Act, or the denial of habeas corpus, or the desertions from the Federal armies, President Lincoln, the Northern government or the people of the Union were all guilty of the most foul, corrupt, and wicked deeds, while the Confederacy remained untouched by all these rank issues.

Throughout the war in America, *The Times* employed the services of James Spence, wealthy merchant, Confederate partisan and financial advisor, from the City of Liverpool. Spence was not paid by *The Times*, although he did receive a special edition of the Britannica as a gift for his services, but both Spence and *The Times*, were well compensated for the relationship. *The Times* provided a platform for Spence to expound his pro-Southern views, and *The Times* received Confederate copy, which pleased their pro–Southern readers, at no expense. Should there be some doubt as to the association of Spence and the Confederacy, it should be noted that Spence was one of the largest subscribers to the Erlanger Confederate Cotton Loan, to the sum of £50,000.

On 29 August 1862, *The Times* published a letter from James Spence on conditions in the North. Spence was shedding crocodile tears over that nation, once the home of liberty, and now suffering all the pains of conscription:

> You have justly observed that the condition of the North excites now a feeling of pity. It is a pitiful thing to see men rushing to escape from a country like rats from a sinking ship. America had once a charm that none denied. Whatever might be wanting in the North, it was the home of liberty. It is now a land of bastilles, passports, spies, informers, censors, conscripts. One cannot realize the idea of an American conscript. We have been so accustomed to believe and revere the principles the North professed that, to see these abandoned in a day — nay, spurned and derided — seems like some grotesque passage of a dream....

The Times followed the Spence letters with the following from Charles Mackay in New York, on the imagined deterioration of the Northern war effort, on 12 May 1863:

> Meanwhile its armies are melting away, and no steps are taken to supply their broken ranks. Nothing whatever has been done to carry out conscription, while in New York, Brooklyn, Philadelphia, Chicago, Boston,

Pittsburgh, Cincinnati, and all the great trading and manufacturing cities of the north and north-west, the working-classes have banded themselves into secret societies to resist the operation of the [Conscription] Act. It is notorious to everybody but the government that it will be perilous, if not impossible to enforce the draught in this city; and that if no soldiers are to be drawn from New York they must be drawn from the newly-arrived immigrants from Ireland and Germany by the offer of high bounties. All ardour for the war is at an end, except among the churches, the contractors, and the ultra Republican revolutionists — men who will not fight, but will pay liberally to fight by deputy.... And while such is the state of feeling in the trading and commercial centres of the Republic the people of the agricultural States of the North-West ... have leagued themselves together into secret societies, the objects of which are not alone to resist the conscription, but to come to terms with the South....

On 6 July 1863, *The Telegraph* followed the lead of *The Times* and reported on the resistance to the draft among the Northern people:

According to recent custom, the endeavours of the Unionists are distracted and hampered by local resistance of their own people. Even in Maine an attempt to arrest deserters has terminated in the shooting of the captors; in Pennyslvania similar embarrassing results are yet more significant, while in Indiana the citizens are understood to be organised round more than one centre for the purpose of resisting the draft.

The Examiner would have treasured the conscription problems of the Federals: "better if they could have forfeited their victories at Vicksburg and Port Hudson and turned their back on conscription," according to the issue of 1 August 1863:

On the whole, it is undeniable that in the field the run of fortune has been against the Confederates, but as a set-off there are the riots against conscription in New York and other places. If the President had his choice he would probably have preferred a repulse at Vicksburg and Port Hudson to the repulse of the Federal authority in New York, and the fierce resistance to compulsory service. Lost battles can be retrieved, but matters look desperate indeed when men show the resolution to die in fighting against their government rather than for it....

The Quarterly Review 117 (1865) 260, could see little that would help the North. The implementation of the Conscription Act was corrupt and failed to involve persons of favor:

The [Northern] armies have been largely composed of German and Irish mercenaries. The most grandiloquent advocates of it have kept themselves and their relations out of it [the war]as in the case of Mr. Everett, who was never weary of inciting others to go to the armies; but when the name of his own son was drawn, bought him out....

On 20 July 1863, *The Times* downplayed the success of the Northern troops at Vicksburg and assured its readers that the Union draft would have little effect:

> even if the 300,000 troops called for by the Northern conscription are enrolled, and armed, they will be slaughtered in another two years of miserable conflict. The Cabinet of Washington are not equal to the task. Every crisis of affairs seems to elicit additional proof that they are in every respect unfit to deal with the events passing around them. The gleam of success that has fallen on the Federal arms in the surrender of Vicksburg and the incidents of the second Maryland campaign [Gettysburg] have exhibited the President and his chief Ministers in a manner most pitiable. With their country torn asunder, and its soil reeking with blood, they only find a voice to make poor and flippant election speeches....

The fertile mind of Charles Mackay found the means of deprecating the workings of the Conscription Act, and the Irish and the German immigrants in one disparaging report to *The Times* published in the paper's 15 June 1863 issue:

> Volunteering has ceased; bounty money attracts none but a few Irish and German immigrants; the enrollment of names for the conscription, which may never, perhaps, be enforced, and certainly not in the State or City of New York, leads to disturbance in places of public resort, which shows how odious in the sight of the labouring classes is compulsory military service; and the armies already in the field are melting away like ice in the summer sun.

On 25 April 1863, *The Times* published the following Mackay letter. Its purpose was a further indictment of Northern conscription. With typical Mackay distortion it became an attack on Northern women, and a means of deceitfully contrasting them with the heroic women of Charleston:

> At the great war meeting held to receive General Butler at the Academy of Music, and to strew with metaphorical roses the pathway of that amiable hero, it was observed at the Cooper Institute a few evenings afterwards only one lady was present. How are these facts to be explained? Are the ladies, the church and chapel going ladies of New York, so thoroughly imbued with the ideas of blood, gunpowder, and extermination, instilled into their minds by their clerical teachers, that they have no hearts for gentle peace? Or do their husbands and fathers make so much money by the war that, in consideration of silks, the satins, the Cashmere shawls, the jewelry, the carriages, the opera-boxes, and the largely augmented pin-money

which they receive from their prosperous natural protectors, their senses are dulled to the consideration of the horrors which the very name of war implies, especially of a war against men of their own race, blood, country and language?... Every woman and child are removed from Charleston, to be out of the reach of danger should the Federals fulfil their threat of not allowing one stone to stand upon another in that doomed city. The women of Richmond clamour for bread, and break open the Government stores to obtain it, or die; and the vast region from the Potomac to the Rio Grande is the scene of privation and suffering to women as well as the heroism of men. But only one woman of New York was to be found to grace with her presence an assembly that met together in the sacred cause of peace and conciliation, while at least 2,000 were glad to come together in their gayest array and with their sweetest smiles to do honour to such a man as Butler. It is bad enough that war should demoralize men — infinitely worse when it demoralizes women — and makes hard those hearts that nature intended should overflow with mercy and all kindly sympathies....

But, as if the North had not its full share of problems with conscription, there was now the problem of Army desertions. Frank Lawley wrote from Richmond on December 20 of 10,000 Federal deserters after the battle of Fredricksburg, in an item that appeared in *The Times*, 23 January 1863:

Since the [Federal] army has withdrawn to the northern bank of the river the Confederate cavalry, hanging constantly on its skirts, reports worse demoralization than has ever been known among the Federals before. Ten thousand deserters have quitted the army since the battle of the 13th [Fredricksburg]....

On 15 April 1863, Charles Mackay and *The Times* had more to say of desertions in the Federal Army:

It was computed a month ago that from 130,000 to 150,000 soldiers of the Federal army were absent from duty without leave. As a necessary preliminary to the enforcement of conscription, Mr. Lincoln issued a proclamation, notifying that deserters returning to their duty by the first of April should incur no other penalty than the forfeiture of their pay and allowance to that date; but that those who, after that warning, persisted in absenting themselves would incur the penalty of death. It does not appear that the proclamation has had much, if any, effect, and the Government in consequence is puzzled what to do. It is strongly urged by its friends and preachers, the lecturers, the contracters, and the rich men, who will pay any amount of money for substitutes rather than shoulder the rifle themselves or submit to the miseries and privations of the camp, by shooting a dozen or two deserters in every State. But Mr. Lincoln hesitates to adopt this course. He is a merciful man, averse to the shedding of blood, and has, perhaps, misgivings as to the expediency of the course recommended. A hundred thousand or a hundred and fifty thousand deserters are not to be easily terrified, or easily reached, more especially if they are supported by the sympathy of the population among whom they have scattered themselves. In the West the desertions are particularly numerous....

The Union was beleaguered with problems of conscription and desertions, or so the British press advised its readers. But then *The Times* and Charles Mackay expounded on President Lincoln and habeas corpus in the predictably negative manner, on 17 March 1863:

This week will be a memorable one in the annals of America. It has sealed the doom of the liberties of the North unless there shall occur in due time a counter revolution to restore Constitutional Government. Three extreme measures have been passed to make Mr. Lincoln Dictator, and have accomplished their purpose. By the first he is authorized to suspend the operation of the law of habeas corpus whensoever he shall deem fit, expedient, or necessary. He or his secretaries may cause to be imprisoned and kept in prison, without trial, for an indefinite length of time, any person, high or low, in any of the States of the Union. He may order a military force to seize the Governor of New York or Connecticut, or any other sovereign commonwealth. He may arrest and hold in Forts Lafayette, Warren, or McHenry, the members of any Legislature whose proceedings he may adjudge to be treasonable or dangerous. He may seize the judge upon the judgement-seat, and carry him off to prison.... He may silence any tongue, or pen, or printing press in the country, and no judge or jury shall question the legality of the act....

The Quarterly Review 117 (1865) 260, wrote of habeas corpus in the Union, and claimed that freedom of the press would be suspended.

The Press will have to be kept under rigourous censorship. The writ of habeas corpus must be permanently suspended; and elaborate staff of police spies must be maintained to conduct the arrest of possible ring-leaders, and to check the first symptoms of revolt....

The problems of the North in matters of habeas corpus, conscription, and desertions had been the subject of much criticism by the ruling class British press. That these problems existed in the Confederacy were ignored. In truth, the Confederacy had brought on conscription a year before the North; habeas corpus, a shield often used by state governors to excuse favorites from serving in the Confederate armies, was sorely needed, but seldom employed or enforced; desertions and peace societies abounded.

The first Confederate Conscription Act, passed April 16, 1862, provided for the enrollment of all white males in the Confederate States between the ages of eighteen and thirty-five and placed them at the disposal of the President during the war. It was the first such law in North American history and preceded a similar act enacted in the North by one year. Unable to pay more than a token bounty to volunteers, faced with a sharp drop in enlistments after the first war enthusiasm had worn off, and with the failure of a state draft, the Confederacy was forced to resort to a nationwide conscription. Its enormous exemptions, however, invited evasion. Lawyers early augmented their incomes by obtaining such exemptions — for fees as high as $5000. Enterprising printers soon had fraudulent exemption papers for sale at $4000 and up. The provision that drafted men could provide substitutes from non-conscript classes gave rise to a flourishing business in which brokers supplied substitutes for $500 and up.[109]

"Some months later the exemption law was amended to include certain industrial workers, newspaper editors, munition workers, farmers who had charge of as many as 500 head of cattle or 250 horses or mules, and an overseer for every plantation having as many as twenty slaves. This last provision became known as the 'twenty nigger' law." State laws had already required the presence of a white man on slave plantations in order to provide police protection, as well as to increase production. But the law was detested by the non-slaveholders who cited it as proof that it was "a rich man's war but a poor man's fight." The exemption acts aroused almost as much opposition as conscription. Many thousands of able-bodied young men sought employment in the deferred classes, or procured substitutes by paying the necessary toll...."[110]

The Confederacy escaped none of the evils that beset a nation engaged in the business of war. The British press did not hesitate to inform its readers of all the ugliness of war — treason, desertion, evasion of duty and profiteering. All of this and more was to be found in the North and the Northern armies. The press was blind, or professed to be, to similar problems which sorely pressed the Confederacy. In truth, these disrupting phenomena harmed the Confederacy far more than they did the Union, because its men and resources, as compared to those of the Federal States, were limited. The North was afflicted by segments in its population who worked against the cause, but it did not contain an extensive minority almost unanimously opposing national effort. The mountain country of the South had always been celebrated for secret organizations, lawlessly engaged in forcing their will in defiance of constituted authorities. In pre–Revolutionary days these bands were known as Regulators. In the early days of the Republic there were the Whiskey Boys — moonshiners bound together to fight the tax gatherer. In the same way, from 1861 to 1865, societies flourished whose business it was to fight the Confederacy and do everything in their power to accomplish its destruction. Scarcely a county in southwestern Virginia, eastern Tennessee, western North and South Carolina, northern Georgia and Alabama was unrepresented in these secret orders. Their object was to prevent recruiting for the Confederacy, to oppose tax measures in Richmond, to fight conscription laws, to stimulate desertion, and to agitate peace on the basis of a return to the Union.

As the Civil War in America progressed the similarities between the measures Lincoln adopted to keep the Northern States afloat and those embraced by Jefferson Davis became similar. Despite the inventions of the English press regarding the homogeneity and patriotism of the Confederate people, large sections of the Southern populace raised objections to the government. When those protests interfered with the military, Davis, as Lincoln, maintained that it was necessary to suspend the writ of habeas corpus. When a community ran riot with spies, deserters, and "peace associations" organized for the purpose of opposing conscription, weakening the Confederacy, and traitorously dealing with the enemy; when cities and counties had been laid at the mercy of treasonable mobs, Davis found that the usual legal procedures of peace times could not be depended upon. Such disaffected individuals, when arrested, were usually discharged by friendly state judges. Habeas corpus, which required their immediate presence in court for trial, became their safeguard. The only way to restore order was to do precisely what Lincoln had done in a similar state of stress—suspend the writ, seize all prospective domestic foes on suspicion, and secure them in jail. In this way Davis became a good Lincolnian, a thoroughgoing nationalist. Lincoln also found that public safety sometimes demanded martial law. So did Davis; and consequently many Southerners who had preached State Rights all their lives perceived with horror the hand of central government reaching over from Richmond, temporarily closing courts and constabularies, and placing in their stead graycoated militarists of the Richmond "oligarchy."[111]

Good morale was harder to maintain in the Confederate army than in the Union. The growing awareness of defeat did little to lift men's spirits. Antietam, Gettysburg, Vicksburg, Atlanta, Chattanooga—these disasters had a cumulative effect, leading men to question risking their lives in an obviously losing cause. Declining morale was reflected in many ways. Cases of drunkenness increased. There was more straggling—the practice through which soldiers sought surreptitiously to avoid combat. Even seasoned veterans now fell victim to panic, as at Missionary Ridge on 25 November 1863, where entrenched Confederates fled in disorder before the advancing Federals. More ominously, secret peace societies began to appear among the troops. In Georgia in 1864 one such group planned to desert and then attempt to win over other soldiers to do likewise in order to end the war. A more organized movement in Alabama planned to mutiny on Christmas Day, 1864, by laying down their arms and calling for peace. Such moves were quickly suppressed; what could not be suppressed was desertion. "The incomplete Confederate records show approximately 100,000 deserters, of whom more than a thousand were officers, but reports of government and military officials indicate that the problem was more serious than these figures suggest. As early as July, 1862, the Secretary of State declared that desertions and illegitimate absences had so weakened the army 'that we are unable to reap the fruits of our victories.'"[112]

Eaton writes: "The breakdown of Southern spirit in the later years of the war was registered in the appalling number of desertions. The official reports fixed the number of defections at 103,400, but actually the number was greater. In addition to the loss of strength from desertion the remarkable laxity of the authorities in granting furloughs depleted the army. Modern studies indicate that there was one desertion to every nine enlistments in the Confederate armies and one to every seven in the Union armies. North Carolina with 23,694 deserters and Virginia with 12,071 led the Southern states; but they also furnished the largest number of troops. The widespread absenteeism in the Confederate armies is indicated by the fact that at the beginning of the war 21 per cent of the soldiers were absent, and by December, 1864, the number had increased to 51 per cent. The Northern armies suffered more extensively from desertions, having more than 200,000 offenders, but their surplus man power made the loss less serious than those of the Confederacy."[113]

Suspension of the writ of habeas corpus was the cause of great anxiety in the Confederacy. The Confederate Congress had first given Davis power to suspend the writ early in 1862, and had later extended the power until February 1863. But a year later, "in February 1864, desertion and treasonable activity in various sections of the country impelled Davis again to ask Congress for the power to again suspend. After a bitter debate Congress granted the power for a period from February 15 to August 1."[114]

The reality that Southerners were not unanimous in supporting the cause was staggering to the readers of the English press. So glamorous had been the routine pictures of Southern loyalty, homogeneity and patriotism in the London journals, that it was trying for the reader to learn that the Confederacy had its squalid side. For its ill-informed readers the English press had painted a sparkling spectacle of nine million people springing to arms in defense of an independent existence. There were no skulkers, bounty jumpers, shirkers, stragglers, deserters, or runaways. In the first year, indeed, there was much in the spontaneous volunteering of the "chivalry of the South" that justified this exalted picture. Hendrick writes: "Secretary Walker reported that he had more than 200,000 volunteers whom he could not use. In that early day Southerners regarded the war as a few months holiday; a single battle, it was believed, would settle the matter; and an eagerness seized everybody to get into the fray. After a few months, however, especially after the victory of Bull Run had been succeeded by Confederate disasters, and the truth dawned that the country was facing a long, bloody war, this popular zeal began to cool. No better proof is necessary than that in April, 1862, about a year after hostilities started, the Confederacy was compelled to resort to conscription. This unexpected method of raising troops gave the 'mountain boys' their opportunity. A conscription agent appearing in their region was about as welcome as a press gang in eighteenth-century London. Such emissaries were frequently met with shotguns. More than one left his dead body on the ground. Why, said these sons of the soil, should they sacrifice their lives for

Virginia 'aristocrats' and wealthy cotton planters? ... That provision which caused so much dissatisfaction in Yankee-land — the purchase of 'substitutes' by rich men — was also a feature of the Confederate conscription law, and was about as popular south of the Potomac as north.... The 'twenty-nigger law' similarly seemed discriminatory to the mountain peasantry. Here were the slave owners, the men responsible for the war, living in safety and comfort at home, while the thrifty, nonslaveowning, small farmers were being dragged from their little cabins to fight the battles of the plutocrats."[115]

There were newspapers in London that rose above the absurdities which were being fed to the reading public. As early as 7 May 1863, *The Daily News* noted the lack of homogeneity in the South:

> It is a common remark that we get next to no direct information of the state of opinion in the Southern States of North America beyond the Federal lines. It cannot be denied, however, that the indirect evidence is abundant and striking. While the outside world has been deluded by protestations of the unanimity of the inhabitants of the revolted States, there is evidence of discord in the flight of rich and poor to the Federal lines; in the resistance to conscription; in the appointment of the cavalry to act in the rear of the infantry, to stop runaways; in the State controversies about State independence; the refusal of State Governments to let their soldiery serve beyond their own frontiers; in the numerous and vehement charges of tyranny on the one side, and disloyalty on the other; and in the recent riots in several of the Southern cities....

Again, 2 September 1863, *The Daily News* reminded the people of England that their hopes of the victory of the South to be produced by the draft riots in New York, which had been fully exploited by the English press, had not materialized.

> The coming revolution in New York, which during the last few weeks has been the solemn burden of Secessionist prophecy, and the sovereign hope of Southern bondholders, appears to have shared the fate of so many other props of Confederate faith in these latter days.... The desponding faithful were repeatedly assured that the draft would never be carried in New York, or that if the attempt was made the result would be a great Southern victory. According to the inspired Spence, the principle of State rights, which by one of the most curious of all Confederate fictions the Southern Government is supposed to represent, would be triumphantly vindicated in the Empire-city; and the Federal Government experience a disastrous defeat in its attempts to enforce the law of the Union.... According to the latest news the drafting under the Conscription Act was going on in the various districts of New York without disturbances or excitement of any kind. The atrocious Copperhead riots had evidently destroyed the influence of the small but desperate faction who being virtually allied with the rebels strove

to give them material aid, and it thereafter became a point of honour with every good citizen, whatever his political sentiments might be, to support the execution of the laws....

General Lee surrendered his army at Appomatox on 4 April. On 22 April 1865 *The Examiner* finally made full disclosure of the problems of the Confederacy:

From the beginning of the year there have been signs not only of the failing resources of the Southerners, but of what is worse for such a cause, failing resolution. Patriotism is never restored by appeals, and President Davis's appeals did nothing but disclose the nakedness of the land. It was one of those cries for help which rather discourage help by the suggestion that it cannot avail, the need being too great. At that time it was stated that the country was swarming with deserters, whose return to the ranks would dispense with any conscription and amply recruit the Confederate armies. Then came the proposal to enlist the negroes, which, if good at all, should have been adopted at first, when the Southern cause was prospering, and when it should not have seemed a measure of the last extremity.... Sherman's unobstructed march was the next bad sign, and the pretence that it was because the men of the country were with the Confederate armies that he encountered no opposition was too preposterously absurd when the complaint was so loud of desertion, and the women were invited to drive back the laggards to the ranks with their broom-sticks. Still the spirit of the South, or that part of it which remained sound, and the conduct of its Generals were much counted upon for the restoration of its fortunes, and a partial success prepared us to expect the ups and downs, the seesaw of victory which has hitherto marked the whole course of the war. But so, it seems, it was not to be. The whole frame-work of the Southern war has collapsed, for nothing less is the effect of the total overthrow of Lee, and the evacuation of Richmond and Petersburg.

Some of the sanguine friends of the Confederates reckon still on the room for their chivalry in the wide territory still open to them. But there is much delusion in that reliance on chivalry. All wars of an upper class are marked with great success at the outset, but it is the fire of straw, and wants the sustaining substance of a lower order of people. The coarse hands will win in the long run against the fair ones, with the ability of leadership equivalent, or nearly so, and numbers on the side of the former. The great quality of the Northerners has been pertinacity. They have shown little skill, have committed many blunders, but they have always been ready to try again, and by the exhaustion of failures made their way to success. Discouragement has certainly not been in their vocabulary. But then it must always be borne in mind that the cost of life was not all their own, and that they were making free with Irish and German blood.

Part Four

The British Press and Abraham Lincoln

15. Insult and Eulogy

The British press in the mid–Victorian era reeked of self-satisfied morality, ethics, and virtue. It was self-aggrandizingly righteous, unprejudiced, unbiased, and dedicated to fair play. Above all, it was honorable and respectable as all things English had always been and would forever be — except when its control of world commerce was threatened by this upstart across the Atlantic. With the additional threat of democracy being imported from America into the island of Britain, the newspapers and journals slowly veered to the wicked, corrupt, and profane. Their target was Abraham Lincoln, president of the United States. Their unprincipled attacks were not only based on his programs, which were fair game for criticism, but were based on the most savage personal calumny, as evidenced in *The Times*, 7 October 1862:

> Mr. Lincoln will, on the 1st of January next, do his best to excite a servile war in the States which he cannot occupy with his arms. He will run up the rivers in his gunboats; he will seek out the places which are left but slightly guarded, and where the women and children have been trusted to the fidelity of coloured domestics. He will appeal to the black blood of the African; he will whisper of the pleasures of spoil and of gratification of yet fiercer instincts; and when blood begins to flow and shrieks come piercing through the darkness, Mr. Lincoln will wait till the rising flames tell that all is consummated, and then he will rub his hands and think that revenge is sweet. That is what Mr. Lincoln avows before the world that he is about to do.
>
> Mr. Lincoln avows, therefore, that he proposes to excite the negroes of the Southern plantations to murder the families of their masters while these are engaged in the war. The conception of such a crime is horrible. The employment of Indians sinks to a level with civilized warfare in comparison with it; the most detestable doctrines of MAZZINI are almost less

atrocious; even Mr. Lincoln's own recent achievements of burning by gun-
boats the defenceless villages on the Mississippi are dwarfed by this gigantic wickedness.

The Times, 4 July 1864, presented another of Mackay's slanders:

> As a President he is the worst failure that America has ever produced,
> and both parties in the State admit him to be so. It is a pity that he can-
> not see himself in the same light, and that he does not earn the respect
> of his true friends and the forebearance of his foes by retiring into pri-
> vate life.

The Times, 28 May 1863: "Although the Government of Mr. Lincoln con-
fessedly has the respect of no body of men in the country; though he himself is
a person of neither ability nor dignity...." It did the same on 17 August 1864:

> re-election to the Presidency [would] send down to posterity the name of
> Abraham Lincoln as the last and worst President of the United States, and
> the unskillful and unlucky pilot who not only made shipwreck of the glory
> but of the liberty of his country.

The Times, 13 September 1864, condemned Lincoln's verbal skills: "Mr. Lincoln has, in a number of speeches, proclamations, and letters, which will rank
among the worst political documents of which history has preserved any
record...." And on 19 October 1863 censured his aesthetic sense and his judgment: "With singular bad taste, and a presumption which augers no good for
the destinies of those over which he presides....

Blackwood's Edinburgh Magazine (January 1862) 122:

> Of course we do not blame Mr. Lincoln for being President. But we ven-
> ture to pity him. No man is more unfortunate than he who is in a con-
> spicuous position for which he is manifestly unfit.... In his public compo-
> sitions he is distinguished chiefly for a disregard of grammar and an
> infatuated fondness for metaphor. He gets laboriously on to a figure of
> speech, which generally runs away with him, and, after exhibiting him in
> various eccentric postures, leaves him sprawling in an attitude highly unbe-
> coming in the President of a great Republic....

The Economist (1 June 1861) 591:

> Nor does the accession of Mr. Lincoln place the Executive power precisely
> where we should wish to see it. At a crisis such as America has never before
> seen, and as it is not, perhaps, probable she will see again, the Executive
> authority should be in the hands of one of the most tried, trusted, and
> experienced statesmen of the nation. Mr. Lincoln is a nearly unknown

man — who has been but little heard of — who has had little experience —
who may have nerve and judgment, or may not have them — whose character, both moral and intellectual, is an unknown quantity — who must,
from his previous life and defective education, be wanting in the liberal
acquirements and mental training which are principal elements of an
enlarged statesmanship.

The following passages further illuminate *The Economist's* wholesale contempt for Abraham Lincoln:

(2 March 1861) 226:

They [the Confederacy] at once seized where they could ... while the obnox-
ious Lincoln is still uninstalled and powerless....

(25 April 1863) 449:

The President means well, but does nothing else well. He is the "accident
of an accident" in quiet times: the inexplicable caprice of a forgotten cau-
cus selected Mr Lincoln as a candidate because no one knew much about
him, and therefore scarcely any one could object to him.

(17 January 1863) 57:

Mr. Lincoln and his advisers will probably continue it [the war]. It is their
war; many of them have grown rich by it, and the rest hope to grow rich.
They will not give up the sweets of office and the profits of contracts to the
Democrats — to the peace party of the future — without a long and eager
contest....

(31 October 1863) 1209:

...educated Englishmen of all classes [are] as plain spoken in their prefer-
ence of the dignified and able State Papers of Jefferson Davis to the feeble
and ungrammatical prolixity of Abraham Lincoln.

(17 September 1864) 1165:

It is undeniable that Mr. Lincoln's administration has given satisfaction to
no one. Its notorious and unprecedented corruption has disgusted the lovers
of public purity and decency; its numerous acts of illegal and stupid tyranny
have alienated the lovers of liberty and constitutional right; its military
incapacity has disgusted all; — while its inconsistent, timid, and tentative
proceedings on the slavery question have alarmed and offended the Democratic masses, without having given confidence or satisfaction to the hearty
Abolitionists.

The Quarterly Review 112 (1862) 551, joined the attack:

> The incompetence of the President is the most conspicuous cause of the present calamities; and the incompetence of the President is a direct result of the mode in which he is chosen.... With a man of Mr. Lincoln's incapacity and obstinacy...

The Saturday Review (30 May 1863) 685:

> Mr. Lincoln's confused grammar and blundering metaphors compared unfavourably with the scholarly compositions of Mr. Davis... .

The Examiner, 5 November 1864:

> His personal honour may be pure, as has been the personal honour of some of the worst scourges of mankind. He may not be corrupt in one sense, not a peculator, but he has been the patron of peculators, and has allowed the worst robbers of the State to enrich themselves. A worse man than Mr.Lincoln would be less mischievous, and his very mediocre virtues lean to vice's side in the unhappy circumstances of his country.

The Examiner, 24 December 1864:

> What the cost in blood may be will not trouble the conscience of a man of Mr. Lincoln's simplicity, who eschews that as an abstract speculation. A list of the weak men worse for the world than the wicked men once proposed by Macaulay, and in it certainly Mr. Lincoln would be entitled to a high place. He means well say his friends, and the Greeks said as much of their Furies. A man of bad character would be incapable of so much mischief. All the mediocrities baneful when armed with vast power are united in him.

The Examiner, 11 October 1862:

> Jealousies of liberty cannot be all dead in America, and people must ask whether they are to submit to the decrees of the poor puppet President as to those of Providence, and to bless his name who giveth and take away; giving liberty to blacks, and taking it away from born freemen.

The Glasgow Herald, 10 October 1862:

> The anti-slavery proclamation of President Lincoln is evidently the last resort of a bewildered statesman. It is the offering of a weak Executive....

The Manchester Guardian, 20 December 1864:

> We judge rather from the fact that the [Lincoln] Message is instilled throughout with a bewilderment and confusion which may most naturally be supposed to constitute the personal mental condition of the unhappy man on whom Fate has imposed a burden and a responsibility so painfully beyond his strength....

The Standard, 30 August 1864:

> The illiterate backwoodsman of Illinois has too long usurped and mis-used an authority to which, in the eyes of the rest of the world, he has never had the least fragment of a moral claim. It is time that he should stand aside, make a place for better men, and retire with what con-science he may to the obscurity from which four years since, and for the punishment of the sins of America, he so suddenly and disastrously emerged.....

The Standard, 7 November 1864:

> His [Lincoln's] re-election will be the signal for a reign of terror. His dis-position has been already shown ... by the illegal arrest and confinement of the leading citizens of many States in the North. The author of so many murders in cold blood is not likely to hold the lives of Democrats much more sacred than those of Southern prisoners; the plunderer of Virginia and New Orleans is not likely to respect the property of opponents in New York and Philadelphia.

Regardless of every vicious attack, the press made something of a turn-around upon Lincoln's death.

The British public was treated to a series of eulogies in honor of Abraham Lincoln. As befitting the British, the writings expressed the standard expressions of grief. But they rendered little else. Lincoln remained an unkempt figure whom they could not accept nor trust; the defeat of the Confederacy was not to be taken lightly; and America continued inept.

The Saturday Review (29 April 1865) 491:

> Mr. Lincoln, though he committed many mistakes, so far exceeded the anticipation of his friends and enemies that his character may perhaps here-after serve as an argument in favour of the American practice of selecting high functionaries at random. He was made President because he had attained local notoriety by the exercise of moderate ability, and his hon-esty was taken for granted. During the arduous experience of four years he constantly rose in general estimation by calmness of temper, by an intu-itively logical appreciation of the character of the conflict, and by undis-puted sincerity. Above all, he showed that he was capable of learning from

his own errors and from the course of events. Having contributed largely to the failure of the campaign of 1862 by his distrust of McClellan, he had the wisdom, during the final advance upon Richmond, to repose unlimited confidence in Grant. On the bearing of slavery on the war he had from the first formed the opinion which became a constitutional ruler. As he said at an early period in the contest, he would have preserved slavery, or destroyed it, or let it alone, if by any of those methods he could have restored the Union. At the beginning of 1863 he issued the Emancipation Decree which looked like a crime, and proved to be only a manifesto. If it had become operative in those unconquered portions of the South to which it was exclusively applicable, Mr. Lincoln would have been condemned as the author of an intolerable servile revolution. As the slaves remained tranquil, the proclamation served the useful and harmless purpose of advertising an inevitable change in the policy and object of the war. The enlistment of negroes was a more practical step in the same direction; and ultimately the President found himself strong enough to make emancipation an indispensable condition of peace. Among Mr. Lincoln's merits may be reckoned his want of natural fluency in speech and writing. He was seldom tempted to commit himself to the vapouring professions of his Ministers and political supporters. He allowed Mr. Seward to bluster to foreign Government, but he never blustered himself. Friendly observers assert, perhaps correctly, that, Mr. Lincoln was the only apparently honest man in Washington. He was also exceptionally determined to preserve peace, notwithstanding the menaces of his subordinates. On the whole, he satisfied the requirements of a difficult position better than any rival who could be suggested. When he was re-elected by a large majority, the choice of the Republican party was generally approved at home and abroad; and if the people of England had shared in the election, the result would probably have been the same. Mr. Lincoln's good qualities cannot add to the horror, which is felt at the murder, but they justify the general regret.

The Saturday Review (6 May 1865) 525:

The universal expressions of sincere regret for the death of Mr. Lincoln, and of indignation against his murderer, are necessary to satisfy the consciences of Englishmen, and possibly they may conciliate American feeling. It is not surprising that strong partisans of the North should have profited by the occasion to proclaim or assert the triumph of their own principles. As Mr. Lincoln fell by the hand of an assassin in the very moment of success, he naturally becomes the symbol as well as the martyr of his cause. Having risen before the eyes of the world from obscurity to greatness, he is, by an easy fallacy, supposed to have been harshly underrated, because he was not appreciated before he was known. The proof of his high qualities consisted in the recognition which he gradually earned in spite of prejudice, or of the unavoidable ignorance of strangers. Unfriendly or neutral observers in England were first impressed in his favour by a reticence which can scarcely be regarded as an American virtue. Mr. Lincoln's homely jests and parables were especially valuable as substitutes for ordinary rhetorical declamation. From the beginning of the war to the close of his life he never vituperated the South, nor is it known that he uttered a menace against any foreign government. His countrymen seem to have respected his exceptional prudence, especially as they felt that, in all his attachments and feeling, Mr. Lincoln was essentially one of themselves. As Mr. Adams justly observed at the American meeting on Monday, he represented the nation the more truly because he always took care rather to follow than to excite a popular impulse. The exclusive advocates of Emancipation do some injustice to his character when they claim Mr. Lincoln as an organizer and leader of their cause. He hated slavery, but he felt that his first duty was to the Union, as his successor prefers the same object of allegiance, although the maintenance of slavery had formerly been his chief political object. In his last inaugural speech Mr. Lincoln rose above the narrowness of a merely sectional politician. In characteristically religious language, he expressed the well-founded conviction that both belligerents, or perhaps their predecessors, were virtually responsible for a conflict arising from the existence of an unnatural institution. The clemency which he was prepared to extend to the defeated party was dictated by a sense of justice, and not by any sentimental weakness. He probably felt that a great civil war must have been caused by motives and circumstances too complicated to correspond with the simple and ready definition of a crime. When the evil of slavery was abolished, he hoped that the passions of its opponents and supporters might also disappear. The intimate connexion of wisdom and goodness of disposition has seldom been more forcibly illustrated. After making allowance for the necessary obliquities of party feeling, there is little to find fault with in the speeches which have been made at various public meetings. It is perfectly clear that the Federal cause is neither better nor worse because the President of the United States has been foully murdered, but it would have been strange if the enthusiastic friends of the North had not profited by the accidental sympathy of the country and the civilized world. Professions of goodwill to the Union were less objectionable, because there is reason to suppose that the war is nearly over. Two or three years ago, aspirations for the success of one belligerent implied gratuitous hostility to the other, but it now seems to be equally the interest of all parties to terminate an unequal contest. The chief objection to the anti-slavery or democratic speeches with which the occasion has been imbued consists in their tendency to disturb the realm of apparent unanimity of the whole English nation. A better mode of expressing the common feeling is provided by the addresses or resolutions of corporations and of public bodies which represent different political opinions. In one large town, a dissentient who foolishly and culpably expressed satisfaction at the death of the President is said to have been summarily ejected from the building by a Southern partisan. The story may perhaps not be literally true, but it symbolizes the real opinion and feeling of the country. The innumerable movers of resolutions and their associated orators have done the fullest justice to their subject when they have abstained from political discussion, and from all but personal eulogy of the victim of assassination. It is not because Mr. Lincoln held this opinion or that, but because he was an upright statesman occupying an extraordinarily conspicuous position, that all men shudder at the crime of the murderer. It is perhaps permissible to combine condemnation of a great crime with expressions of general goodwill to the United States, although there is an obvious risk of misconstruction on one side, and of compromise of dignity on the other. It was not surprising that Lord Russell should remember the difficulties which beset the relations of England and the United States, but the death of the President was an event apart from the perplexities and distractions of diplomacy....

The Manchester Guardian, in the midst of a cotton starved textile industry, expressed its true feeling and was unforgiving on 27 April 1865:

> It is far more easy to speak of this point (the assassination of Lincoln) with a certainty of commanding general assent than to predict the effect of this astonishing political catastrophe on the American struggle. One consideration of a painful nature, which though possibly not the most pressing, is among the first to rise in the mind, is the too probable tendency of such an event still further to embitter what remains of the contest. If the subjugation of the South be only a matter of time, it seems inevitable that the concluding passages of the process should be made even more sanguinary and relentless than they otherwise might have been by the rage which the murder of the President will inspire. This inference is the more to be regretted as Mr. Lincoln had shown signs of a moderate and conciliatory disposition which seemed to promise an endeavour so far as lay in him to improve by a liberal policy the advantage which had been attained by force alone. Of his rule we can never speak except as a series of acts abhorrent to every true notion of constitutional right and human liberty; but it is doubtless to be regretted, for the sake of his country as well as our own, that he had not an opportunity of vindicating his good intentions by his manner of consolidating the power he had appeared to have gained....

The Examiner, 29 April 1865, manipulated its comments on the assassination of President Lincoln to justify its continual harangue on the war in America, a war it attempted to convince its readers was the responsibility of the free states, a war in which the Confederacy was fighting for freedom. If The Examiner managed some faint approval of Lincoln, it was to voice disapproval of democracy. The Examiner, 29 April 1865:

> The events of the last four years, however, have so heated and poisoned the current of the nation's blood that things seem to have become possible that were not so before. More than a half a century has gone by since a Prime Minister of England was struck down by the hand of an assassin in the lobby of the House of Commons.... For the first eighty years of its existence the great Republic of the West had been spared the grief and shame

of harbouring in its bosom any man base or mad enough to put in execution the cowardly design. The events of the last four years, however, have so heated and poisoned the current of the nation's blood that things seem to have become possible that were not so before. Far be it from us to endorse or sanction the sentiment which we hear with loathing muttered inarticulately in some quarters, and openly avowed by Mr. Mason, the Confederate agent here, that to shoot an unarmed man through the head while sitting in his box in the theatre [... is] "the necessary results" of civil war. If anything can approach in heinousness the acts themselves, it is the deliberate extenuation of them, and the attempt to divert public execration by imparting to them the dignity of political vengeance. The cause of the South has earned itself many friends in England, and now that the cause is lost, it signifies comparatively little what blunders may be made by its agents or advocates. The game has been played out, and must soon come to an end, as far as the open struggle is concerned. But for the sake of the vanquished it is a frightful blunder to add by wanton words of seeming palliation to the just rage of a victorious people, whose chief councillor and guide has been suddenly butchered before their eyes in cold blood, and whose principal Minister of State has hardly escaped a similar fate.... Public morals are outraged whenever the theory of ruffianism is gravely discussed. On no pretence will we have it; nor shall we tolerate equivocation or evasion in the matter. The leaders of the unsuccessful attempt at Secession owe it to themselves and to their followers to wash their hands of President Lincoln's blood. Erring he may have been in their eyes as a politician; guilty he may have been in their judgment of great faults as a statesman. But it is an indecency we will not endure that these faults or errors should be debated over his bleeding corpse.... A nation does not load itself with £400,000,000 of debt within the brief space of four years, does not submit to have its mercantile marine destroyed, and does not send from every household the prime of its youth to suffer or to perish in the field of battle, to humour the whims of two or three ambitious politicians. It is beyond question that, rightly or wrongly, the people of the Federal States were animated by an indomitable purpose throughout the struggle; and then in the civil as well as in the military executive, if one set of men failed to achieve their purpose, they would have called on another. In point of fact, Mr. Lincoln and Mr Seward occasionally risked popularity and influence by prudent efforts to moderate the temper of the multitude.... For the honour of England we are glad that from the highest to the lowest in the land there has been heard only one voice of horror at the crime, followed by the calm and unreserved expressions of national condolence. This is as it should be.... The people of America are nearer to us than we have sometimes remembered of late; nearer in their fundamental laws, and ideas of order and authority; nearer in their religious sentiments and observances; nearer in their habits of thought and effort; nearer in their intellectual culture and the great sanctions of domestic life, than any other great people in the world. We cannot if we would, and assuredly we would not if we could, dissociate ourselves in sympathy or interest from them. We have interchanged national charities in days of need; in the present dark hour of America's grief our fitting place is that of chief among the mourners. It is not the man, but the Chief Magistrate of the Republic, whom the spirit of England follows to the grave.

Three articles appeared in *The Times* observing the assassination of Abraham Lincoln. Each represented the total lack of morality of *The Times* establishment. After spending four years in the utter degradation of the President of the United States, *The Times*, without blinking an eye, filled its columns with Lincoln the Great.

The Times, 28 April 1865:

> Besides our national abhorrence of assassinations we have also a profound respect for rulers, by whatever way they come to their high place. President Lincoln ranked in our minds with Kings and Emperors, and was as much "the Lord's anointed" to simple English loyalty as any crowned head in Europe. There might have been reasons which, in the great distance and greater differences that divide us, might have tended to lessen our sympathy with the President. There are American statemen of much higher abilities, and more educated for rule, who have done all they can to repel our sympathies, and have to some extent succeeded. But no American of Mr. Lincoln's vigorous character, resolution, earnestness, and free humour has ever been so simple and inoffensive to this country. While we could not but regard the selection of such a man to be the ruler of some thirty-five millions, a third of them on the eve of secession, as highly characteristic of Republican institutions, we yet all wondered to see him there. We wondered all the more because he did not personally illustrate any principle upon which either Union could be enforced or Separation justified. President Lincoln was a man evidently anxious to do his duty, and prepared, with what most Englishmen would think recklessness, to undertake any post. He was anxious to keep well with everybody, and have not a foe in the world. But he wished, also, to keep things as they were. He brought no policy to a position of almost absolute power and fearful responsibility except a stubborn determination worthy of an old English Conservative.

What greater tribute could *The Times* bestow on a mere mortal?
The Times, 1 May 1865:

> A few minutes before midnight, on Friday, the 14th of April, the telegraphic wires announced to the people of America that the genial, kind-hearted, honest Abraham Lincoln, President of the United States, has been murdered in the theatre....

In death the "barge-man" and uneducated President of the United States became a man of integrity.

The Times, 1 May 1865:

> Though in power and influence something more than a king, Mr. Lincoln had never ceased to be a citizen; he did not belong to the race of crowned heads who, intermarrying exclusively with each other, are said to form a nation apart — being of every country and none. Mr. Lincoln had risen, by his own exertions, through a course of honourable and successful industry, to the highest office his fellow-citizens had to bestow. There was a homeliness and simplicity about him, a quaint humour, a genial nature, and a sterling rectitude of character peculiarly calculated to conciliate to him the sympathy and regard of great masses of mankind. For the last four years his name has been constantly in our mouths; his every act, thought, and word has been the subject of criticism and comment. We have traced his motives, we have speculated on his intentions, till we really seemed to have established a sort of intimacy, and to have with him something like personal acquaintance. It has been a matter of curious speculation how such a man would acquit himself under circumstances always so difficult and often so depressing and disheartening. At last fortune seemed to become weary of testing any further his patience and his constancy; the tremendous obstacles which had held him at bay for four years gave way with almost threatrical suddenness, and he found himself — what at one time seemed scarcely within the reach of probability — victorious in the final and conclusive conflict of a great civil war. He was a prominent figure in a great historical picture, and, as far as we can judge, was prepared to play a most noble part. He was animated by the spirit of conciliation, and the last and, perhaps, the happiest day of his life was spent in wishes and plans for healing the wounds of a prolonged and frightful contest. Without an instant's notice, without the slightest apprehension or foresight of his fate, he was plunged by the hand of an assassin into a state of insensibility from which he never rallied.... There is in such a tale everything that can excite the tragic passions of pity and terror.... The feeling which the death of Mr. Lincoln has excited in En-gland is in no degree confined to the advocates of the Northern cause; it has shown itself just as strongly among the friends of the South, and has carried away with it indiscriminately Whigs, Tories, and Radicals. A knowledge of England and of her institutions, and of the thoroughly popular element which underlies their aristocratic form, is not so widely spread in America as we could wish; but we feel confident that a sorrow in which both nations may without exaggeration be said to share cannot pass without leaving them better acquainted with each other, and more inclined to friendship and mutual allowance for each other's faults, than they were before.

Perhaps history will reward Charles Mackay as the premier scoundrel of the Victorian era. After occupying his time as the spokesman for *The Times* in demeaning and villainizing the character of President Lincoln, he produced this hypocritical paean:

Mr. Lincoln was among the most merciful of men, and had he lived to reconstruct the Union, which his armies had restored, would, if any forecast could have been made from his recorded utterances, his whole course of action, and the general benignity of his character, have done his best to efface animosities, and make the North and South shake hands like noble brothers, each proud of the other, though they had been temporarily estranged....[116]

Notes

1. B.D., *Federals and Confederates, for What Do They Fight? [...]* (London: Caldwell, 1863) 3.

2. Thomas Ellison, *Slavery and Secession in America [...]* (London: Low, 1862) 14.

3. *Ibid.* 223.

4. A.J.B. Beresford Hope, *A Popular View of the American Civil War* (London: Ridgway, 1861) 8.

5. *Ibid.* 10.

6. A.J.B. Beresford-Hope, *England, the North, and the South* (London: Ridgway, 1862) 31.

7. A.J.B. Beresford-Hope, *The Social and Political Bearings of the American Disruption* (London: Ridgway, 1863) 27.

8. *Ibid.*

9. *Ibid.*

10. Anonymous [Balme, Joshua R.], *The American War Crusade: Plain Facts for Earnest Men* (London: Hamilton, 1863) 5.

11. B.D. 16.

12. *Ibid.* 23.

13. Samuel Garratt, *The Bible and Slavery* (London: Morgan, 1863) 43.

14. Gustav Gottheil, *Moses versus Slavery [...]* (London: Simpkin, 1861) 10.

15. Frances P. Cobbe, *The Red Flag in John Bull's Eyes* (London: Faithfull, 1863) 2, 3.

16. Count Agénor de Gasparin, *The Uprising of a Great People: The United States in 1861* (London: Low, 1861) 17.

17. Count Agénor de Gasparin, *America Before Europe: Principles and Interests* (New York: Scribner's, 1862) 395.

18. Frederick Douglass, *Narrative of the Life of Frederick Douglass — An American Slave* (Boston: Anti-Slavery Office, 1845) 67.

19. *Ibid.* 120–125.

20. John E. Cairnes, *Who Are the Canters?* (London: Faithfull, 1863) 7.

21. Dan Gow, *Civil War in America [...]* (Manchester: Heywood, 1862) 27.

22. James W. Massie, *The American Crisis, in Relation to the Anti-Slavery Cause [...]* (London: Snow, 1862) 8.

23. Gasparin, *America Before Europe* 159.

24. B.D. 13.

25. Steven E. Locke, *English Sympathies & Opinions [...]* (London: Bosworth, (1866) 12, 13.

26. Hugo Reid, *The American Question in a Nut-Shell [...]* (London: Hardwicke, 1862) 30, 31.

27. Beresford-Hope, *Social and Political* 27.

28. Beresford-Hope, *Popular View* 9.

29. Charles Mackay, *The Founders of the American Republic [...]* (Edinburgh: Blackwood, 1885) 398.

30. Beresford-Hope, *Popular View* 18.

31. E.B. Long and Barbara Long, *The Civil War Day by Day [...]* (Garden City, N.Y.: Doubleday, 1971) 374.

32. *Ibid.*

33. *Great Issues in American History*, ed. Richard Hofstadter. Vol. 1 (New York: Vintage, 1958) 414.

34. *A Cycle of Adams Letters, 1861–1865*, ed. Worthington C. Ford (Boston: Houghton, 1920) 35.

35. Brian Jenkins, *Britain and the War of the Union* (Montreal: McGill-Queen's University Press, 1974) 51.

36. *Ibid.* 149.

37. Ephraim D. Adams, *Great Britain and the American Civil War*, vol. 1 (London: Longmans, 1925) 302.

38. Douglas A. Lorimer, *Colour, Class, and the Victorians [...]* (Leicester, England: Leicester UP 1978) 179.

39. Karl Marx and Friedrich Engels, *The Civil War in the United States*, ed. Richard Enmale (New York: International, 1937) 191–194.

40. Donald Featherstone, *Colonial Small Wars, 1837–1901* (Newton Abbott, England: David, 1973) 209.

41. *The History of the Times*, ed. Stanley Morrison (London: The Times, 1939) 372, 373.

42. L.C.B. Seaman, *Victorian England [...]* (London: Methuen, 1973) 149.

43. Brian Jenkins 83.

44. John W. Burgess, *The Civil War and the Constitution, 1859–1865* (New York: Scribner's, 1901) 291–295.

45. Ephraim D. Adams, *British Interests and Activities in Texas, 1838–1846*, vol. 2 (London: 1925) 116.

46. Adams, *Great Britain*, vol. 2, 143, 144.

47. Frank L. Owsley, *The South: Old and New Frontiers [...]* ed. Harriet C. Owsley (Athens: University Press of Georgia, 1969) 118.

48. John E. Cairnes, *England's Neutrality in the American Contest* (London: Emancipation Society, 1864) 12, 13.

49. Grosvenor P. Lowrey, *English Neutrality — Is the Alabama a British Pirate?* (Philadelphia: Ashmead, 1863) 32.

50. Gasparin, *America Before Europe* 15.

51. *Ibid.* 43

52. *Ibid.* 46.

53. Count Agénor de Gasparin, *A Word of Peace on the American Question* (London: Low, 1862) 20, 21.

54. Gasparin, *America Before Europe*, 15.

55. Adams, *Great Britain*, vol. 1, 245.

56. Adams, *British Interests*, vol. 1, 252.

57. D.P. Crook, *The North, the South, and the Powers, 1861–1865* (New York: Wiley, 1974) 48.

58. Burton J. Hendrick, *Statesmen of the Lost Cause [...]* (Boston: Little, 1939) 274.

59. Adams, *Great Britain*, vol. 2, 1–4.

60. Frank L. Owsley, *King Cotton Diplomacy [...]* (Chicago: University of Chicago Press, 1931) 23.

61. Adams, *Great Britain*, vol. 2, 9.

62. Owsley, *The South* 118.

63. Owsley, *King Cotton* 554.

64. Mary Ellison, *Support for Secession [...]* (Chicago: University of Chicago Press, 1972) 172.

65. Gasparin, *America Before Europe* 66–71.

66. Adams, *Great Britain*, vol. 1, 257, 258.

67. Richard I. Lester, *Confederate Finance and Purchasing in Great Britain* (Charlottesville: University Press of Virginia, 1975) 90.

68. Owsley, *King Cotton*, 554.

69. Crook 173, 174.

70. Allan Nevins, *The War for the Union* (New York: Scribner's, 1971) 338, 339.

71. James R. Soley, *The Blockade and the Cruisers* (New York: Scribner's, 1883) 44.

72. *History of The Times* 359.

73. *Ibid.* 366.

74. Brian Jenkins 48.

75. *History of The Times* 387.

76. Charles Mackay, *Life and Liberty in America [...]*, vol. 1 (New York: Harper, 1859) 241.

77. Mackay, *Life and Liberty*, vol. 1, 310.

78. *Ibid.* vol. 2, 57.

79. *Ibid.* 63.

80. Mackay, *Founders* 398.

81. Leslie Stephen, *The "Times" on the American War: A Historical Study* (London: Ridgway, 1865) 22.

82. *History of The Times* 387, 388.

83. *Ibid.* 389.

84. *Ibid.* 384.

85. Adams, *Great Britain*, vol. 2, 196.

86. Stephen 81.

87. Kingsley B. Smellie, *Great Britain Since 1688 [...]* (Ann Arbor: University of Michigan Press, 1962) 165.

88. Adams, *Great Britain*, vol. 1, 28.

89. Hendrick 254.

90. T.A. Jenkins, *The Liberal Ascendancy, 1830–1886* (New York: St. Martin's, 1994) 104.

91. Adams, *Great Britain*, vol. 1, 55.

92. G.M. Young, *Victorian England: Portrait of an Age* (London: Oxford University Press, 1936) 24.

93. Jack Gratus, *The Great White Lie [...]* (London: Hutchinson, 1973) 78.

94. Eric E. Williams, *Capitalism & Slavery*. 1944. (London: Deutsch, 1964) 3.

95. *Ibid.* 138.

96. Lorimer 128.

97. A Creole of Louisiana [Eugene Musson], *Letter to Napoleon III [...]* (London: Kirkland, 1862)

98. Brian Jenkins 72.

99. Owsley, *King Cotton* 182.

100. Crook 22.

101. John E. Bright, *Speeches of John Bright [...]* (Boston: Little, 1865) 24.

102. William Russell, *My Diary North and South*. 1863. Ed. Eugene H. Berwanger (Philadelphia: Temple University Press, 1988) 106.

103. *Ibid.* 107.

104. Robert Trimble, *Slavery in the United States of North America [...]* (London: Whittaker, 1863) 8.

105. Arthur M. Schlesinger, Preface, *The Cotton Kingdom* [...] 1861. (New York: Modern Library, 1984) ix.

106. Frederick Law Olmsted, *The Cotton Kingdom [...]* 1861. Ed. Arthur M. Schlesinger (New York: Modern Library, 1984) 475.

107. *Ibid.* 8.

108. *Ibid.* 476.

109. Robert Cruden, *The War That Never Ended [...]* (Englewood Cliffs, N.J.: Prentice-Hall, 1972) 125.

110. Albert D. Kirwan, ed., *The Confederacy* (New York: Meridian, 1959) 197.

111. Hendrick 414.

112. *Ibid.* 124.

113. Clement Eaton, *A History of the Southern Confederacy* (New York: Free Press, 1965) 271.

114. Kirwan 209.

115. Hendrick 334.

116. Charles Mackay, *Forty Years' Recollections of Life [...]* (London: Chapman, 1877) 449.

Works Cited

Primary Sources

Newspapers

The Daily News (London: Bradbury, 1846–1912).
The Daily Telegraph (London: Ellis, 1856–1937).
The Examiner (London: Hunt, 1808–1881).
The Glasgow Herald (Glasgow, Scotland: Publisher varies, 1805–1992).
Lloyd's Weekly Newspaper (London: Lloyd, 1849–1902).
The Manchester Guardian (Manchester: Taylor, 1828–1959).
The Morning Post (London: Nott, 1803–1937).
Once a Week (London: Bradbury, 1859–1880).
The Standard (London: Baldwin, 1827–1916).
The Times (London: Times Newspapers, 1788–).

Magazines and Journals

Blackwood's Edinburgh Magazine (Edinburgh: Blackwood, 1817–1905).
The Economist (London: The Economist Newspaper, 1843–).
The Edinburgh Review (London: Longmans, 1802–1929).
Macmillan's Magazine (London: Macmillan, 1859–1907).
The Quarterly Review (London: Murray, 1809–1967).
The Saturday Review of Politics, Literature, Science and Art.
(London: Saturday Review, 1855–1931).

Books and Pamphlets

Anonymous. [Balme, Joshua R.] *The American War Crusade: Plain Facts for Earnest Men.* London: Hamilton, 1863.

B.D. *Federals and Confederates, for What Do They Fight?: The True Issue of the American Civil War*. London: Caldwell, 1863.

Beresford-Hope, A.J.B. *England, the North, and the South*. London: Ridgway, 1862.

_____. *A Popular View of the American Civil War*. London: Ridgway, 1861.

_____. *The Social and Political Bearings of the American Disruption*. London: Ridgway, 1863.

Bright, John. *Speeches of John Bright, M.P., on the American Question*. Boston: Little, 1865.

Cairnes, John E. *England's Neutrality in the American Contest*. London: Emancipation Societiy, 1864.

_____. *Who Are the Canters?* London: Faithfull, 1863.

Cobbe, Frances P. *The Red Flag in John Bull's Eyes*. London: Faithfull, 1863.

A Creole of Louisiana [Eugene Musson]. *Letter to Napoleon III on Slavery in the Southern States*. London: Kirkland, 1862.

A Cycle of Adams Letters, 1861–1865. Vol. 2. Ed. Worthington C. Ford. Boston: Houghton, 1920.

Douglass, Frederick. *Narrative of the Life of Frederick Douglass, an American Slave*. Boston: Anti-Slavery Office, 1845.

Ellison, Thomas. *Slavery and Secession in America, Historical and Economical*. London: Low, 1861.

Garratt, Samuel. *The Bible and Slavery*. London: Morgan, 1863.

Gasparin, Count Agénor de. *America Before Europe: Principles and Interests*. New York: Scribner's, 1862.

_____. *The Uprising of a Great People: The United States in 1861*. London: Low, 1861.

_____. *A Word of Peace on the American Question*. London: Low, 1862.

Gottheil, Gustav. *Moses versus Slavery, Being Two Discourses on the Slave Question*. London: Simpkin, 1861.

Gow, Dan. *Civil War in America: A Lecture Delivered in Aid of the Lancashire Relief Fund, on November 24th, 1862, in Sydenham Chapel, Forest Hill*. Manchester: Heywood, 1862.

Locke, Steven E. *English Sympathies & Opinions Regarding the Late American Civil War*. London: Bosworth, 1866.

Lowrey, Grosvenor P. *English Neutrality: Is the Alabama a British Pirate?* Philadelphia: Ashmead, 1863.

Mackay, Charles. *Forty Years' Recollections of Life, Literature and Public Affairs, from 1830 to 1870*. Vol. 2. London: Chapman, 1877.

_____. *The Founders of the American Republic: A History and Biography*. Edinburgh: Blackwood, 1885.

_____. *Life and Liberty in America, or, Sketches of a Tour in the United States and Canada in 1857–8*. New York: Harper, 1859.

Marx, Karl, and Friedrich Engels. *The Civil War in the United States*. Ed. Richard Enmale, from articles originally published in the *New York Daily Tribune*, the *Vienna Presse*, and from correspondence between the authors, 1861–1866. New York: International, 1937.

Massie, James W. *The American Crisis, in Relation to the Anti-Slavery Cause: Facts and Suggestions Addressed to the Friends of Freedom in Britain*. London: Snow, 1862.

Olmsted, Frederick Law. *The Cotton Kingdom: A Traveller's Observations on Cotton and Slavery in the American Slave States; Based Upon Three Former Volumes of Journeys and Investigations by the Same Author.* 1861. Ed. Arthur M. Schlesinger. New York: Knopf, 1953.

Reid, Hugo. *The American Question in a Nut-Shell, or, Why We Should Recognize the Confederates.* London: Hardwicke, 1862.

Russell, William H. *My Diary, North and South.* 1863. Ed. Eugene H. Berwanger. Philadelphia: Temple University Press, 1988.

Soley, James R. *The Blockade and the Cruisers.* (Vol. 1 of *The Navy in the Civil War.*) New York: Scribner's, 1883.

Stephen, Leslie. *The "Times" on the American War: A Historical Study.* London: Ridgway, 1865.

Trimble, Robert. *Slavery in the United States of North America: A Lecture Delivered in Liverpool, December, 1861.* London: Whittaker, 1863.

Secondary Sources

Adams, Ephraim D. *British Interests and Activities in Texas, 1838–1946.* Baltimore: Johns Hopkins, 1910.

_____. *Great Britain and the American Civil War.* 2 vols. London: Longmans, 1925.

Burgess, John W. *The Civil War and the Constitution, 1859–1865.* Vol. 2. New York: Scribner's, 1901.

Crook, D.P. *The North, the South, and the Powers, 1861–1865.* New York: Wiley, 1974.

Cruden, Robert. *The War That Never Ended: The American Civil War.* Englewood Cliffs, N.J.: Prentice-Hall, 1972.

Eaton, Clement. *A History of the Southern Confederacy.* New York: Free Press, 1965.

Ellison, Mary. *Support for Secession: Lancashire and the American Civil War.* University of Chicago Press, 1972.

Featherstone, Donald. *Colonial Small Wars, 1837–1901.* Newton Abbott, England: David, 1973.

Gratus, Jack. *The Great White Lie: Slavery, Emancipation, and Changing Racial Attitudes.* London: Hutchinson, 1973.

Great Issues in American History. Ed. Richard Hofstadter. New York: Vintage, 1958.

Hendrick, Burton J. *Statesmen of the Lost Cause: Jefferson Davis and His Cabinet.* Boston: Little, 1939.

The History of the Times. Ed. Stanley Morrison. Vol. 2. London: The Times, 1939.

Jenkins, Brian. *Britain and the War of the Union.* Vol 1. Montreal: McGill-Queen's University Press, 1974.

Jenkins, T.A. *The Liberal Ascendancy, 1830–1886.* New York: St. Martin's, 1994.

Kirwan, Albert D., ed. *The Confederacy.* New York: Meridian, 1959.

Lester, Richard I. *Confederate Finance and Purchasing in Great Britain.* Charlottesville: University Press of Virginia, 1975.

Long, E.B., and Barbara Long. *The Civil War Day by Day: An Almanac, 1861–1865.* Garden City, N.Y.: Doubleday, 1971.

Lorimer, Douglas A. *Colour, Class, and the Victorians: English Attitudes to the Negro in the Mid-Nineteenth Century.* Leicester, England: Leicester University, 1978.

Nevins, Allan. *The War for the Union.* Vol. 3. New York: Scribner's, 1971.

Owsley, Frank L. *King Cotton Diplomacy: Foreign Relations of the Confederate States of America.* University of Chicago Press, 1931.

_____. *The South: Old and New Frontiers: Selected Essays of Frank Lawrence Owsley.* Ed. Harriet C. Owsley. Athens: University of Georgia Press, 1969.

Schlesinger, Arthur M. Preface. *The Cotton Kingdom: A Traveller's Observations on Cotton and Slavery in the American Slave States; Based Upon Three Former Volumes of Journey and Investigations by the Same Author.* By Frederick Law Olmsted. Ed. Schlesinger. 1861. New York: Modern Library, 1984.

Seaman, L.C.B. *Victorian England: Aspects of English and Imperial History, 1837–1901.* London: Methuen, 1973.

Smellie, Kingsley B. *Great Britain Since 1688: A Modern History.* Ann Arbor: University of Michigan Press, 1962.

Williams, Eric E. *Capitalism & Slavery.* 1944. London: Deutsch, 1964.

Young, G.M. *Victorian England: Portrait of an Age.* London: Oxford University Press, 1936.

Index